Anatolian Livestock Trade in the Late Ottoman Empire

Middle East Environmental Histories

Middle East Environmental Histories seeks to publish the best work on the environmental history of the Middle East from late antiquity to the present. People in the Middle East, as everywhere, have lived in, with, and against the natural world. The multiple engagements of these peoples with environments over time helped to produce ideas, states, cultures, literatures, families, and societies. This series aims to further elaborate these histories. It will examine the Middle East in its global context while always keeping the particularities of the Middle East and its various environments in focus—the region's historic role as the crossroads of trade between the Mediterranean and Asia, its cultural and religious diversity, the place of Islam, the balance between settled and sown, and the role of oil, to name a few. Although a series about the history of the Middle East, it will lean on interdisciplinary influences from other fields. Overall, it desires to mark the best of this growing field and help shape its future.

Other titles in this series:

Richard W. Bulliet, *Exploring Animal Energy in the Arid Zone: More Camels, Fewer Wheels*, 2024

ANATOLIAN LIVESTOCK TRADE IN THE LATE OTTOMAN EMPIRE

Yonca Köksal Özyaşar and Can Nacar

Leiden University Press

Cover design: Andre Klijsen
Cover illustration: Nicholas V. Artamonoff / National Museum of Asian Art Archives, Smithsonian Institution, Myron Bement Smith Collection, FSA_A.04_2.06.55.268
Lay-out: Crius Group

ISBN 9789087284350
e-ISBN 9789400604759 (e-PDF)
https://doi.org//10.24415/9789087284350
NUR 696

Printed and bound by CPI Group (UK) Ltd, Croydon, CR0 4YY

Contents

List of Figures

List of Photographs

List of Maps

Acknowledgements

Several institutions provided support for this study. We extend our sincere gratitude to the Scientific and Technological Research Council of Turkey (TÜBİTAK) for its generous funding and support, which made this project possible. We thank the College of Social Sciences and Humanities at Koç University for providing infrastructural and administrative support.

We are deeply thankful to our assistants, whose dedication, hard work, and expertise have been indispensable throughout the project. Yalçın Göktaş, Onat Ozan Ata, Süleyman Ergüven, Evren Çakıl, Ayberk Özdemir, Deniz Özeren, Muratcan Zorcu, Onur Çezik, and Semih Burak Örs worked in different stages of this project. Their contributions have been invaluable, and this work would not have been possible without their hard work and commitment.

We would like to extend our gratitude to the staff of the various archives and libraries that facilitated this project: Presidency of the Republic of Türkiye Directorate of State Archives, Istanbul Atatürk Library, Istanbul Beyazıt Library, Center for Islamic Studies in Istanbul, SALT in Istanbul, National Library of Turkey, Suna Kıraç Library at Koç University, National Museum of Asian Art, and Austrian National Library.

We are thankful to our colleagues in the Department of History at Koç University, particularly Dilek Barlas, late Zafer Toprak, and Kerem Tınaz for their continued support, insightful discussions, and encouragement. Their collective knowledge and expertise have enriched this project and helped shape its outcomes. We also warmly thank our students at Koç University, particularly Burak Burkay Maktav, Erhan Saçlı, and the members of the History Club for their comments and questions that influenced this text.

We have discussed many of the ideas in this book with our friends and colleagues. They have generously given their time to listen to us and provide invaluable comments and suggestions. We thank them all: Nikos Kontogiannis, İrfan Kokdaş, Yahya Araz, Cahit Telci, Hülya Canbakal, Semih Çelik, Sherry Vatter, Yener Koç, Yaşar Tolga Cora, Önder Eren Akgül, Zozan Pehlivan, Anıl Aşkın, Samuel Dolbee, and Özge Samancı.

At Leiden University Press, we are thankful to Alan Mikhail, the editor of the Middle East Environmental Histories series, as well as Saskia Gieling, Lisa van Vliet, and two anonymous reviewers for all their efforts in making the book possible in its present form.

To our family members, we owe an immeasurable debt of gratitude. Tina Alaca Nacar, and Başar and Ayşe Su Özyaşar's unwavering love, encouragement, and understanding have sustained us through the challenges and triumphs of this journey.

Parts of Chapter 3 were previously published in "Marketing Sheep in the Ottoman Empire: Erzurum and Its Trade Networks (Circa 1780s–1910s)," *Archiv Orientalni* 91, no. 1 (2023): 41-67, reprinted with the permission of the journal's editorial office, © 2023.

CHAPTER 1

Introduction

Abstract

This chapter introduces major concepts -including ecosystems, provisionism, and free trade- along with key themes such as disease outbreaks, migratory movements, and land conflicts, and poses questions to be addressed in the subsequent chapters. It identifies human and non-human actors that will take the center stage in the narrative and discusses some notable developments in livestock and meat industries during the nineteenth and early twentieth centuries. This discussion illustrates that, similar to its counterparts in Europe and America, the Ottoman Empire witnessed increased meat consumption in urban areas, driven by population growth and advances in communication and transportation technologies. The chapter then briefly traces the evolution of Ottoman urban provisioning networks from the eighteenth to early twentieth centuries, highlighting the growing importance of Anatolia as a source of sheep for Istanbul's slaughter needs. Finally, it introduces the primary sources utilized for this study and provides an overview of the next five chapters.

Keywords: Ottoman Empire; Anatolia; livestock trade; meat; ecosystem; provisionism; free trade

> Trades intimately connected with that of cooks are those of butchers, bakers, and poulterers. Meat, principally mutton, is supplied by the neighboring districts of Roomelia and Anatolia, except about the time of Beiram, when numerous flocks are driven towards the capital from distant provinces. The sheep are of various kinds. Those of the European districts are small, long-horned, long-woolled, and resembling the coarse breeds of England....
>
> The Anatolian breeds of sheep are larger and coarser than those of Roomelia. Their heads are heavy and strongly arched, their legs long and bony, and their fleeces extremely coarse. Their weight averages from fifty to sixty pounds, but they are not preferred for the kitchen. The broad-tailed doomba is not uncommon. It is a large, unwieldy animal, with superabundant offal. Its tail-fat, sometimes weighing twelve or fourteen pounds, is esteemed for culinary purposes.[1]

This is how Charles White, an English journalist and military officer, narrated his impressions of the sheep and meat trade in Istanbul in the early 1840s.[2] Although his account highlights the role of Anatolia as an important supplier of sheep for slaughter, literature on the food provisioning of Istanbul has paid little attention to examining this role. While works dealing with the period from the seventeenth to mid-nineteenth centuries focus primarily on shipments from Rumelia (the European part of the empire),[3] the period from the 1850s to World War I remain overall little studied.[4] In this book, we follow a different path and trace the growth of livestock, particularly sheep trade from Anatolian provinces to Istanbul and other major urban markets in the nineteenth and early twentieth centuries. This growth, we argue, unfolded within the broader framework of economic, social, political, environmental, and technological shifts. A myriad of factors, ranging from administrative practices and policies to the impacts of wars, financial crises, and environmental challenges such as epidemics and famines, intricately shaped the political economy of livestock trade. While these factors had considerable impact on the lives of both human and non-human actors involved in the trade, they were also influenced by them.

From the early nineteenth century onwards, the gradual territorial losses experienced by the Ottomans in Rumelia, the primary supplier of meat to Istanbul, threatened a decline in sheep and cattle shipments. The situation was compounded by the displacement of populations due to these territorial losses. Combined with migration from the countryside to port cities, this contributed to a significant increase in urban populations and drove up the demand for food, including animal products like meat. Consequently, the demand for livestock from various regions of Anatolia surged, catering not only to the capital but also to other major urban centers. However, these population movements and increase in livestock trade also created conditions ripe for the outbreak and spread of epidemics and epizootics, further exacerbated by the strain on resources in various parts of Anatolia. This resource pressure, in turn, laid the groundwork for social tensions and conflicts across Anatolia, involving a multitude of human and non-human actors with diverse interests.

Meanwhile, the modernizing Ottoman state implemented two policies that significantly impacted the livestock and meat trade. First, liberal economic reforms introduced from the 1830s onward led to the relinquishment of government regulatory control over livestock markets by the late 1860s. Consequently, the Ottoman ruling elites entrusted the provisioning of their capital to free market forces. However, this shift towards free trade was not abrupt; it involved a gradual transition, often oscillating between provisionist concerns – especially during environmental, economic, and political crises – and liberal policies. Second, as part of nineteenth-century centralizing reforms, the government undertook the settlement of nomadic and semi-nomadic tribes, crucial sources of livestock in Anatolia. Contrary to expectations, sedentarization did not lead to a decline in tribal livestock. Instead, the role of tribes in the livestock trade remained significant, albeit in altered forms after settlement.

In the subsequent pages, this book analyses the evolution of livestock production and trade in Anatolia within the context of these and other emerging developments. It focuses on three key regions: central, northeastern, and northwestern Anatolia, and four eastern Mediterranean ports: İzmir (Smyrna), İskenderun (Alexandretta), Mersin, and Antalya (Adalia). These regions were chosen due to their status as major suppliers of sheep to Istanbul in the nineteenth and early twentieth centuries, while the ports served as outlets for exports to Istanbul and other markets, particularly Egypt. Rather than using conventional units of provinces or categorizations that view Anatolia, the Balkans, and Arab lands as holistic entities, this book defines regional economies through the interactions of goods, services, and human interventions in ecosystems. These economies were characterized by the features of their geographical locations, ecosystems, and human activities, which brought about economic growth often accompanied by social tensions and conflicts.[5] A separate chapter will scrutinize Istanbul as the central hub of livestock trade networks, with a focus on state policies regarding meat provisioning of the city and regulation of the urban market and landscape for animal slaughter and sale.

By highlighting diverse ecosystems and socioeconomic dynamics, the subsequent chapters aim to address several key questions, ultimately contributing to the literature on Ottoman environmental and socioeconomic history: How did the ecosystems and socioeconomic dynamics of the aforementioned regions and ports change in the nineteenth and early twentieth centuries? What were the repercussions of these changes on livestock production and trade? How did they impact the organization of livestock and meat trade in Istanbul?

Setting the Ottoman Experience in a Broader Context

While the Ottoman Empire witnessed a major transformation in livestock and meat trade, marked by a gradual shift towards liberal policies and an increasing reliance on supplies from Anatolia, its contemporaries also underwent significant changes. The time period covered by this study witnessed a major expansion in the livestock trade and meat industry in different parts of the world, which was encouraged by a whole host of factors. One was the upward trend in meat consumption in many Western countries, from the United States, Britain, and Germany to Denmark and Spain, due mainly to urbanization.[6] In major nineteenth-century cities, such as New York, Mexico City, and Paris, this paved the way for the liberalization of meat provisioning.[7] Still, another factor was improved communication, transportation, and cooling technologies that, in the words of Gergely Baics and Mikkel Thelle, "enabled the expansion of regional supply chains to national, international, and global markets."[8] For example, in the United States, the rapid extension of the railroad network led to the emergence of Chicago and Kansas City as two major livestock markets, each with strong connections to Midwest cattle towns. Moreover, the advent of refrigerated train cars in the 1870s allowed Chicago meat packers to make dressed-beef shipments to distant markets.[9] At around the same time, transoceanic shipment of frozen meat also became feasible. The first such shipment was made in 1877 from Buenos Aires to the French port of Le Havre. Only a few years later, steamers began to carry frozen beef and mutton from Australia and New Zealand to England.[10]

These developments went hand in hand with important changes in the butchering industry and livestock production. In Europe and the Americas, artisanal butchery was gradually giving way to industrial processes in abattoirs and meatpacking plants.[11] Meanwhile, livestock raisers in these and other parts of the world showed willingness to benefit from the increased demand for meat. In the United States, for instance, merino sheep production increased significantly during the Civil War, from 1861 to 1865, as wool from it was used for manufacturing military uniforms. When wool prices fell sharply following the end of the war, American producers began to crossbreed merino with French and English varieties known for their good meat quality. The resulting breeds generated a new market for mutton and lamb.[12] Likewise, as Rebecca Woods notes, raisers in New Zealand saw an opportunity in the burgeoning frozen meat trade "to revitalize a pastoral economy that, because of its emphasis on a single product, wool, was very much at the mercy of the vicissitudes of international markets." The crossbreeding experiments they engaged in resulted in the formation of new breeds, such as Corriedale, producing high-quality mutton for British consumers.[13]

As it became increasingly integrated into the capitalist world economy and experienced some degree of urbanization in its last century, the Ottoman Empire did not remain isolated and untouched by these developments. Until its demise, the empire maintained a predominantly agrarian society, with rural dwellers comprising about 80 percent of the total population by the early twentieth century. However, between 1840 and 1914, several cities underwent rapid growth, particularly due to migratory flows and capitalist expansion. While, for instance, İzmir's population nearly tripled and reached 300,000, that of Damascus doubled to around 240,000. Meanwhile, Istanbul, the largest urban center in the empire, exceeded a million.[14] Although it is difficult to determine whether this growth was accompanied by a rise in per capita meat consumption, total urban demand increased alongside the growing number of consumers. James Grehan, for example, estimates that in the late eighteenth century, Damascene butchers slaughtered between 60,000 and 75,000 sheep annually. By the eve of World War I, this number had apparently increased to around 85,000.[15] Likewise, as detailed in Chapter 6, Istanbul's demand for slaughtered animals doubled from the 1840s to the early 1910s.

During this period, modern transportation technologies that enabled the expansion of the livestock trade and meat industry in different parts of the world also became available in the Ottoman Empire. Istanbul and İzmir became better connected to major centers of livestock raising in Anatolia and beyond, thanks to the introduction of trains and steamships. In Anatolia, the first railroad tracks were laid from İzmir to Aydın in the early 1860s, and shortly afterward a second line was opened to this booming port city through Kasaba. About two and a half decades later, the German-financed Anatolian Railroad Company built a line from Istanbul to Ankara, with a branch to Konya.[16] Yet, the effect of these efforts on the Anatolian livestock trade remained limited. Similar to their counterparts in the Russian Empire, many merchants from the provinces of Ankara and Konya continued to drive their sheep to market on foot.[17] That was partly because the rates charged by the railroad companies seemed high to them, and partly because they wanted to choose their destination en route by comparing prices in major urban markets. However, the story of steamships that began to appear in Ottoman waters in the 1820s evolved differently.[18] While, unlike many cities in the United States and Europe, shipments of frozen meat did not become accessible in Istanbul, steamers became widely used for transporting live sheep, cattle, and lambs from northeastern, northwestern, and western Anatolia to the city. During the same period, Egypt emerged as a major consumer of Anatolian sheep and cattle as well, due to a combination of factors such as the growth of urban populations, the introduction of mandatory military service, the spread of cash crop farming, and loss of a large number of animals to epizootics.[19] As Egyptian consumers increasingly depended on imports, steamers laden with sheep and cattle began to frequently travel from the ports of İzmir, İskenderun and Mersin to Alexandria and Port Said.

To gain deeper insights into these developments, it is essential to delve into the political economy of the livestock trade. This exploration could begin by examining alterations in the state policies and supply networks serving the empire's major urban centers, notably the capital, and how they provided fresh meat from the late eighteenth to the early twentieth centuries.

State Policies: Provisionism, Free Trade, and Interventions in Times of Crises

Like various other early modern urban centers in Europe, Istanbul, where mutton was the main meat consumed, depended on a complex and regulated sheep supply chain.[20] As early as the late fifteenth century, state authorities established a system called *celepkeşan* to provide for the needs of the imperial palace and troops, state dependents, and the general populace in the city.[21] The system was based on the registration of a group of wealthy people from Rumelian provinces to annually supply the capital with a certain number of sheep. Once a *celepkeş* (registered sheep merchant) collected and brought the animals required of him to Istanbul, he was to sell them under the supervision of *koyun emini* (overseer of the provision of the sheep for the state) to the city's butchers at a price fixed by the government.[22] This practice, however, began to decline in the late sixteenth century when the empire fell into a severe crisis characterized by long-lasting wars fought on both eastern and western fronts, skyrocketing inflation, adverse climatic conditions of the Little Ice Age, and frequent internal uprisings.[23] As the registered merchants failed to fulfill their deliveries to Istanbul under these conditions, the government turned the *celepkeşan* in-kind obligation into a cash tax in some regions and used the revenues generated by it to organize the collection and transportation of sheep from Rumelia to Istanbul.[24] This system remained in force until the early 1780s, when a new in-kind tax, called the *ondalık ağnam* (one-in-ten sheep tax), was introduced in Rumelian provinces, except for Moldavia (Boğdan), Wallachia (Eflak), Scutari (İşkodra), and Bosnia. The *ondalık ağnam* required herders to hand over one-tenth of their sheep to the state at prices far below their market value in order to ensure a regular supply of meat to soldiers, state dependents, and other residents in Istanbul. By the early nineteenth century, the number of animals collected through this tax had reached significant levels – hundreds of thousands annually.[25]

The *celepkeşan* system and the *ondalık ağnam* tax were mainly applied in Rumelia,[26] because the Istanbul populace preferred the mutton from thin-tailed *Kıvırcık* sheep raised in this region over that of the fat-tailed *Karaman* breeds in Asia Minor.[27] This, however, does not mean that from the late fifteenth to early nineteenth centuries the capital exclusively relied on provinces to its north and west for the provision of meat. Especially at times when shipments from Rumelia appeared insufficient, Ottoman ruling elites turned to Anatolian provinces for supplies. One such period was the 1590s, when the Ottomans were then engaged in a prolonged war against the Habsburgs in central Europe. Since meat supplies in Rumelia were reserved primarily for the fighting troops, demand for Anatolian sheep peaked. Authorities in the imperial capital issued frequent orders to provincial officials and tribal leaders in Anatolia, instructing them to direct flocks of sheep from their localities to Istanbul.[28] To give but one example, in 1596, the governor-general (*beylerbeyi*) of Karaman in central Anatolia was ordered to collect and send 200,000 heads to the capital, a move that triggered a major rural uprising.[29] As will be demonstrated in Chapters 2 and 3, a similar surge in demand occurred in the late eighteenth and early nineteenth centuries, as wars, territorial losses, and other calamities disrupted supply networks in Rumelia. By the 1840s, annual sheep shipments from Asia Minor to Istanbul had reached about 150,000 heads per year, but this was still less than one-fourth of the number of animals slaughtered in the city.[30]

Both the number and percentage of these shipments increased substantially in the latter half of the nineteenth century. In the early 1870s, a British consular official reported that the annual consumption of meat for Istanbul necessitated the slaughter of 1,140,000 animals: 1,120,000 sheep and lambs, and 20,000 oxen. Of these, about 300,000 came from the Anatolian provinces of the empire.[31] In the following two decades, the annual slaughter increased by about 30 percent, while shipments from Anatolia rose by 45 percent.[32] This upward trend had, however, little to do with the state's provisionist policies, many of which – as will be further discussed in the following chapters – were abolished before the 1870s due to inflationary pressures on meat prices. The shift to liberal policies accelerated after the Crimean War (1853–56) when meat prices in Istanbul and other cities increased significantly. Parallel to the adoption of free trade policies in other sectors of the economy after the Anglo-Ottoman Treaty of Baltalimanı (1838), the abolition of *ondalık ağnam* in 1857 and the removal of price ceilings (*narh*) by 1862 virtually ended government regulation of the livestock trade to Istanbul. Yet, state authorities did not completely withdraw from the market. The Tanzimat reforms required government involvement in urban life, particularly through new institutions such as municipalities that addressed sanitation and health issues in the livestock trade. Because the capital lacked a centralized abattoir until the early 1920s, the Istanbul Municipality, for instance, took steps to tighten regulatory oversight over slaughterhouses to ensure the wholesomeness of meat supplies. Meanwhile, the state remained the primary buyer of beef and mutton, distributing them to military troops, board schools, orphanages, hospitals, and dervish lodges in the city. Provisionist concerns also required its intervention in the market during times of political, economic, and environmental calamities through various means, such as import restrictions.[33]

The Ottoman state's role extended beyond crafting regulatory market policies. As a modernizing state, it sought to tap the resources of its population more effectively. For this purpose, the government pursued different policies in major centers of sheep export in Anatolia, tailored to the specific political, demographic, and environmental circumstances of each region. In central Anatolia, where pastoralist tribes constituted a very large part of the population, the government initiated a sedentarization campaign in the early nineteenth century. This move posed a serious threat to the livelihoods of tribes, as it aimed to restrict and ultimately end their seasonal migrations between winter and summer pastures. Considerable progress in that direction had already been made by the 1860s; however, as Chapter 2 will demonstrate this did not mean that tribal groups were powerless in the face of the sedentarization campaign. Instead, the fact that Istanbul relied considerably on their sheep for meat gave them negotiating power. Thus, some among them could continue to engage in long-distance seasonal migration with their animals, at least until the 1900s, with approval from state authorities.

Eastern Anatolia, with its large tribal population, too had become the scene of state efforts at sedentarization. When the Hamidian government established tribal cavalry units called the Hamidiye Light Cavalry Regiments (*Hamidiye Hafif Süvari*

Alayları) in this region in 1890, one of its goals was the permanent settlement of nomads. While this was only partly accomplished, the formation of the regiments significantly reconfigured the socioeconomic and political landscape of the region. Tribal chiefs who joined the Hamidiye expanded and consolidated their power, and thus, as Chapter 3 points out, they managed to appropriate a portion of the wealth generated by increased sheep exports to Istanbul.[34] The state also played a role in this increase by launching infrastructure projects to improve the channels of trade. A major initiative was the construction of an extensive telegraph network within a relatively short span of time, which allowed some provincial merchants to relocate their headquarters to Istanbul and establish connections with diverse interior regions.[35]

Meanwhile, some infrastructure projects deliberately aimed to change the ecosystem of major livestock-raising regions. As will be discussed in Chapter 4, in the middle section of the south Marmara littoral that comprised part of Hüdavendigar province, there were various attempts from the mid-nineteenth century to the 1900s to drain wetlands in order to facilitate the settlement of refugees arriving in large numbers from the Caucasus, Crimea, and Rumelia.[36] The reclamation of wetlands, we argue, was part of a larger process of increased state intervention in the lives of non-human actors.[37] This process also involved introducing quarantine measures and vaccines to combat animal diseases, as well as the use of crossbreeding to improve the wool or meat quality of local sheep breeds. However, these efforts proceeded unevenly among the provinces. They were more noticeable in Hüdavendigar than in central and northeastern Anatolia. One factor behind this was that Hüdavendigar housed a state farming enterprise which, for a while, actively engaged in crossbreeding merino sheep with native stock to supply fine-quality wool to state-run textile factories.[38] Apparently, due to this enterprise and Hüdavendigar's vital role in the meat provisioning of Istanbul during winter months, some sanitary measures intended to control epizootics were also first experimented within this province in the 1890s.

Ottoman state policies affected the functioning of livestock trade and the material conditions of both human and non-human actors, while at the same time being negotiated and reconfigured by them, as seen in the above examples from different regional economies of Anatolia. The following two sections introduce these actors in detail, highlighting their role in shaping not only trade but also social and political dynamics in their regions and beyond.

Human Actors of Livestock Trade

As it traces trade networks that connected different parts of rural Anatolia to Istanbul and other major urban markets, this study represents an effort to contribute to the small but growing body of scholarly work that highlights the economic and commercial dynamism of the Ottoman Empire's interior regions.[39] In addition to examining state policies, it emphasizes the agency of both human and non-human actors in the formation and evolution of these networks. Among human actors were entrepreneurs who sought to capitalize on the increased demand for meat by setting up trading, livestock raising, and grazing ventures. They included a wide range of people, from state elites (including Sultan Abdülhamid II) and prominent Istanbul bankers to local notables such as tribal chiefs, large landholders, and merchants.

The expansion of the livestock trade contributed to capital accumulation in the hands of these actors, transforming some into major capitalist entrepreneurs. An early example was the Chalikov family, whose story Andreas Lyberatos has recounted. In the early nineteenth century, the family employed more than 2,000 people in the *ondalık ağnam* tax collection network in Rumelia and in the delivery of collected sheep to Istanbul.[40] A later one was Christakis Zografos, who will be discussed in Chapters 4 and 6. He worked as a contractor in the late 1850s and early 1860s, providing cheap meat supplies to state institutions. Through this venture, he accumulated a considerable fortune, which enabled him to become one of the notable Galata bankers and a prominent figure in Istanbul's Greek community. However, livestock business was not solely the domain of non-Muslim merchants. Contrary to the argument that Muslim capital was missing in the late Ottoman Empire and that trade was predominantly controlled by non-Muslims, this book highlights the active role of Muslim entrepreneurs in Ottoman economic life.[41] As will be discussed in Chapters 2, 3, 4, and 6, some of these entrepreneurs managed not only to accumulate economic capital but also to extend their political influence beyond the borders of their provinces over time. Figures like Çayırlızade Hilmi Efendi and Emin (Sazak) Bey accumulated large landholdings in central Anatolia, where they raised large flocks of sheep and goats for wool and meat. Their growing economic power granted them significant political influence both at the local and central administration levels. When the Grand National Assembly was convened in Ankara in 1920, both were present as deputies, alongside a prominent sheep merchant from northeastern Anatolia, Mühürdarzade Asım.

While highlighting such 'success stories,' this study will also shed light on the unequal social dynamics that underpinned them and the inherent economic risks associated with the livestock and meat trade. In the United States, continental Europe, and Australia, advancements in animal healthcare emerged alongside the development of transportation networks, refrigeration technologies, and the establishment of centralized modern slaughterhouses equipped with industrialized butchering, packaging, and sanitation facilities. However, despite widespread discussions about refrigeration and centralized abattoirs among the Ottomans, these facilities were not introduced in Istanbul until the end of the empire due to a lack of state funds and strong resistance from merchants and butchers. This financial shortfall also resulted in the operation of the Istanbul livestock and meat markets on a credit basis, making them vulnerable to breakdowns. Under these conditions, bankruptcy and penury were constant threats, especially for small-scale butchers and merchants. As Chapter 6 will detail, these actors became increasingly vocal in demanding the establishment of a regulated market for livestock and meat. In the late nineteenth century, this demand led to intense debates and conflicts between various government bodies, including the Council of State, the Ministry of Interior, and the Istanbul Municipality. Meanwhile, due to the increased commercialization of pastures, driven by the growing sheep exports to Istanbul and other markets, the threat of dispossession became imminent for rural populations, particularly in northwestern and western Anatolia. This development, in turn, triggered long-lasting land conflicts, some of which will be discussed in Chapters 2, 4, and 5.

Non-Human Actors

Sheep, cattle, and goats were not only commodities or 'cash crops,' as termed by Sarah Shields, to be traded; they were also active agents, influencing and being influenced by the social, economic, environmental, and political conditions in their localities and beyond.[42] An important non-human agent with the power to affect their lives was the climate. Together with geographic factors, such as altitude and soil, the climate had a major impact on the distribution of breeds. Chapters 4 and 5 demonstrate that during the winter months, the provinces of Hüdavendigar and Aydın, located in northwestern and western Anatolia respectively, hosted large numbers of *Kıvırcık* sheep from Rumelia. This was due to their mild climate and availability of large pastures, which provided a stimulus for the growth of export trade from these areas. Meanwhile, central and eastern Anatolia specialized in raising different varieties of *Karaman* sheep, which were resistant to the colder and longer winters of these regions thanks to fat stored in their tails. Although the cold winters with considerable snowfall posed a serious challenge for livestock flocks and their raisers in the northeastern Anatolian province of Erzurum, several high mountain ranges created favorable conditions for spring and summer grazing. To fatten their cattle and sheep for export to different parts of the empire, the raisers could rely on fertile mountain pastures exposed by the melting snow.[43] Without these pastures, Erzurum's role as a hub of interregional trade, connecting northeastern Anatolia with Russia, Iran, Syria, Egypt, and Istanbul – a topic that will be discussed in Chapter 3 – might not have been sustainable.

Although well adapted to local conditions in Anatolia, sheep and other livestock populations were vulnerable in the face of extreme climate events, such as severe cold winters and droughts, which depleted their forage and ultimately led to many casualties. Additionally, the weakened survivors became more susceptible to diseases like anthrax and cattle plague. Throughout the late nineteenth and early twentieth centuries, the Ottoman Empire witnessed frequent outbreaks of epizootics, some of which took a heavy toll. During this period, the government's tribal settlement process further complicated the lives of animals. While they used to freely move from one pasture to another depending on weather and forage availability, their mobility became limited, causing considerable suffering. As detailed in Chapter 2, thousands of sheep in central Anatolia, denied access to their customary pastures, starved to death. Moreover, animals experienced considerable difficulties on their marches to markets. Even with the introduction of railroads and steamships, their journeys remained arduous. Packed tightly in wagons and on decks, they were not properly fed, resulting in considerable weight loss; many also fell victim to accidents, such as ship collisions.

As some recent studies have shown, the sufferings of livestock populations had significant consequences for human communities. Zozan Pehlivan, for example, points out that the decimation of the nomads' flocks by a series of droughts and severe cold waves associated with the El Nino Southern Oscillation was one of the underlying causes of the rise of violence in Ottoman Kurdistan during the late nineteenth and early twentieth centuries.[44] Similarly, this book reveals that some central Anatolian tribal groups, subjected to sedentarization, encountered serious economic difficulties, as their sheep died in large numbers. However, since this situation also had the potential to endanger Istanbul's meat supply, the government occasionally had to reconsider the limitations imposed on tribal mobility and allow their flocks access to their customary pastures. Moreover, deaths caused by diseases, cold weather, and droughts pressured the government to intervene in the livestock and meat trades through the implementation of price controls and export limitations, due to their impact on economic life in both rural and urban areas. In the latter, the scarcity of sheep and cattle for slaughter led to rising meat prices for consumers and increased tensions between butchers and government meat contractors, who relied on these animals to sustain their businesses.

The book delineates major periods of strain during the nineteenth and early twentieth centuries, often marked by concurrent extreme climate conditions, disease outbreaks, military conflicts, and economic downturns. Each chapter examines how these difficulties influenced and were responded to by the livestock trade networks in Anatolia. The initial period spanned from the early 1840s to the early 1860s. During this time, the three export regions – central, northeastern, and northwestern Anatolia – faced serious climatic and environmental challenges. Central Anatolia grappled with a devastating famine in the mid-1840s, which also affected parts of northeastern Anatolia. Moreover, in the latter region harsh winters struck first in 1847, followed by an outbreak of animal disease, and again in

1852, with both instances causing losses among sheep and cattle. Meanwhile, parts of northwestern Anatolia endured severe floods in the 1830s, with lingering effects into the 1840s and beyond, particularly on landholding patterns. Additionally, the period witnessed the Crimean War, which not only led to the diversion of livestock for slaughter supplies to support Ottoman forces and their allies but also exacerbated the financial problems of the empire. To address these problems, the government issued vast amounts of paper money (*kaime*), resulting in a major inflationary surge in the early 1860s.

These developments profoundly impacted the organization of animal trade and supply networks. First, as will be discussed in Chapter 2, the famine led to a severe debt crisis among the primary sheep suppliers in central Anatolia. This crisis, persisting into the 1850s, hastened the tribal settlement process and contributed to the abolition of the quota system, which required the Cihanbeyli and affiliated tribes in the region to supply a certain number of sheep to Istanbul. Similarly, the environmental calamities of the 1840s and early 1850s compelled the government to reduce the export quotas imposed on provincial actors in northeastern Anatolia for the capital. Second, as will be detailed in Chapter 6, meat prices in Istanbul, already on an upward trend, soared during the Crimean War and continued to rise in the early 1860s, marked by the state's increasing financial difficulties. Notably, many of the liberal reforms mentioned throughout the study, such as the abolition of the *ondalık ağnam* tax, the guild butchers' monopoly, and *narh* system in Istanbul, were introduced during this period, along with abolition of export quotas.

After a generally quiet 1860s, the second wave of strain struck between the early 1870s and early 1890s, marked by a harsh period of successive environmental disasters across a wide geography. Central Anatolia experienced a severe famine from 1873 to 1875, followed by a 'violent winter' in 1879–80 that decimated thousands of sheep in this region, as well as in northeastern and northwestern Anatolia. A similar situation emerged when drought hit central Anatolia, along with the Cilicia region, from 1886 to 1888 and northeastern Anatolia in the early 1890s. To make matters worse, these calamities were often followed by animal disease outbreaks, threatening the lives of weakened sheep and cattle. Moreover, during the early 1890s, cholera swept across the Ottoman Empire, compelling the government to establish a vast network of quarantine stations where many livestock en route to markets had to spend days, and sometimes weeks, together with their human guardians. The period in question also saw significant turmoil due to financial crisis caused by Great Depression of 1873 and the Ottoman-Russian war of 1877–78, which resulted in substantial territorial losses for the Ottomans and large-scale population movements into the capital and the Anatolian peninsula. These movements played an important role in the commercialization of pasture lands and escalation of land conflicts, particularly in Hüdavendigar province. Meanwhile, in eastern Anatolia, where tensions between Kurds and Armenians were on the rise, there were increasing complaints about animal theft and the appropriation of locals' livestock by powerful political actors, such as Kurdish tribal chiefs who joined the Hamidiye regiments.

These developments had a considerable impact on the livestock and meat markets as well as state policies. The devastating wave of famine, war, severe winters, and disease outbreaks not only threatened agricultural production but also created inflationary pressures in urban markets in the late 1870s and early 1880s. During this period, there were widespread complaints about high meat prices in both Istanbul and İzmir. In response to such conditions, state interventions in the market continued and even intensified. To prevent an agricultural crisis, the export of farm animals was temporarily banned in various provinces across Anatolia. Moreover, in Istanbul, a guild of livestock merchants was established to allow the government closer control over the capital's meat market. Meanwhile, municipal officials in İzmir persisted in the practice of setting fixed prices for beef and mutton. The state's interventionism, however, extended beyond human actors. The late 1880s and early 1890s saw increased efforts by the government to safeguard animal welfare by containing the spread of contagious diseases. These included the introduction of quarantine regulations and undertaking studies to develop vaccines.

However, these efforts did not prevent a major outbreak of animal disease in Anatolian and Syrian provinces in the early twentieth century, marking another period of strain. This outbreak had mixed consequences. Similarly affected, Egypt experienced an increased demand for livestock, which led to a growing volume of exports from Ottoman ports, including İskenderun and İzmir. Combined with the large casualties caused by the outbreak and the harsh winters that struck Anatolia, particularly its central parts, in the 1900s, this situation also heightened concerns about the scarcity of farm animals and rising meat prices. Under such conditions, the government once again had to impose a temporary export ban on plough cattle. It also sought to utilize the guild of livestock merchants to ensure affordable prices in Istanbul. Yet, despite these hardships, the book demonstrates that Anatolian livestock trade significantly expanded, and the peninsula became an important supplier for both Istanbul and other markets during the last century of the empire. The following chapters will highlight the various factors that made this expansion possible, such as the introduction of new transportation technologies, changes made by merchants in the organization of the trade, and state policies.

Overall, as the above account suggests, this study not only examines how sheep and cattle were exchanged as commodities but also traces their experiences as living beings. Few studies consider animals as playing active roles in the making of Middle Eastern and Ottoman history. One, by Richard Bulliet, argues that because the cost of raising animals was lower in the Middle East and North Africa, it became more advantageous to rely on animal power instead of using water and wind-based power mills in the eleventh and twelfth centuries.[45] Alan Mikhail's pioneering work similarly assigns agency to animals in shaping social and economic relations in Ottoman Egypt. He identifies a major transformation in agricultural production when landless peasants replaced animal power as the new labor force in the late eighteenth and early nineteenth centuries, a period when disease and extreme weather killed large numbers of animals.[46] Studies examining the interactions between human and animal actors are even more limited. In one such study, Semih Çelik demonstrates how state policies changed human-buffalo relations in the district of Kocaeli in northwestern Anatolia. When the Ottoman state, in the mid-nineteenth century, pressured peasants there to use their buffaloes for supplying timber to the imperial dockyards and government construction projects, most responded by selling the animals.[47] Likewise, Onur İnal studies camels as historical actors contributing to the incorporation of western Anatolia into the world market as they facilitated the transportation of goods and people.[48] The following chapters aim to contribute to this literature by exploring how livestock suffered during times of drought, famine, and sickness; how the settlement of tribes and commercialization of pastures affected their lives; how they travelled from their grazing grounds to Istanbul and other markets; and what awaited them in the capital. Meanwhile, they also examine how their experiences, particularly sufferings, affected the lives of human actors with whom they interacted. To answer these questions, the book draws on a variety of primary sources, which will be briefly introduced below.

Sources

One of the major primary sources underpinning this study is the collection of documents from the Ottoman state archives in Istanbul. These documents include imperial decrees issued by the sultans, official correspondences from ministries, state councils, governors, provincial councils, and municipalities, reports compiled by diverse official commissions, and petitions submitted by livestock raisers, merchants, and butchers from different provinces. They offer a wealth of detailed information on the lives of animals, as well as various aspects of the livestock and meat trade. For example, they discuss the effects of environmental and other calamities on livestock populations, the volume of sheep and cattle exports from different Anatolian provinces to Istanbul and other urban markets, the routes taken by merchants and their shepherds en route to Istanbul, and the difficulties encountered by animals during these journeys. These documents also detail the dynamics of supply and demand influencing fluctuations in livestock and meat prices, and the sources of tension and conflict among different market stakeholders, including consumers, butchers, and municipal officials.

It is important to note here that given the extensive time span covered by this book – which coincided with significant administrative reforms within the empire – numerous state institutions played roles in regulating the livestock trade, and their functions evolved over time. Before its dissolution during the Tanzimat period, the office of the head butcher (*hassa kasapbaşı)* oversaw the organization of sheep supply from provinces to Istanbul. Typically, the head butchers relayed their requisition orders to the *kadıs* (judges) of provinces, making sharia court records important archival sources for the early nineteenth century. However, administrative restructuring led to the emergence of new institutions in the following decades, which supplanted the role of the head butcher. Ministries such as the Interior and Finance, the Council of State (*Şuray-ı Devlet*), and municipalities, particularly the Istanbul Municipality (*Şehremaneti*), gained prominence in regulating aspects of the livestock trade. Conflicting perspectives among these entities were not uncommon. While, for instance, municipalities often advocated for regulatory measures to ensure a sufficient meat supply for cities, the Council of State was concerned with the economic ramifications of such measures and favored free trade, as will be discussed in the following chapters.

The other Ottoman state documents we consulted are the sharia court registers for Ankara and the provincial yearbooks (*salnames*) of Ankara Aydın, Erzurum, Hüdavendigar, and Konya provinces. The court registers, whose importance was mentioned above, meticulously record the *narh* prices for meat, allowing us to track price fluctuations from the 1780s to the 1850s. These registers also offer valuable insights into Ottoman provisionist policies and the challenges faced by merchants and their flocks en route to Istanbul. The provincial yearbooks, published in the latter half of the nineteenth and early twentieth centuries, contain noteworthy descriptions of the environmental and geographical conditions of their respective localities. Additionally, they feature data on livestock populations and sheep tax revenues, serving as indicators of the government's capacity to enumerate and tax animals. Since local resistance to taxation was commonplace, we do not assert the absolute accuracy of the data. Nonetheless, the yearbooks provide a means to observe trends and variations in the size of livestock populations in the aforementioned provinces.

Another major corpus of primary sources consulted for this study is the British consular documents, particularly the annual trade reports for Adana, Aleppo, Ankara, Bursa, Damascus, Erzurum, Istanbul, İzmir, Konya, and Trabzon. These reports often share the same limitation as provincial yearbooks: the figures they provide on the size of livestock populations and the volume of sheep and cattle exports represent approximate estimates. However, they can still be used to trace changes in the volume and direction of livestock trade in Anatolia from the mid-nineteenth century to the early 1910s. In addition to trade figures, these reports furnish information on extreme climate events, epidemics, and epizootics, detailing their impacts on the livelihoods of sheep, goats, cattle, and other livestock. It is important to note that to increase the reliability of our analysis, we have cross-checked Ottoman and British state documents against each other and other primary and secondary sources, whenever possible. We observed that, although at times slightly varying in particulars such as export figures, they often verify and complement each other.

In addition to state documents, this study draws on newspapers (*Bursa*, *Sabah*, *the Levant Herald*, and *the Levant Herald and Eastern Express*) and ego-documents such as memoirs and travel accounts. The newspapers contain reports on the movement of meat prices in Istanbul, the spread of diseases in both humans and livestock, and the measures adopted by the government to contain prices and diseases. They also provide information about the rules of exchange in the Istanbul livestock and meat markets, as well as the dangers encountered by merchants and their flocks on their way to urban markets. Likewise, the memoirs and travel accounts of Ottoman subjects and foreigners offer insights into life in Ottoman cities and the countryside in the nineteenth and early twentieth centuries. While some of these accounts, like the one by the aforementioned Charles White, discuss in detail how the residents of Istanbul were supplied with meat, others provide vivid descriptions of the geography, climate, people, and trade networks of the major livestock-raising and export centers in Anatolia.

Organization of the Book

This book examines how different ecosystems, regional social and economic dynamics, and state policies shaped the livestock trade in late Ottoman Anatolia, as detailed in the five chapters that follow. While doing so, it takes the reader on a journey from the Caucasus to the Mediterranean, following the footprints of animals over a period of major social, political, demographic, environmental, and economic transformations for the empire. Chapter 2 focuses on central Anatolia (mainly Ankara and Konya provinces), a region that, thanks to Ottoman provisionist policies, had become one of the major suppliers of sheep to Istanbul by the early nineteenth century. The second half of the century brought multiple changes to the region. While the government abandoned its provisionist policies, considerable progress was made in the settlement of tribes. Moreover, famines, droughts, disease outbreaks, and locust invasions repeatedly struck Ankara and Konya. The chapter examines how state and local actors – tribal chiefs and commoners, livestock populations and merchants, large landholders, and small peasants – were affected by and responded to these developments. It argues that their responses enabled the maintenance of a high level of exports from central Anatolia to Istanbul, İzmir, and Bursa.

Chapter 3 focuses on northeastern Anatolia, which by the early twentieth century was mostly covered by Erzurum province. It highlights the dynamic nature of Erzurum's trade networks that extended from the Caucasus in the east, to the Syrian provinces and Egypt in the south, and Istanbul in the west, showing how both their significance and organization changed from around the 1880s onward. Whereas in earlier decades, most of the sheep exports of this province went to Syrian cities and towns, Istanbul gradually became its major market. The chapter argues that this shift was influenced by various factors, including the Ottoman-Russian rivalry in the Black Sea, improvements in transportation technologies, and changes made by merchants in the organization of trade. Chapter 4 moves to Hüdavendigar province, which stretched from the northwestern to central Anatolia. Despite the differences in ecosystems between the eastern and western parts of the province, both served as important centers for livestock raising and as stop-over points for non-local sheep merchants on their way to Istanbul, İzmir, and Bursa. Thanks to these factors, Hüdavendigar experienced significant growth in sheep exports to the capital between the 1860s and 1900s. The chapter argues that this growth had several important consequences for the province. First, when combined with demographic factors – the influx of tens of thousands of refugees – it led to growing disputes over land among a diverse group of actors, including large landholders, local villagers, sheep merchants, and refugees. Second, it triggered increased state intervention and involvement in the spheres of economy and animal healthcare.

Chapter 5 analyses eastern Mediterranean ports as major gateways for Anatolian sheep and cattle. Among them, İzmir had conflicting functions: it was both a major export port for these animals and an important consumer of beef and mutton, with its dense and growing population. The chapter shows how government officials, merchants, and butchers negotiated and struggled with each other to respond to these conflicting demands. The development of İzmir's role as an export port was closely related to the increased demand from Egypt, which also affected several coastal towns and cities in southern Anatolia. Premier among them was İskenderun, with annual exports to Egypt amounting to about 100,000 sheep and cattle in the 1890s, followed, though far behind, by Mersin and Antalya. Although, as this chapter demonstrates, Istanbul had rivals, it maintained its position as the largest importer of sheep for slaughter until the end of the Ottoman Empire. Chapter 6 examines the organization and operation of the livestock and meat markets in the capital. It highlights their dynamic nature by showing how the deregulation and (re)regulation of the markets, along with the rise in fortunes of a few entrepreneurs and the decline of many small-scale butchers and merchants to the brink of bankruptcy, went hand in hand.

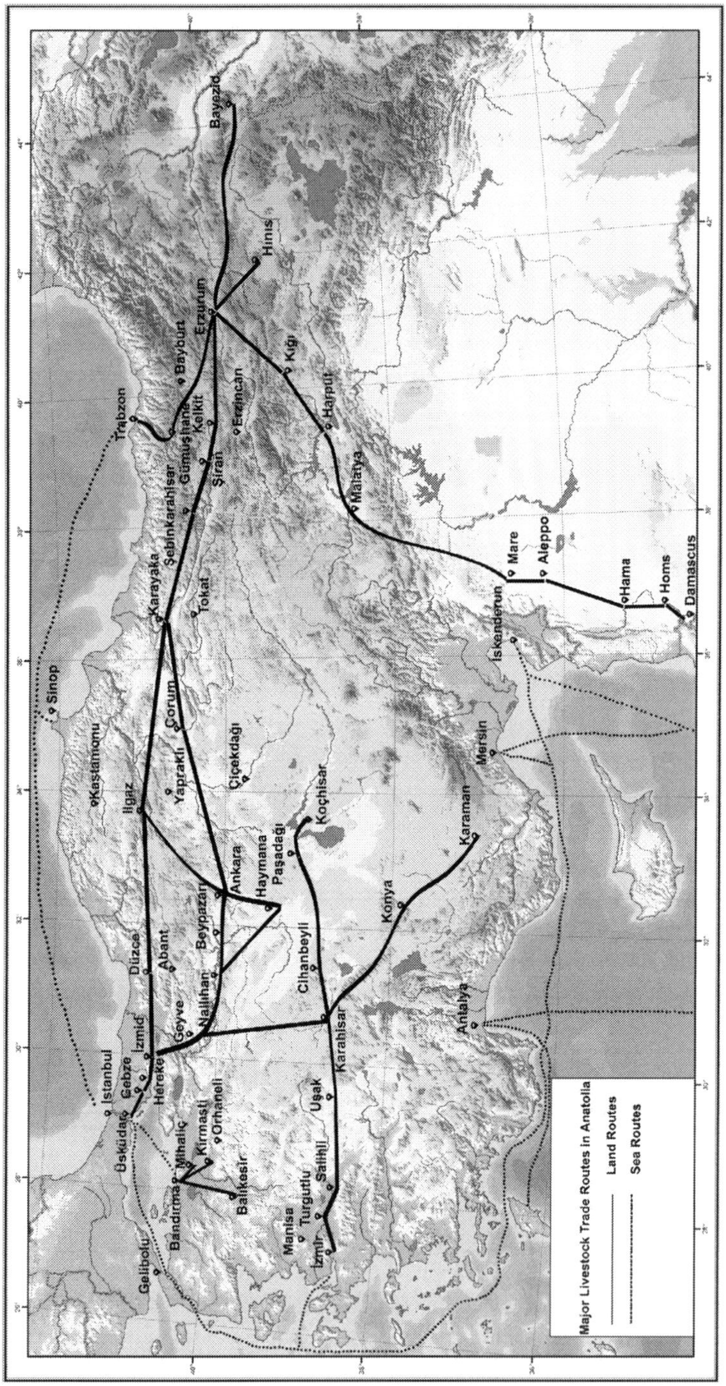

Map 1.1. Major Livestock Trade Routes in Anatolia

CHAPTER 2

Central Anatolia: An Established Supplier of Livestock to Istanbul

Abstract

This chapter examines the formation and operation of trade networks that connected central Anatolia, particularly the provinces of Ankara and Konya, to major urban markets through livestock exports. It demonstrates that from the late eighteenth century onwards, central Anatolian tribes had become one of the major suppliers of sheep to Istanbul. As part of its provisionist policies, by the 1790s, the government began assigning annual export quotas to the Cihanbeyli who controlled the livestock trade of its seven affiliated tribes and formed a sophisticated trade network to fulfill their quota requirements. This system remained in place until the late 1860s, when considerable progress was made in the settlement of the Cihanbeyli and other tribes, and in liberalizing trade. Despite frequent environmental calamities, affecting both human and non-human inhabitants, central Anatolia remained a major exporter of sheep in the late nineteenth and early twentieth centuries. The chapter argues that this enduring role was due, on one hand, to government policies that allowed tribes to sustain their mobile ways of life and trade networks and, on the other hand, to the resilience and adaptability of local livestock raisers and merchants to changing socioeconomic conditions. In addition to tribal trade, the chapter also presents examples of local landholders and their capital accumulation in livestock trade.

Keywords: Ankara; Konya; the Cihanbeyli; the Reswan; tribal settlement; famine; trade networks

Among the centers for animal trade in Asia Minor, central Anatolia emerged as the most well-known as it was famous for its Angora goats and mohair (*tiftik*), a soft fabric produced from the hair of these goats.[1] While both had commercial value on a global scale, they were not the only source of wealth in the region. As the nineteenth century unfolded, sheep, together with wheat, gained importance, and this did not go unnoticed by Ottoman and foreign observers.[2] A French traveler to the district of Haymana in 1861, for instance, noted that tribes there were heavily involved in the export of horses and sheep to Istanbul and various Anatolian cities.[3] About a decade later, in 1873, the head of the butchers' guild in Istanbul listed Ankara and Konya provinces among the major suppliers of meat to Istanbul.[4] Likewise, British consular officials reported an upward trend in sheep shipments from Ankara between the early 1880s and late 1890s.[5]

With this background, the current chapter examines the formation and operation of trade networks that connected central Anatolia, particularly the provinces of Ankara and Konya, to Istanbul through livestock exports. It first focuses on the period from the 1790s to the mid-nineteenth century, when the Cihanbeyli and the seven affiliated Kurdish tribes (Şeyh Bezenli, Mikailli, Zeyveli, Atmanlı, Seyfanlı, Terkanlı, and Geygel) were incorporated into Ottoman provisionist policies through a quota system.[6] Then it explores how this system ran into difficulties starting from the 1840s because of successive environmental and financial calamities and was finally abolished in the 1860s. Thereafter began a new era, one in which trade was liberalized but not unbounded. Its rhythms were, to a considerable extent, determined by weather extremes, disease outbreaks, and the sedentarization policies of the government. Although the first two caused serious disruption to trade, central Anatolia remained a major supplier of sheep to Istanbul during the half century preceding World War I. The chapter argues that this owed much to changes in trade networks and their organization, highlighting the roles of both human and non-human actors, such as tribal merchants, large landholders, and sheep. But before proceeding to these issues, an overview of the ecosystem including topography and transportation routes of central Anatolia is provided.

Landscape, Climate, and Roads

Central Anatolia occupies a critical region amid the Anatolian plateau, with its high mountains, aquatic systems, and vast plains and steppes. To the north, it is surrounded by mountains including Ilgaz, Aluç, Abant, and Bolu which has large areas of forest. In its west, the Sakarya River irrigates a large tract of country between Ankara and Eskişehir. There are also two major water bodies in the east and the south: the Kızılırmak River and the Salt Lake (Tuz Gölü). While the former set a natural boundary for the mobility of pastoralists and their animals, the latter replenished salt to the soil surface. To the south lie plains, both upland and lowland, stretching from Haymana to Karaman.

Central Anatolia has a semi-arid climate with low rainfall and cold winters.[7] These climatic conditions had two important consequences. First, the natural vegetation of the region was dominated by steppe plants. Second, life there was vulnerable to natural calamities, especially during times of reduced precipitation. Between the mid-1840s and mid-1870s, two major famines occurred, causing the death of tens of thousands of people and livestock in Ankara and Konya. Lack of adequate water supplies had been a sensitive issue not only during such calamities. Throughout the nineteenth century, one major complaint in the city of Ankara was the lack of fountains and regular water and irrigation networks. Several attempts were made to provide regular irrigation for farmlands in the countryside and water supply to the city.[8] But the impact of these attempts remained limited. In 1907, land under cultivation in Ankara and Konya provinces did not exceed 8 percent of the total land surface.[9]

As a large portion of rural populations in these provinces could not solely rely on agriculture for their living, they used steppes that spread across the region as pastureland to raise livestock. For instance, in the Haymana district of Ankara, an important supplier of sheep to Istanbul during the late Ottoman and early Republican periods, meadows and pastures amounted to 270,000 *dönüms* (67,500 acres), or about 16 percent of the district's land at the turn of the twentieth century.[10] Pastures also occupied a large area in the northern and western parts of the Konya province.[11] After touring the Axylon plain, close to Salt Lake, in 1909, an American geographer named Ellsworth Huntington wrote as follows: "The soil was strongly impregnated with salt, and the water of the brooks was somewhat saline. Irrigation concentrated the salt, as it always does, and after a few years rendered the ground unfit for plants of any kind except for coarse grasses."[12] These grasses formed a verdant plain that stretched "indefinitely on every side" and was thus used as grazing ground by herders.[13]

In the region's agriculturally more fertile areas to the east and west, there were large pastures and meadows fed by the Kızılırmak and Sakarya Rivers. After visiting Nallıhan in 1909, located on the shores of the Sakarya River, Ahmed Şerif, an Ottoman journalist, wrote that its lands were productive and fertile. Villagers, he continued, used a large portion of these lands as pasture for their animals.[14] In the district of Sivrihisar, located to the south of Nallıhan, there were plenty of pastures that spread over the sides of the Sakarya valley too.[15] Likewise, the northern parts of the region, particularly the mountainous border zone between Ankara and Kastamonu provinces, had fertile highland pastures used mostly during the spring and summer seasons. These highland and lowland pastures supported large populations of goats and *Karaman* sheep, which were well-adapted to the local climate conditions.

According to the official Ottoman statistics and British consular reports, during the forty-year period between 1873 and 1913, the total number of these animals ranged mostly from 2 to 3.5 million in Ankara province (see Figures 2.2 and 2.3). The situation was similar in Konya. Local authorities reported the sheep and goat population of the province in 1879 as 2.6 million.[16] According to the British vice-consul there, by 1905, this number had increased to some 3 million but then declined about one-third over the following years due to natural calamities.[17] As will be discussed in detail below, some of these animals were driven to Istanbul from spring to autumn to be sold for slaughter. The route they followed varied depending on their place of departure. For instance, those from the northern districts of central Anatolia, such as İskilip, were headed westward along the southern edges of Kastamonu province, and passing through Ilgaz, Gerede, Düzce, Hendek, brought to Gebze and ultimately to Üsküdar (see Map 1.1).[18] During this journey lasting for more than a month, merchants who wanted to keep their animals from losing weight took them for a few days, sometimes weeks, to highland pastures along the route.[19]

Likewise, merchants from Haymana and nearby districts often drove their flocks, weakened by winter hardships, north to the fertile highland pastures of Abant, Ilgaz, and Susuz in Kastamonu province.[20] When, after a certain grazing period, the journey to Istanbul started, there were two routes available. The first followed a northerly course and connected to the route from İskilip. The latter, and more popular one, which lasted about forty days, went south-westward, and after passing through Mudurnu, Nallıhan, and Taraklı, reached Geyve. From there, it proceeded northwest to İzmid, Gebze, and finally to Üsküdar.[21] Meanwhile, merchants exporting sheep from both northern (i.e. Cihanbeyli and Koçhisar) and southern (i.e. Bozkır, Ereğli, Karaman, and Karapınar) districts of Konya province used the district of Karahisar-ı Sahib (Afyonkarahisar in present-day Turkey) as a stop-over point. There they obtained information about meat prices in three major consumer markets – Istanbul, Bursa, and İzmir – to determine their eventual destination. Those who opted for the capital headed northward to Geyve and, once there, they began to follow the route taken by their Ankara counterparts.[22]

While these journeys could, for a long time, only be undertaken on foot, the arrival of the railroads in the latter half of the nineteenth century provided an alternative for central Anatolian merchants. The Anatolian Railway reached Ankara in 1892 and Konya four years later. In 1893, the Ankara line carried 8,550 head of sheep to the capital. The following year, this number increased to around 9,000, but in 1893 and 1894 rail shipments accounted for less than 5 percent Ankara's total sheep exports .[23] Over the following years, although railroads remained a minor mode of transportation, they began to play a more important role in connecting the Ankara and Konya merchants with the capital and other markets, thanks partly to the lowering of freight rates by the Anatolian Railway Company.[24] While, for instance, the sheep shipments from Konya aggregated over 100,000 heads in 1905, trains running on this line carried 20,000 of these animals to Istanbul. The rest were driven on foot to Karahisar and, as mentioned above, from there some headed to İzmir, passing through Salihli, a town in the district of Manisa with a station on the İzmir-Kasaba Railway. After a few days' stop-over in this town, some of the animals continued their journey on foot, while the others were loaded on İzmir-bound trains.[25] Thus, overall, rail shipments accounted for over 20 percent of Konya's exports in that year. This ratio, however, went down during the following several years, as harsh winters and poor harvests, combined with outbreaks of epizootics, decimated large numbers of sheep in central Anatolia. The British consular officials in Konya reported that in 1908, live sheep had been "much less exported than usual, only 5,000 going by train to Constantinople and Smyrna and 70,000 by road."[26]

While discussing trade routes and means of transportation, it is important to highlight the role of central Anatolia as a transit point. This role dated back to earlier centuries of the Ottoman Empire, thanks partly to the fact that Ankara was located on the ancient Silk Road. Although the previous importance of the Silk Road went through a relative decline in the period under study here, Ankara continued to serve as a center connecting several trade routes. For instance, in the 1780s, the Ottoman state authorities divided animal trade routes from Istanbul to Anatolia into three branches (*kol*), one reaching to Erzurum, another to Adana, and the third to Diyarbekir; and all passed through the province of Ankara.[27] While shipments from Adana and Diyarbekir declined to negligible levels in the following decades, the situation was different for Erzurum as will be discussed in the next chapter. Many merchants from northeastern Anatolia continued to drive their flocks through Ankara province on the way to Istanbul until steamship transport redirected the trade away from overland routes to the Black Sea in the late nineteenth century.

Through strong trading networks for sheep, central Anatolia remained well connected with Istanbul. In what follows, this chapter discusses the establishment and maintenance of these networks over a timespan of more than a century. It examines the role of a broad range of human and non-human actors such as government authorities, local notables, tribal chiefs and merchants, sheep, locusts, weather, and diseases in these processes. For this purpose, it focuses, first, on how Ottoman provisionist policies unfolded in central Anatolia from the 1790s to the mid-nineteenth century, a period when Istanbul came to increasingly depend on this region for meat supplies.

The Emergence of Central Anatolia as a Major Supplier for Istanbul

The increased role of central Anatolia in provisionist policies stemmed to a significant extent from the fact that Rumelia became a frequent scene of wars in the late eighteenth and early nineteenth centuries. During the Ottoman-Russian War of 1787–92, central state authorities issued orders to the *kadı* of Ankara to supply a certain number of sheep for the consumption of the troops collected by Cabbarzade Süleyman, a prominent local notable and the subprovincial governor of Bozok, when they were on their way to Istanbul.[28] Moreover, in 1792, the *kadı* received another order stating that as supplies from Rumelia had been used for provisioning the troops there, the population of Istanbul faced the threat of a meat shortage, which could be overcome by increasing shipments from Anatolia. To this end, the order concluded that sheep driven by Anatolian merchants to Istanbul should not be taxed en route.[29] This measure appeared effective in stimulating exports from central Anatolia. According to official reports, by August 1792 the Cihanbeyli tribe had brought 8,300 Karaman sheep to the capital.[30]

In the early 1820s, another military conflict flared up in Rumelia, resulting in the establishment of an independent Greek state. This also triggered a confrontation between Sultan Mahmud II (r. 1808–39) and his governor of Egypt, Mehmed Ali Pasha, that would last through the 1830s. After invading Syria in 1831, Egyptian forces under the command of Mehmed Ali's son İbrahim Pasha advanced into Anatolia and defeated the Ottoman troops in Konya only a year later. After the defeat, the Ottomans continued to maintain large numbers of troops in southeastern Anatolia to keep an eye on the movement of Egyptian troops and pacify uprisings in the region. Available evidence suggests that the district of Ankara was assigned an important role in the provisioning of these troops. In 1834, for instance, the head butcher in Istanbul was instructed to purchase 10,000 sheep from there at below-market prices for the imperial army.[31] Such purchases continued until the settlement of the conflict with Mehmed Ali Pasha in 1841, resulting in a steep rise in meat prices in Ankara in the late 1830s (See Figure 2.1). It is important to note here that the 1830s was not the first time that the office of head butcher collected sheep from Ankara. From 1805 onwards, the government ordered the population of this district to provide 1,200 sheep or their cash equivalent for use in royal shipyards. These orders, however, met with strong resistance. Ankara's residents often appealed to the sharia court, arguing that they did not have the means to fulfill what was expected of them.[32]

Meanwhile, central Anatolian tribes had already been integrated into provisioning networks that supplied the imperial capital with food. There were reports as early as 1795 that the head of the Cihanbeyli tribe undertook to bring 80,000 head of sheep to Üsküdar annually. In the following years, the government took a number of steps to formalize the role of the Cihanbeylis (and seven tribes under their leadership) in the provisioning of the capital and to facilitate their shipments. By the early 1820s, for instance, the sultan issued an order allowing merchants from the Cihanbeyli and affiliated tribes to use pastures en route to Istanbul free of charge. This order was preceded by an imperial certificate (*berat*) that established a new post of head trader (*tacirbaşı*), whose holder would be responsible for ensuring that the merchants in question supplied 80,000 sheep annually to the butchers of the capital.[33]

While the first head traders were appointed from among the chiefs (*mir*) of the Cihanbeyli, the heads of other tribes, who realized that the new post could endow its holder with political and economic power, soon began to emerge as rivals to them.[34] One such rival was Mehmed Bey, the head of the Şeyh Bezenli tribe. In 1816, he applied to the government for appointment as the head trader, arguing that while the current holder of the post, Halil Bey, the head of the Cihanbeyli tribe, was unable to fulfill the annual quota, he could organize the shipment of 120,000 sheep to Istanbul. Although his demand was accepted, Mehmed Bey's tenure did not last long. After failing to deliver the promised number of animals, he was replaced by Halil Bey with an order dated 1817. The order also established that, from that year on, the Cihanbeyli and affiliated tribes was to supply Istanbul with 100,000 sheep per annum.[35]

The competition and conflict between the Cihanbeyli and Şeyh Bezenli leaders continued in the following years until the murder of Mehmed Bey in 1825. Both sides mobilized their supporters to complain about the other party. While some merchants from the Şeyh Bezenli and several other tribes were claiming that they were oppressed by Halil Bey, the opponents of Mehmed Bey accused him of appropriating the sheep and goats of the poor members of his tribe.[36] Although the sources we consulted do not mention the reason for Mehmed's murder, it was possibly related to his rivalry with the head of the Cihanbeyli tribe. His inventory records suggest that the late Şeyh Bezenli chief collected sheep for shipment to Istanbul from not only nearby areas but also from eastern Anatolian tribes. According to these records, some of the animals in Mehmed Bey's possession belonged to a certain Abdulhayoğlu who was the head of the Merdisi tribe and one of the leading sheep merchants from Erzurum.[37] Quite possibly the succeeding leaders of the Şeyh Bezenli continued such relations after 1825, but unlike Mehmed Bey, they did not seek appointment to the post of head trader.

As the Cihanbeyli leaders consolidated their dominant position within the tribal hierarchies, central Anatolia's role in provisioning the capital increased further. By the early 1840s, the Cihanbeyli's sheep export quota was raised to 120,000 heads per year.[38] Meanwhile, several other tribal groups in the region were also involved in trade to Istanbul. Prominent among them were the Reswans. Some members of this Kurdish tribe migrated from eastern Anatolia and northern Syria to central Anatolia and maintained there a semi-nomadic existence with their flocks, moving between the Uzunyayla pasture near Sivas and Paşadağı between Ankara and Kırşehir.[39] While the Reswan merchants were not required by the government to satisfy a shipment quota, some of them collaborated with their Cihanbeyli counterparts and drove their sheep to the Istanbul market, simultaneously contributing to the provisioning of Bursa and nearby markets.[40]

The 1840s not only witnessed an increase in sheep exports to Istanbul but also presented a number of challenges to the human and non-human actors in central Anatolia. The Cihanbeyli and other tribes, who moved seasonally between upland and lowland pastures for their survival and livelihood, faced the threat of being deprived of their mobility. One of the main objectives of the Tanzimat reforms, beginning with the Gülhane Edict of 1839, was the settlement of tribal populations to increase agricultural production and tax revenues and to accelerate the trend toward universal military conscription. To make matters worse for tribes and other local actors, the early years of the settlement process coincided with a time of ecological stress in central Anatolia, as a famine struck in the mid-1840s. The following section explores the impact of these on local populations, both human and non-human, and on the livestock trade to Istanbul.

Settlement of Tribes and Accompanying Difficulties

Tanzimat policies towards tribes spread across a large area from Syria and Kurdistan to Cilicia and central Anatolia aimed at settling them permanently in many regions. This was part of a centralization policy where state control was expanded in provinces. Historically pastoralist tribes had close connections with the Ottoman state and urban markets, as suppliers of live animals and animal products such as leather and wool. They also at times served for the Ottoman army and security forces. With the Tanzimat reforms, however, their established ways of life came under serious challenge. While nomadism was identified with savagery in both government and intellectual circles, civilization increasingly came to mean permanent settlement.[41] That was largely because the centralizing and reforming Tanzimat state needed to extract increased tax revenues to finance its reform projects and conscript soldiers for the newly expanding army. Moreover, the elimination of criminal activities often associated with tribes, such as robbery and banditry, would increase security in the countryside and encourage both agriculture and trade.

One of the first targets of the sedentarization policy was the Reswan tribe, some members of which were accused of disturbing local security, production, and trade through criminal activities. In 1830, the governor of Konya, Esad Muhlis Pasha, suggested settling Reswan units in the provinces of Ankara and Konya, but plans along this line did not bear much fruit.[42] A second, and more successful, attempt came in 1848 when 3,000 households from this tribe were settled in Bozok, Ankara, and Sivas districts, and 500 households in Esbkeşan (today's Cihanbeyli) by military units.[43] According to a population survey in 1859–60, there were 463 Reswan households settled in forty-three villages in Haymana. Two decades later, this number dropped to 300. Meanwhile, however, Reswan settlements in Esbkeşan grew considerably, reaching 1,200 households in 1880.[44]

The 1840s also saw the beginning of efforts to sedentarize the Cihanbeyli tribe, whose current head, Alişan Bey, had been subject to complaints of unruly behavior.[45] In 1844, Rüstem Pasha, the inspector of the reforms in Anatolia, proposed a plan to settle the Cihanbeyli households by shifting authority away from Alişan Bey and toward the leaders of smaller tribal units.[46] In the years following this report, the sedentarization process of the Cihanbeyli and affiliated tribes seemed to

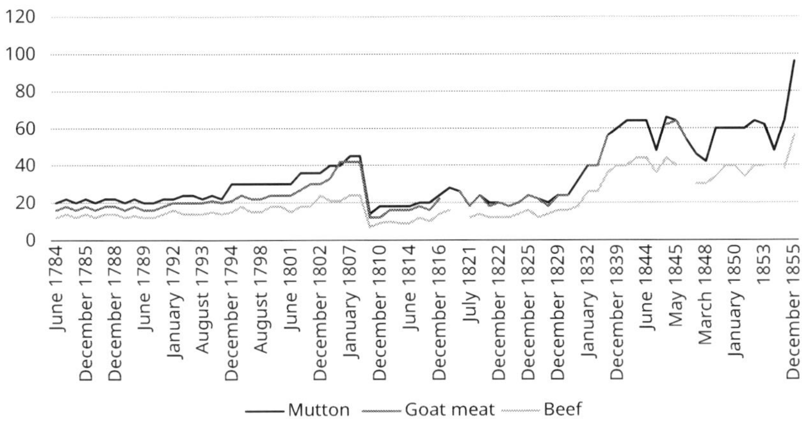

Figure 2.1 Ankara *Narh* Prices for Red Meat (in *paras* per *kıyye*)

proceed apace. By 1851, about 1,000 households from the Cihanbeyli, Şeyh Bezenli, and Mikailli tribes were settled in villages in the districts of Ankara, Konya, and Karahisar.[47] It is important to highlight here that this process coincided with a debt crisis facing the Cihanbeylis. In the early 1840s, Alişan Bey received a loan worth 2.1 million piasters (approximately 19,000 British pounds) from an influential Russian merchant named David Savalan, probably to organize the collection of sheep that the Cihanbeyli and affiliated tribes had to send to Istanbul annually, but he failed to repay it.[48]

This failure resulted, in part, from ecological stress. The dryness that began in central Anatolia in the late 1830s climaxed in a serious drought in 1845, causing poor harvests and famine in that and the following year.[49] While many people died of starvation, many others sought to flee from the famine-stricken areas to ones that they thought were safe. British consular officials reported that at least 6,000 people perished en route from Ankara to Bursa. Likewise, according to Ottoman official records, of the total of 516 Cihanbeyli households settled in Konya and Karahisar, 123 resorted to migration to survive the famine. Livestock herds in the region also suffered greatly. For instance, in just one year, from 1845 to 1846, the oxen population in the district of Kangırı decreased by half.[50] A similar fate befell the large sheep populations across the region, resulting in a surge in prices. According to the *narh* registers of Ankara, the retail price of mutton was forty-eight *paras* per *kıyye* (1.28 kg.) in June 1844, with forty *paras* equivalent to one piaster. In May of the following year, however, it reached sixty-four *paras* (See Figure 2.1).

Under these conditions, it became quite difficult for merchants from the Cihanbeyli and affiliated tribes to maintain the flow of livestock exports to Istanbul.

Shipments likely experienced a sharp decline in 1845 and 1846, leading to the insolvency of Alişan Bey. This, in turn, triggered a long-lasting conflict between tribal merchants and David Savalan. Determined to recover his loan, Savalan, through his agents in the capital and other cities such as Bursa and İzmir, began to confiscate sheep marketed not only by tribes affiliated with the Cihanbeyli but also by the Reswan merchants. In response, tribal leaders threatened to stop sending sheep to Istanbul and thus forced the government to appoint officials to oversee debt payments and prevent the escalation of the situation. Despite that, in the late 1850s, there were still merchants who complained of the confiscation of their animals by the agents of the Russian merchant.[51]

This debt crisis had two major consequences for the Cihanbeyli and affiliated tribes. First, it contributed to the loss of prestige for Alişan Bey, thereby accelerating the sedentarization process. In 1852, Alişan was dismissed from his position as tribal head, and about eight years later, the autonomous administrative status of the Cihanbeyli was abolished. Thereafter, households from this and affiliated tribes began to be incorporated into the towns and villages where they had settled over the preceding two decades.[52] Second, recognizing that the debt crisis had the potential to disrupt the meat supply of the capital, the Ottoman central authorities began to question the efficacy of the quota system imposed on the Cihanbeylis. Their uneasiness grew in the latter half of the 1850s and early 1860s when meat prices in Istanbul showed a marked upward tendency because of the Crimean War and subsequent monetary crises. At least several times during this period, exports from central Anatolia remained quite low.[53] In response, the government abolished the quota system by the late 1860s.[54]

These developments marked the beginning of a new era, in which market forces would play a greater role in determining the organization and level of sheep trade between central Anatolia and the capital. Until then the government had carefully monitored the movements of the Cihanbeyli merchants to prevent them from diverting their exports to markets other than Istanbul, such as Bursa and İzmir. With the abolition of the quota system, this practice was abandoned.[55] Merchants were now free to choose where to sell their animals. However, the new era also brought its challenges and difficulties. The decreased mobility of tribes due to sedentarization had the potential to result in a reduction in the size of their flocks. To make matters worse for tribes, the process of sedentarization went hand in hand with the enclosure and commodification of pastures on which they had customary rights. In 1889, a certain Abdullah – identifying himself as a member of both the Cihanbeyli and Zeyveli tribes – petitioned the office of the Grand Vizier, complaining that the imperial order that allowed merchants from these two tribes to use pastures along their route to Istanbul free of charge was ignored by both the government and private landholders.[56] Besides all these, livestock populations and trade were threatened by calamities that plagued the region from the early 1870s to the 1900s, a period that the following section will focus on.

Droughts, Severe Winters, Diseases, and Other Calamities

In the early 1870s, central Anatolia was hit by a severe famine, resulting from a wave of drought that affected many parts of Eurasia. Hot and exceedingly dry summers followed by harsh winters led to harvest failures and, ultimately, famine in the region in 1873–75. Between 100,000 and 250,000 people died of starvation and many survivors migrated to distant places such as Adana and Maraş in search of food.[57] The famine also proved disastrous for livestock populations. According to British consular officials, in 1872 there were more than 3 million sheep and goats in Ankara province, but this number decreased to around 800,000 in 1875 (See Figure 2.2).[58] Likewise, in the fall of 1874, the governor of Konya reported that the famine claimed the lives of about 2 million sheep and goats and many camels in his province. To save their animals, some herders and merchants drove them to places, such as Aleppo, Diyarbekir, and the Taurus Mountains, which were untouched, or less affected, by the famine.[59] Meanwhile, some others tried to convert their flocks into money before they perished. In October 1874, the *Levant Herald* reported that there were large numbers of sheep and goats brought to Istanbul from Anatolia by Kurdish shepherds. Due to "drought and scarcity of forage," the report continued, "they are in such a condition as to be but of indifferent use in supplying the butchers of the capital."[60] However, their owners could still realize large profits from the sale of these animals. They purchased them at low cost from local herders desperate for cash to meet their daily needs, while meat prices in Istanbul rose with the outbreak of famine.[61]

In the famine-stricken provinces, a recovery in the number of sheep and goats began in 1876 but slowed down in the early 1880s because of abnormal weather conditions that struck central Anatolia, along with eastern and northwestern parts of the peninsula (see Figure 2.2). A British military official traveling from Sivas to Ankara in the winter or early spring of 1880 wrote the following about the situation in Ankara province: "The winter has told severely upon the goats which produce the mohair. Whilst at Angora I was informed that between thirty and forty percent had died and the heavy snowstorms which I met with afterward on my journey from Angora to Ismid must have killed many more. There are no kids this year, and the cattle and sheep have also suffered."[62] This severe winter was followed by a locust invasion in the region. In June, the British vice-consul in Konya wrote the following about the situation in the province: "The locusts are making considerable progress in this vilayet. They have now spread as far as … a village to the north-west of Bor in the east of the vilayet."[63] The same month, his counterpart in Ankara reported that in the districts of Mihalıçcık and Beypazarı, one-fourth of the growing crops had been destroyed by a plague of locusts, leaving little forage for livestock.[64] According to a later report from Ankara, by the end of the year, the locusts "took almost entire possession of the province, destroying all vegetation."[65]

While their livestock were suffering from cold weather and food shortages, herders and merchants also found themselves hard-hit by the financial crisis facing the Ottoman Empire. Desperate for cash following its default in 1875, the government issued large sums of paper money, especially during the Russian War of 1877–78. This monetary expansion caused a sharp fall in the value of paper money and an inflationary spike. As a result, livestock merchants began to show a strong reluctance to bring their animals to the market. In response to these troubles, the government announced in 1879 that it would withdraw the paper currency from circulation by requiring 80 percent of taxes to be paid in coins. Because of this decision, trade remained disrupted for several more years, after which there came a recovery.[66] However, the situation turned bleak again when a drought struck Ankara and Konya provinces in 1886–88. The shortage of fodder, due to dry weather conditions, resulted in the death of many livestock. It also made survivors weak and vulnerable to diseases. In the late 1880s and early 1890s, cattle plague, which was a contagious and commonly fatal disease of cattle, goats, and sheep, was reported to be prevalent in central Anatolia. These conditions exerted a disruptive effect on trade flows. In November 1887, three merchants – one of whom was from the Cihanbeyli tribe and another from the Reswan – filed a petition complaining that because of the drought, the number of sheep exported from Ankara and Konya provinces to Istanbul remained small in that year.[67]

Central Anatolian trade suffered another blow when cholera hit the region in 1894. The disease entered the Ottoman Empire a few years before, during the Fifth Pandemic that swept through Asia and Europe and caused an immediate decline in shipments of live sheep from the Black Sea coast to Istanbul.[68] As Ankara and Konya provinces were by then largely untouched by it, merchants from there seemed to play an increasingly important role in the provisioning of the capital. In September 1893, for instance, the Istanbul Municipality proposed that the government award decorations to three Reswan merchants (Osman Efendi, İskender Bey, and Mustafa Ağa) for their efforts to keep meat prices in the city from rising.[69] Shortly thereafter, however, things changed. Before the autumn of 1893 had ended, cholera appeared in Eskişehir and then spread over a broad area. In response, the government, began to enforce a cordon sanitaire in the region through quarantine stations.[70] In the summer of 1894, those driving sheep from Ankara and Konya to Istanbul had to undergo an eleven-day quarantine before leaving these provinces and again at Adapazarı. The lifting of this measure following the retreat of the

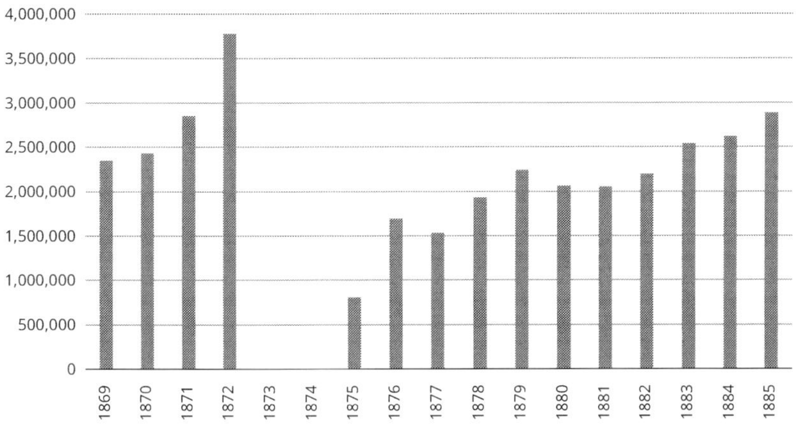

Figure 2.2 The Number of Sheep and Goats in Ankara Province, 1869–1885 (According to British Consular Reports)

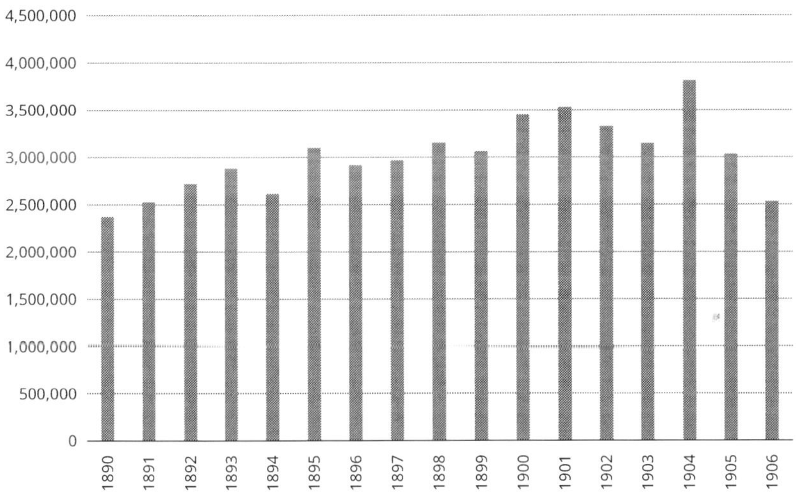

Figure 2.3 The Number of Sheep and Goats in Ankara Province, 1890–1906 (According to the Provincial Yearbook of 1325 [1907])

disease from central Anatolia in September of that year brought sheep merchants and their shepherds some relief. Yet, it was short-lived. In early November, an outbreak of cholera took place in İzmid, and all persons passing through this district en route to the capital began once again to be subjected to eleven days' quarantine. These restrictions caused a substantial decline in trade volume. According to Istanbul municipal officials, between mid-March and mid-October 1894, about 273,000 head of sheep and goats were brought to the city for slaughter, a decline of 35 percent from the same seven-month period in the previous year.[71]

This calamity was soon followed by an epizootic outbreak. In the early 1900s, cattle plague ravaged many parts of the empire, including Ankara and Konya. As a result, sheep and goat populations in both provinces suffered heavy losses (see Figure 2.3).[72] To make matters worse, there were at least two severe winters during this period. In May 1907, the Ministry of Interior noted that in total about 1.5 million sheep and goats in Ankara and Konya were decimated by cold, starvation, and disease.[73] The livestock trade did not remain unaffected by these developments. According to British consular officials, sheep shipments from Konya fell from around 123,000 heads in 1906 to 75,000 in 1908.[74]

Notwithstanding such setbacks, central Anatolia maintained its role as one of the major suppliers of meat to Istanbul and İzmir during the late nineteenth and early twentieth centuries. In the mid-1880s, it was sending nearly 200,000 sheep to the capital annually.[75] Between 1893 and 1898, average annual exports from Ankara were about 126,500 heads.[76] Available evidence suggests that shipments continued at a high level during the following years. In November 1902, the governor of Ankara sent a telegram to the Ministry of Interior, noting that in the following spring 50,000 sheep could be sent from Haymana to the capital. In the same month, his counterpart in Konya reported that the province was supplying a large number of sheep for the butchers in Istanbul, İzmir, and Bursa. From 1903 to 1906, its annual exports to these markets did not seem to fall below 100,000 heads.[77] Although the trend was reversed in the next several years, sheep remained one of the province's major export commodities.[78] This dynamism owed much to the continued importance of animal husbandry to rural livelihoods, even after the settlement of the large tribes in the region, as well as to the efforts of local merchants and the government to maintain trade networks.

Tribal Populations after the Settlement

The early days of the settlement were traumatic both for tribes and their animals. Even though the state provided some incentives to encourage tribe members to engage in agricultural production such as land for cultivation and the right to keep their cattle and sheep, a major complaint among tribes was the lack of pastures for feeding their livestock and land for agriculture.[79] Tribal units were sometimes settled next to villages where farmlands and pastures were available. However, local villagers were unlikely to share their limited resources with the newcomers. For example, the Reswan notables settled in Bozok frequently appealed to the state authorities about their inability to feed their livestock and demanded resettlement in the Haymana region where pastures were abundant.[80] The Reswan and Cihanbeyli units, who were settled in a scattered area ranging from the provinces of Sivas to Konya, frequently deserted their settlements and escaped to their former pastures. This led the Ottoman state to resort to military force to prevent their movement.[81]

The settlement process, however, did not completely eliminate the mobility of tribes. Tribal units that were fortunate enough to be settled in the vicinity of their former pastures could still use them. After a visit to Katrancı village, a major Mikailli settlement in the district of Haymana, in 1861, French archaeologist Georges Perrot wrote that its residents spent the entire summer in pastures not far from the village. These people, he concluded, made a living mainly through livestock breeding and exports.[82] An early twentieth century traveler to Ankara likewise noted that Kurdish tribal populations settled in villages in Bala, Haymana, and Cihanbeyli still spent almost half the year in highland pastures.[83]

Some tribal units with well-established trade networks to Istanbul were allowed to undertake longer seasonal migrations. Among them were 250–300 households from the Zeyveli, a major supplier of sheep to the capital within the Cihanbeyli's sheep supply network in the early nineteenth century.[84] These households were settled in Kuruçay, a village in the district of İskilip, and its environs. They spent their winters there and set off in early spring for the Karakaya and Yapraklı highland pastures in the district of Kangırı. After staying in these pastures for one and a half months, from mid-May to late June, to graze their animals, they headed northwest to the Ilgaz Mountains to spend the rest of the summer and early fall. While leaving Ilgaz in mid-September, the members of the tribe were divided into two groups. Some among them drove their sheep to Istanbul for sale, and the rest headed back to İskilip for the winter season.[85]

The Zeyveli households could for a long time maintain cordial relations with settled populations along their migration route. According to an official report, there were, by the late nineteenth century, strong trade ties between them and the residents of Tuht, a town located on the southern foothills of the Yapraklı Mountain. Moreover, some tribal children were allowed to pursue religious education in Tuht in return for donations to mosques and madrasas there.[86] However, things soon turned sour as competition over land suitable for cultivation and grazing intensified, particularly with the arrival of thousands of refugees from the Caucasus, Crimea, and Rumelia to central Anatolia from the 1850s onward.[87] Although the Zeyvelis had an imperial order dating to 1824 that granted them grazing rights to the aforementioned highland pastures, the residents of Tuht and nearby villages mobilized to prevent their entry to Yapraklı. They obtained a decision to that effect from the local administrative council of Kangırı in 1901 and quickly engaged in the appropriation of the tribal pasture lands for their own use.[88] In response, the Zeyvelis appealed this decision to higher government authorities, complaining that their flocks, now forced to spend the entire year in Kuruçay and its environs, were being depleted due to the lack of water and forage during the dry summer seasons.[89] Ottoman official records indicated that this complaint was well-founded. In the four-year period between 1901 and 1904, the number of sheep possessed by the Zeyveli households decreased sharply from around 10,500 to 3,790.[90]

Eventually the issue came before the Council of State. In 1903, it ruled that in accordance with long-established custom and the imperial order dated 1824, the Zeyveli households should be allowed to graze their animals on the pasture of Yapraklı.[91] This decision, however, did not go uncontested. When the Zeyvelis headed to Yapraklı in early spring 1904, they found their way blocked in Yüklü, a village close to Tuht, by the residents of this town and nearby villages. As local government officials failed in their efforts to mediate the dispute, a violent clash broke out between the two sides, resulting in one casualty and thirty-one injuries.[92] Although tensions continued over the following years, both central and local authorities permitted the Zeyveli households to maintain their grazing rights on Yapraklı and Ilgaz pastures, at least until the end of the Hamidian period, so as not to endanger the meat supplies of Istanbul.[93]

It is important to note here that even long after their customary rights to grazing were removed, some central Anatolian tribes continued to undertake long seasonal migrations. In an interview in the 1940s, a tribal leader from Konya stated that because forage became increasingly scarce there in winter, they rented pastures in the district of Aydın. Their animals were grazed on these pastures for six-seven months and then driven to markets in Istanbul and İzmir.[94] This continued (short- and long-distance) mobility helped tribal populations, particularly their elites, maintain large flocks of livestock. Perrot, for instance, noted that the chief of Katrancı village possessed great wealth in sheep and pack animals.[95] Likewise, by the early 1920s, a Reswan notable from Haymana, named Mustafa Bey, reportedly had tens of camels and thousands of sheep and goats. He also possessed large tracts of land, like most of the major livestock producers in the region.[96]

The sedentarization of tribes influenced the organization of the sheep trade and threatened especially the role of head traders as well. With the abolition of the tribal chief position, the Cihanbeyli leaders lost their monopoly on the post of head trader, which was not eliminated outright after the end of the quota system in the 1860s. The post remained in operation until 1882, but over the preceding two decades, duties assigned to its holders were changed to ensure that tribal merchants continued their trade with Istanbul. In the 1860s, head traders, still appointed from among the Cihanbeyli members, began to function primarily as Istanbul agents for central Anatolian (tribal and non-tribal) merchants, who brought their flocks to Uzunçayır, the major marketplace for Anatolian sheep driven overland to the capital. They, or in their absence their deputies, were expected to find customers for these flocks and to take an active part in negotiating the sale price and other contractual terms. Once a deal was struck, merchants often received advance payment from the purchasing butchers and returned to their home provinces.[97] Then it fell to the head trader to settle their accounts with the butchers.[98]

Although some of them claimed the contrary, head traders did not provide these services without pay.[99] In 1861, a group of Cihanbeyli merchants filed a petition complaining that contrary to the established rules, the head trader Ali Ağa had recently taken forty of their sheep without payment.[100] Documents from the 1870s and 1880s identify the relationship between a sheep merchant and his head trader as a contractual arrangement. For example, in a report dated May 1874, the Istanbul Municipality noted that head traders who guided merchants in handling their business in Istanbul received payment in-kind, one sheep from every flock brought into Uzunçayır.[101] This arrangement, agreeable to many of the merchants as it allowed them to continue their trade with Istanbul, rendered the position of head trader lucrative.

Consequently, intense competition rose among various actors, including not only Cihanbeyli members but also non-tribal entrepreneurs, for the position.[102] To gain an advantage against their rivals, these individuals often encouraged the Cihanbeyli notables and Anatolian merchants to submit petitions in their favor. In mid-1867, five Cihanbeyli merchants filed a complaint against the incumbent head trader, Süleyman Ağa, advocating for his replacement with Ali Ağa, an itinerant butcher in Istanbul. A few months later, another petition proposed a certain Süleyman Efendi as an alternative candidate. In response, the Istanbul Municipality noted that these petitions represented only a minority of sheep merchants, delaying a decision until the spring of 1868, when a new head trader would be appointed with the majority's consent.[103]

By the late 1870s, head traders began to face intense criticism from municipal officials in Istanbul for their alleged role in surging meat prices, as will be discussed in detail in Chapter 6. In a report to the Ministry of Interior in December 1882, the officials ultimately proposed abolishing the post and transferring its responsibilities to the municipality. The Council of State approved the proposal, which was forwarded by ministry bureaucrats, leading to the dismissal of the incumbent head trader, Ömer Bey of the Cihanbeyli tribe.[104] Notwithstanding the protests of some tribal merchants, the government persisted with its decision.[105] Despite their significant role in this development, municipal authorities failed to promptly fill the resulting vacuum. A certain Hacı Ali Rıza Efendi from Eğin, who had been the tenant of the Uzunçayır meadow since 1884, took advantage of the situation, claiming to replace Ömer Bey and receiving payments from merchants for his services.[106] Despite complaints voiced against him, Ali Rıza managed to establish himself as a de facto head trader, aided by his relationships with Anatolian merchants and his previous experience as the steward (*kethüda*) of the butcher's guild.[107]

One factor that aided Ali Rıza in establishing himself as a de facto head trader was that even experienced merchants sometimes required assistance while conducting business in Istanbul.[108] Additionally, prior to becoming the tenant of the Uzunçayır meadow, he had earned the trust and support of Anatolian merchants, particularly those from Ankara province. In his earlier career as the steward of the butcher's guild, Ali Rıza likely provided valuable services to them, such as offering information about butcher reputations and market conditions in exchange for payment. This, in turn, influenced nine Ankara merchants, seven of whom were Muslims and two non-Muslims, to petition in December 1873 for his appointment as head trader.[109] However, this proposal was declined by the Istanbul Municipality on the grounds that Ali Rıza had improperly served as guild steward and was consequently dismissed from office.[110]

Following his dismissal, Ali Rıza began (or resumed) a career in the civil bureaucracy. Within several years, he became the district governor (*kaymakam*) of Haymana where he stayed until the fall of 1879. This position allowed him to forge closer relations with sheep merchants from Ankara province.[111] Upon his return to Istanbul in the early 1880s, these merchants regarded him as a reliable intermediary in their dealings with butchers. In April 1887, sixty of them, mainly from tribes such as Mikailli, Şeyh Bezenli, Atmanlı, Reswan, Seyfanlı, and Hecibanlı, petitioned for Ali Rıza's appointment as head trader, citing his defense of their rights.[112] In response, the municipal council of Istanbul, acknowledging the vulnerability of Kurdish merchants from Anatolia to fraudulent practices by the city's butchers, recommended reinstating the post of head trader and appointing Ali Rıza, who enjoyed connections with Hamidian bureaucrats active in the Istanbul sheep market.[113] However, this decision was challenged when three merchants, two of whom being also from central Anatolian tribes, submitted a petition to the Grand Vizierate in November 1887, accusing Ali Rıza of various wrongdoings, which included charging high grazing fees and misguiding provincial merchants in the capital.[114]

The Istanbul Municipality initiated an investigation committee to probe these allegations, interrogating twenty-one individuals, including sheep merchants, butchers, and municipal officials. Testimonies revealed instances where Ali Rıza induced merchants to sell their sheep to deceitful butchers, resulting in their financial loss.[115] Consequently, the municipal investigation committee released a report in March 1888 highlighting the need to protect sheep merchants against Ali Rıza's exploitative practices. This led the Istanbul Municipality to reverse its decision concerning the reinstatement of the post of head trader, leaving Ali Rıza's ambition to be appointed as its holder unfulfilled.

Testimonies from this investigation show that, apart from complaints against Ali Rıza, an important factor behind the municipality's decision was that by the 1880s, some tribal merchants had established themselves in Istanbul and begun operating without the need for an outside agent. Prominent among them were two brothers named İbrahim and Abdullah. Residing in Konya in the mid-1880s, İbrahim made sheep purchases in and around this province and arranged for their shipment to the capital. When a shipment reached Istanbul, it was the responsibility of Abdullah, who had settled there a while ago, to take care of the arriving animals, undertake their sale, and keep accounts of all expenditures and revenues. This division of labor enabled the brothers to engage in large-scale trade. According to Abdullah's testimony, from March 1884 to February 1885, İbrahim sent more than 5,000 sheep to Istanbul.[116] The following years saw the rise of numerous other central Anatolian merchants, who reached and even exceeded this level by operating in the same way as İbrahim-Abdullah or working through outside agents. As discussed above, three of them caught the attention of Istanbul municipal officials during the cholera outbreak in 1893. Not long after, in 1900, two others, Derviş Bey from the Cihanbeyli tribe and Haydar Bey from the Seyfanlı tribe, received decorations from Sultan Abdülhamid II (r. 1876-1909) for their efforts to keep meat prices down in Istanbul.[117]

At the turn of the twentieth century, a major supplier for these merchants was large landholders, involved in extensive livestock raising. The following stories of two such figures, Çayırlızade Hilmi Efendi and Emin (Sazak) Bey, show that their land accumulation practices often resulted in heightened social tensions and conflicts.

The Rise of Two Local Entrepreneurs

Çayırlızade Hilmi, who was born in 1867 into a wealthy farmer family in Beypazarı, began acquiring large tracts of land in the nearby district of Nallıhan, an important center for the production and trade of mohair and livestock, in his early twenties.[118] Within about a decade, he made considerable progress in this undertaking. In the late 1890s, thirty-four signatories from eleven villages in Nallıhan submitted a petition to the sultan, stating that Çayırlızade was an oppressor (*mütegallibe*) who seized their pasture lands, cut down their mulberry trees, and destroyed their livestock pens.[119] The petition did not go unheeded. In early 1901, the government appointed a committee composed of three officials to investigate complaints against Hilmi Efendi. Moreover, around the same time, it issued an order for his removal from Beypazarı to Ankara until the completion of the investigation.[120]

During the investigation, the committee interrogated about forty persons from Beypazarı and Nallıhan, including local notables, merchants, villagers, and police and gendarme officers. In their testimonies, most villagers reiterated the claim that Çayırlızade sought and often succeeded in seizing their farming and pasture lands. According to his opponents, much of Hilmi's success stemmed from his ability to develop close relations with higher government authorities. For instance, the testimony of Galatalızade Hacı Mehmed, a prominent merchant from Beypazarı, called attention to Hilmi's contacts with Memduh Pasha, who served as the governor of Ankara province in the early 1890s. Mehmed alleged that during a visit to Beypazarı, the pasha received a bribe of 150 liras from a mohair merchant for turning a blind eye to the handsome profits he made by selling his stock at inflated prices. According to Mehmed, this deal was struck with the mediation of Hilmi Efendi.[121]

Shortly after this visit, in 1895, Memduh Pasha was appointed as the Minister of Interior and remained in this position until 1908. During that fourteen-year period, Hilmi Efendi took full advantage of his connections with the pasha to extend his political influence. According to the testimony of a gendarme sergeant, he could remove those local officials who acted against his wishes. Likewise, a police officer stated that when his house was robbed, Çayırlızade had several people arrested, imprisoned, and interrogated at his residence under torture for about a month. Upon being asked by the investigation committee why he did not intervene in this lawless state of affairs, the officer replied that Hilmi held the reins of the government of Beypazarı in his hands, as he enjoyed protection from the Minister of Interior.[122] Despite such testimonies, however, Hilmi was not subjected to punishment by the aforementioned committee. In 1902, he submitted a series of petitions, asking for permission to return Beypazarı on the grounds that allegations against him were without merit and his absence, especially during harvest seasons, resulted in significant economic losses for him. The Ministry of Interior and the Grand Vizierate acceded to this demand and ended his forced stay in Ankara.[123]

After Hilmi's return to Beypazarı, land disputes between him and Nallıhan villagers continued unabated. For instance, the residents of Çayırhan village, located on the shores of the Sakarya River, filed petitions complaining that they did not have sufficient land for grazing their animals. This was because a few years ago Hilmi forcibly seized two large areas of pasture open to their use. In response to these petitions, the government appointed a new commission in 1904, composed of an official from the Ministry of Interior, another from the Office of Imperial Registry, and an engineer, to settle the case. After its investigations in the field, the commission ruled that since Hilmi held deeds to the disputed pasture lands, amounting to about 30,000 *dönüms* (7,500 acres), the villagers could not claim usufruct rights over them. However, this does not mean that the latter were deprived of their livelihoods. The land they held in their possession, totaling about 65,000 *dönüms* (16,250 acres), was more than sufficient for their grazing needs. Hence, the commission concluded, they were renting a portion of it to non-local herders.[124] The dispute in Çayırhan was halted after this ruling, but only temporarily. The Young Turk Revolution of 1908 ushered in a new phase of it.

The revolution, with its promises of liberty, equality, fraternity, and justice, gave Çayırhan villagers hope that notable figures, like Hilmi Efendi, would lose their grip on power.[125] During the latter half of 1908, they tried to win the support of the new government by identifying their foe with the old regime. In a petition addressed to the parliament, they argued that Hilmi Efendi illegally seized the pasture lands of their village with the backing of Memduh Pasha and the sultan's former first secretary, Tahsin Pasha.[126] However, rather than backing down in the face of such attacks, Çayırlızade quickly contrived to accommodate himself to the new regime and its ruling elites. When journalist Ahmed Şerif visited Çayırhan in December 1909, the villagers complained to him that Talat Bey, the Minister of Interior, was on the side of their foe.[127] Over the following years, similar complaints were made by other local figures, including government officials, who became involved in conflict with Hilmi Efendi.[128]

His connection with Talat Bey (later Pasha) allowed Hilmi to rise rapidly in politics. By March 1909, he had become a member of the Provincial Council of Ankara.[129] In 1912, he was elected to the Ottoman parliament as a candidate for the Committee of Union and Progress (CUP). Until the occupation of Istanbul by Allied forces in 1920, he served as a deputy of Ankara. Then he joined the nationalist movement under the leadership of Mustafa Kemal. He became a deputy in the Grand National Assembly and retained his seat there for about seven years, until 1927.[130] These positions further empowered him in his struggles against Nallıhan villagers. When his opponents in Çayırhan attempted several times in late 1908 and early 1909 to graze their animals on the village's disputed lands, the gendarmes intervened with force and dispersed them.[131] Around the same time, the governor of Ankara sent a report to his superiors in Istanbul noting that, according to the findings of the 1904 commission, Hilmi Efendi was the legitimate owner of these lands. Thus, no other person could claim grazing rights on them.[132] With this strong backing, Çayırlızade solidified his position as a notable landowner and became involved in large-scale agricultural and pastoral production. In a petition addressed in 1916 to the Ministry of Interior, he described himself as a farmer who was employing some 500 laborers, planting about 6.5 to 7.5 tons of seed annually, and herding ten flocks of sheep and goats.[133]

At the time this petition was penned, another major figure in the economic and political life of Ankara province was Emin Bey. Born in 1882 to a well-off family in the district of Mihalıççık, he grew into an entrepreneur with investments in different areas.[134] One of these was tax farming. For fifteen years, from 1903 to 1917, he farmed the tithes of several villages in Mihalıççık, Sivrihisar, and Nallıhan, often making handsome profits. Together with a partner, he also obtained a concession to exploit the Sazak and Karasakal forests for timber and established several sawmills in Mihalıççık.[135] Besides these ventures, Emin Bey continued the family business of animal husbandry and mohair production. Although the famine of 1873–75 decimated his flocks, Emin's father, Abdurrahman Ağa, was able to recover his losses within a relatively short period of time. By the end of the century, he possessed large tracts of land and 700–800 sheep and goats.[136] After taking over the business from his father, Emin managed to further expand the family's landholdings. In his memoirs, he noted that after the Young Turk Revolution, he began to seize the pastures of a Mihalıççık village, which had long been enclosed by several Armenian notables. Emin was able to do so in large part because he had been a notable member of the CUP branch in Mihalıççık since July 1908. This position allowed him considerable influence in local politics. Like Hilmi Efendi, he became a member of the Provincial Council of Ankara and served there for a long time. After World War I, he joined the nationalist movement, becoming a deputy in the Grand National Assembly.[137] With the political and economic power to appropriate new pasture lands, he was able to considerably expand his flocks. According to his memoirs, in the early 1920s, he had more than 2,700 head of livestock.[138]

The cases of Hilmi Efendi and Emin Bey serve as clear illustrations of the relationship between the evolution of market forces and the privatization of land tenure, which often led to conflicts. As market-driven production expanded, landowners sought to appropriate village pastures to bolster their profits from animal husbandry and agricultural activities. As Yücel Terzibaşoğlu and Alp Yücel Kaya argue, this encroachment on village pastures by large landholders was a deliberate strategy to steer peasant labor toward agricultural endeavors by restricting their ability to engage in animal husbandry.[139] Consequently, this trend exacerbated land tenure disputes across various regions of the Ottoman Empire. Chapters 4 and 5 will provide further examples of land tenure cases, particularly in northwestern and western Anatolia, shedding more light on this dynamic.

Conclusion

This chapter has shown that trade links between central Anatolia and Istanbul became firmly established by the early twentieth century. Policies adopted by the government played a key role in this process. From the late eighteenth century onwards, central Anatolian tribes had become one of the major suppliers of sheep to Istanbul. As part of its provisionist policies, the government began by the 1790s to assign annual export quotas to the Cihanbeyli and affiliated tribes. These eight tribes formed a sophisticated trade network to fulfill their quota requirements.

This system remained in place until the late 1860s, when considerable progress was made in the settlement of the Cihanbeyli and other tribes, facilitated by the 1845 famine.

What followed was an uneasy period for sheep, goats, and other livestock. Between the 1870s and 1910s, the region was hit by a series of often overlapping calamities, including droughts, famine, locust invasions, and diseases. Although these events led to many deaths and occasional contractions in trade, central Anatolia remained a major exporter of sheep to Istanbul. This was due, on the one hand, to government policies that allowed tribes to sustain their mobile ways of life and maintained the post of head trader, and on the other hand, to the activities of pastoralists and merchants in Ankara and Konya provinces. Some politically powerful local entrepreneurs had become owners of large flocks by accumulating landholdings at the expense of both peasants and notables. They, as well as smaller-scale livestock producers, were well connected with Istanbul and several other urban markets, thanks in large part to tribal merchants. Having developed different methods of running their ventures, these merchants significantly contributed to the growth of trade between the capital and its Anatolian hinterlands, together with their counterparts from neighboring regions. The next chapter focuses on the story of the eastern neighbor, where tribes likewise occupied a dominant position in livestock trade.

CHAPTER 3

Northeastern Anatolia: An 'Excluded' Region

Abstract

This chapter focuses on northeastern Anatolia, particularly the province of Erzurum, a major exporter of sheep and cattle to different parts of the Ottoman Empire, including Aleppo, Damascus, Egypt, and Istanbul, from the eighteenth to the early twentieth century. It highlights the dynamic nature of the region's trade networks, demonstrating how their direction and organization evolved over time. While exports to Istanbul increased by the early 1900s due to advancements in transportation technologies and heightened demand, shipments to the Syrian provinces experienced some decline. A confluence of demographic, economic, environmental, political, and technological factors also influenced changes in the organization of the trade. By the late nineteenth century, some Erzurum merchants began to run their businesses from Istanbul, coordinating through a network of agents and partners in northeastern Anatolia and other parts of the empire. This move allowed them to pursue their interests more effectively, thereby ensuring the continuation of trade networks between Erzurum and Istanbul. Alongside these issues, the chapter also explores how Erzurum's role as a major livestock exporter affected the lives of animals, specifically highlighting the difficulties they encountered at times of extreme weather and disease outbreak, as well as en route to markets.

Keywords: Northeastern Anatolia; Erzurum; the Hamidiye Light Cavalry; famine; disease; trade networks

A good portion of the literature on late Ottoman economic history examines the integration of the empire into the capitalist world economy. Studies on this topic draw attention to the role of major port cities and various export commodities, including mohair, in connecting the Ottoman hinterlands to imperial metropoles in Europe and America in the nineteenth century. Yet, they often fail to emphasize sufficiently the commercial and economic dynamism of regions such as eastern Anatolia, which were difficult to reach from metropoles and port cities and were not heavily involved in the production of such commodities. One leading scholar has hence asserted that eastern Anatolia "remained largely excluded from domestic and foreign markets."[1] Focusing on northeastern Anatolia, most of which was encompassed by the province of Erzurum, the current chapter seeks to challenge this view. It shows that, from the late eighteenth to the early twentieth century, this region maintained and even reinforced its position as a major supplier of sheep to

Ottoman urban markets. That was largely because provincial merchants managed to develop lucrative trade networks connecting Erzurum with transborder areas in the Caucasus, the Black Sea port of Trabzon, and major consumption centers in the southern and western parts of the empire. Following a brief overview of the historical literature on Erzurum, the chapter traces the evolution of these networks and shows that they were flexible enough to respond to changes in economic, political, and technological conditions and to calamities like severe winters, famine, and disease outbreaks.

Erzurum: A Story of Decline?

The historical narrative of Erzurum unfolds the rise and subsequent decline of a city and province located on the border with Russia and Iran. Both were reported as enjoying economic and demographic growth and prosperity under Ottoman rule starting in the 1520s. Being located on the Silk Road, the province served as a conduit for trade from the Caucasus and Iran to port cities with linkages to Europe such as İzmir, Trabzon, and Istanbul. This position, combined with stable Ottoman rule, made the province and the city of Erzurum a growing trade center in the period between the sixteenth and the eighteenth centuries. Transit trade which involved a complex set of actors – such as Ottoman officials, Turcoman and Kurdish tribes, and merchants of Armenian, Persian, Arab, and Caucasian origin – as well as customs revenues, constituted the major sources of income for the city. In this period, Erzurum also housed several manufacturing industries, including weapons production and iron casting. Industries based on animal husbandry such as textiles, tanning, and shoemaking were also important sectors in the region.[2]

Frequent eruptions of tension and conflict between the Ottoman and Russian Empires turned the situation upside down in the nineteenth and early twentieth centuries. The Ottoman-Russian wars of 1828–29 and 1877–78 caused considerable damage to the region. During the former conflict, Erzurum was occupied by the Russian army, causing damage to buildings and people. When the Russian troops withdrew at the end of the war, about 20,000 Armenians from the city and its surrounding regions left with them.[3] This had serious consequences because Armenians played an important role as traders and artisans in the economic life of the city. The 1877–78 war also resulted in the Russian occupation of the province, which dampened economic activity for a while. The ceding of Kars, Ardahan, and Batum to the Russians following the war made Erzurum an unstable border city. The fear of reoccupation among Ottoman officials, and their consequent prioritization of investment in security and the military over social, political, and economic reforms, continued until the end of Ottoman rule in the region. According to the dominant historiographic view, because of these developments Erzurum fell into stagnation and economic decline.[4]

However, the findings of recent studies have challenged this argument. Tolga Cora, for instance, demonstrates that there was an economic revival following the war of 1828–29. The Armenian merchants who left with the withdrawing Russian army after the war returned to the province a few years later, bringing with them their trade connections with Russia. Moreover, studies by Cora, Sarah Shields, and Yener Koç have illustrated that over the course of the nineteenth century, Erzurum maintained strong trade relations with the empire's Anatolian and Syrian provinces. All these scholars emphasize the pivotal role of livestock and livestock-related goods, such as dried meat (*pastırma*), leather, and soap, in the export trade of the province.[5] This chapter seeks to contribute to this body of scholarly work by examining how a group of human and non-human actors interacted to build and sustain networks of trade between northeastern Anatolia's ecosystem and major urban markets to the south and west. It provides a detailed (three-stage) analysis of the Erzurum sheep trade. The first section investigates how the livestock trade worked from the eighteenth to the mid-nineteenth century. It highlights the role of Erzurum as a major supplier to Syrian provinces and discusses the impact of Ottoman provisionist policies in connecting northeastern Anatolia and its environs to Istanbul. Then, the chapter explores the evolution of the region's trade networks from the 1860s to World War I, a period marked by important economic, political, and technological transformations, as well as environmental disruptions. The concluding section discusses the growing importance of Istanbul as a major market for northeastern Anatolian livestock from the 1880s onward and the resulting impact of this development on the organization of trade.

Trade Networks to the South and West

In the eighteenth century, the province of Erzurum covered the city and surrounding districts, and its governors had a right to exercise authority over the neighboring provinces of Kars, Çıldır, Van, and Muş. Following the promulgation of the Tanzimat, the borders of the province changed several times. It covered most of eastern Anatolia, including the above-mentioned areas, by the early 1870s, but thereafter gradually diminished in size.[6] First, the sub-provinces (*sancak*s) of Van, Bitlis, and Muş were administratively separated from it; then, following the Ottoman-Russian War of 1877–78, the Kars and Çıldır *sancak*s were ceded to Russia. Consequently, in the period from the early 1880s to 1914, the province was composed of the *sancak*s of Erzurum, Erzincan, Bayezid, and Bayburt in northeastern Anatolia.[7]

Even with its reduced size, the province of Erzurum was an important source of livestock in Anatolia. Its fertile upland pastures, scattered across the landscape and watered primarily by rainfall and melting snow, made the region suitable for animal husbandry.[8] A British military officer, for instance, noted in the early twentieth century that the Bingöl Mountains, located to the south of the Erzurum district, were "in winter as forbidding an abode as in summer ... a very paradise for the wandering nomad and his flocks."[9] With the term nomad, the officer was referring to pastoralist tribes with large flocks of sheep, goats, and cattle. These nomadic or semi-nomadic tribes based in the region took their animals between winter and summer pastures, just as their counterparts in central Anatolia and other parts of the empire. While doing so, they often passed the borders between Iran, Russia, and the Ottoman Empire.

During the sixteenth to early eighteenth centuries, various tribes shifted from their traditional migration patterns in Upper Mesopotamia. Instead, they began spending the entire year in the summer pastures and winter quarters of the north-eastern frontiers of the Ottoman Empire. Reasons for this change include tensions between the Ottomans and Safavids, over-taxation, and environmental factors such as the Little Ice Age, which caused droughts and famines. Additionally, the expansion of animal husbandry due to diminished cultivated land and oppression by local rulers played a role. The nomadic pastoralist tribes, lacking agricultural knowledge, relied on outsiders during snowy winters. By the early nineteenth century, many lacked permanent structures and depended on Armenian and Kurdish peasants for stables and hay. However, this reliance often led to strained relationships as nomads would coerce peasants into providing resources without proper compensation. One of these tribes was the Zilan.

In 1848, the Zilans forcibly established their families as guests in several villages in the Kagizman district. They appropriated straw, forage, and livestock from the locals and further expelled inhabitants from multiple villages, occupying their homes for winter.[10] Around the same period, 1,650 families from this tribe were spending winters in Revan (Erivan) in Russia and summers around Bayezid. Similarly, during the 1870s and 1880s, some Jalali households engaged in seasonal migrations between summer pastures in Bayezid and Van and winter encampments in Iran and Russian territory.[11] Like these tribes, sheep merchants travelled across borders to make purchases for shipment to Ottoman lands. Much of this inter-imperial trade passed through the Erzurum customs and pastures.

With relatively easy and secure access to large supplies, northeastern Anatolia became a major center of the sheep trade and sheep exports. During the period from the late eighteenth to mid-nineteenth century, Erzurum was a major supplier to Syrian and, at times, Egyptian markets.[12] Sheep marching from Erzurum to the south often followed the route through Kığı, Harput, and Mare to Aleppo (see

Map 1.1). While some remained there to be slaughtered, others continued further south.[13] James Grehan notes that most of the sheep sold in the Damascene markets in the 1700s came from Erzurum.[14] Likewise, according to a British consular report from 1839, Aleppo annually consumed between 55,000 and 60,000 sheep; about a third of this quantity was imported from Erzurum. Sheep from this district, so the report continued, were also sold in large numbers in Hama, Homs, and Damascus.[15] During this period, other important export markets of Erzurum were Istanbul and western Anatolia. As part of its provisionist policies, the government encouraged and sometimes forced the region's sheep merchants to bring their animals to the capital. Thus, a vibrant trade network began to take shape from at least the 1760s onwards. Below is a series of case stories that give insight into the relative importance of Erzurum for the Ottoman provisionist economy and offer a snapshot of the experiences of those merchants trading with Istanbul.

In 1768, the *kadı* of Erzurum reported that, as had been the case in previous years, herdsmen in the province would send a large number of sheep to the imperial capital.[16] It is, however, worth noting that when sheep merchants set out on a westward journey from northeastern Anatolia, they did not necessarily consider Istanbul their final destination. They often decided where to sell their animals based on information collected en route about prices in different cities and towns. In 1770, for example, the Ottoman central authorities received reports stating that when merchants driving 40,000 sheep from Erzurum and Iran to the imperial capital arrived in İzmid, they began to divert their herds to Aydın based on a rumor that prices were low in Istanbul.[17] According to another report in 1797, two merchants bringing 22,000 sheep from Erzurum diverged from the route to the capital and moved their flocks to Haymana, probably to make sales to the Cihanbeylis and other tribes.[18] Such reports caused grave concern among the authorities, especially at times when a sharp decline in shipments from Rumelia was causing shortages in the capital.

At such times, Erzurum, like the central Anatolian provinces, played a more important role in the supply of animals to the Istanbul market. In 1791, for example, the government issued a decree ordering the shipment of red (*kızıl*) sheep from Erzurum and Bayezid to Istanbul because the supplies in Rumelia were reserved for the use of the troops fighting against the Russians.[19] The early years of the nineteenth century also saw a marked decline in the number of Rumelian sheep reaching the Istanbul market because of consecutive wars with Russia, the Napoleonic wars, and the resulting territorial losses.[20] To alleviate the shortage, the sultan issued a decree to the governor of Erzurum, ordering the shipment of 60,000 to 70,000 sheep from there to the capital. In March 1802, the governor communicated this order to twenty-one prominent local sheep merchants who in turn pledged to supply the largest possible number of animals. One of these merchants was Ali Bey from the Abdulhayoğlu branch of the Merdisi tribe in Erzurum.[21] In this period, he, along with several other tribal and non-tribal merchants, was in the business of collecting sheep from Iran, Erzurum, and its nearby districts (Bayezid, Kars, and Van) and exporting them to Istanbul.[22]

However, in carrying out these activities, Ali Bey and the other merchants often encountered problems and difficulties. A major problem was competition from merchants based in the southern provinces. For example, the sultan's above-mentioned 1802 decree remained ineffective, as merchants from Aleppo, Raqqa, and Diyarbekir made large purchases in Iran, likely in the districts around Maku and Khoy, and deprived their counterparts trading with Istanbul of an important source of supply.[23] Another important problem was the poor transport infrastructure. The overland journey from northeastern Anatolia to Istanbul was a long one, lasting several months.[24] Sheep from the Iranian border and Van were first driven to Erzurum through Hınıs and Pasinler. The route from Erzurum to Istanbul went north-westward and, after passing through Kelkit, Şiran, and Karahisar-ı Şarki (Şebinkarahisar), reached the Karayaka district in Tokat. From this district, which served as a stop-over for sheep from the eastern provinces, the route forked. One branch continued northward and reached Üsküdar after passing through Gerede, Düzce, İzmid, Hereke, and Gebze.[25] As mentioned in the previous chapter, the rich pastures of Susuz, Ilgaz, and Yapraklı were located on this route. The other branch proceeded south to Çorum and Ankara, then moved northwest along Nallıhan and Geyve, merging with the former branch around İzmid (see Map 1.1).

Such a long journey could be undertaken only in certain seasons of the year. Harsh weather conditions during the winter months were prohibitive. In 1834, the Erzurum merchants, who were reported to have 44,000 sheep in their possession, stated to the government that if they were required to make shipments to Istanbul in winter, all their animals would perish en route.[26] To avoid such an outcome, merchants oftentimes drove their flocks, which varied in size from several hundred to 2,000, to the capital under the guidance of several shepherds from spring to autumn, when the roads were in better condition and plants for foraging were not scarce.[27] Even then, however, they had to deal with a variety of problems and threats, such as the loss of their sheep due to tribal raids on the way. In 1792, a group of Merdisi merchants complained that while passing through the district of Çerkeş in north-central Anatolia, they were not safe from raids by the Cihanbeyli or other tribes. In response, the government ordered the head of the Cihanbeylis to ensure safe passage for these merchants.[28]

As compensation for this long and arduous journey, merchants asked for tax exemptions, which were often granted by the government in order to ensure a steady supply of meat for the residents of Istanbul. The above-mentioned decree of 1791 ruled that the flocks of sheep moving from Erzurum and Bayezid to Istanbul would be exempt from taxes levied on the road.[29] Similar orders continued to be issued in the following years and decades, mainly because local officials and tax farmers acted contrary to them. For example, in 1803, a group of merchants filed a complaint against Mehmed Ağa, a senior tax official in Erzurum, for charging a transit tax on sheep driven from the districts of Malazgird and Diyadin, located between Van and Bayezid, to Istanbul. To urge the government to act, they argued that if Mehmed continued to have a free hand in taxation, the following year only a few merchants would make shipments to the capital. This argument proved persuasive, leading to the issuance of an imperial decree stating that flocks driven to the capital should be exempt from customs and various other taxes en route.[30]

Despite such regulations, in the following decades, local officials and tax farmers continued to levy various dues on sheep destined for Istanbul. This, in turn, elicited cries of protest from merchants. The governor of Erzurum, in order to appease them, asked for the exemption of those driving their flocks to Istanbul from all taxes levied on the road once they had paid the *ruhsatiye* (license tax) and *ihtisabiye* (market tax) dues, each amounting to two piasters per head of sheep. The central authorities responded positively to this demand and even went one step further by relinquishing the collection of the *ruhsatiye* in 1845.[31] Hence, until these two taxes were abolished in the early 1860s, merchants trading with Istanbul paid half as much as their counterparts driving sheep to other parts of the empire.[32] Such incentives played an important role in maintaining a steady flow of exports to Istanbul. By the early 1830s, the government required Erzurum province to supply the imperial capital with a minimum of 20,000 sheep per annum.[33]

However, over the course of the following two decades, fulfilling this shipment quota remained an uneasy task because of recurrent environmental hazards. The severe drought that struck central Anatolia in the mid-1840s also affected the northeastern parts of the peninsula. Cattle and sheep populations weakened by it suffered another blow in 1847 when the dry summer season, which resulted in a shortage of straw and hay crops in Erzurum, was followed by a severe winter and an outbreak of animal disease. Shortly afterwards, in 1852, an abnormally long winter exhausted the fodder supply in the province and caused considerable losses among cattle and sheep. In response, the government lowered Erzurum's minimum shipment requirement to 15,000 sheep, and it remained at this level until the 1860s when central authorities abandoned the practice of imposing annual quotas on Anatolian provinces.[34]

Nevertheless, this does not mean that Erzurum's sheep exports followed a downward trend during this period. On the contrary, Erzurum solidified its role as the primary supplier to the Syrian markets. According to a British consular report, in 1855, Aleppo imported 200,000 sheep from Erzurum, half of which were then forwarded to Damascus.[35] Merchants found these markets attractive mainly because the prices there were often higher than in the capital. To take one example: in the late 1830s, the price of sheep ranged between sixty-five and eighty piasters in Hama, Homs, and Damascus, while the Istanbul price varied from twenty-four to fifty piasters.[36] Even in years when this trend was reversed, shipments to Istanbul remained far below those to Syria.[37] This was mainly because merchants from Aleppo and Damascus had established a strong presence in Erzurum and nearby districts. One of them, Mehmed Ağazade Süleyman Ağa, is mentioned in an Ottoman archival document dated 1856. His story was likely representative of many merchants: He was originally from Erzurum but had settled in Damascus. Together with his shepherd(s) and several other assistants, he was traveling to his home district, most likely annually, to arrange the purchase of sheep and have them driven to Damascus.[38] Like many of his counterparts from the south, he probably had networks in Erzurum that enabled him to finance purchases on credit or through loans from prominent local creditors.[39]

Liberal Reforms, Military Defeat, and Environmental Disruptions

The above-mentioned abolition of the quota system in Erzurum (and central Anatolia) went hand in hand with liberal economic reforms concerning the organization and administration of consumer markets. As will be discussed in detail in Chapter 6, in Istanbul, the liberalization of regulations on the trade of principal foodstuffs, including meat, occurred mainly in the mid-nineteenth century. By the early 1860s, the government had abolished first the restrictions on entry to the butchery trade and then the practice of imposing a price ceiling on meat.[40] These moves were made with the expectation that free market conditions, combined with an upward trend in prices, would lead to an increase in sheep exports from the provinces to Istanbul, which in turn would bring down prices.[41] They, however, did not have an immediate effect on the volume of the sheep trade between northeastern Anatolia and Istanbul.

Over the course of the 1860s and 1870s, Erzurum's animal trade remained oriented towards the southern provinces. For instance, in his report for the year 1866, the British consul John George Taylor noted that the province of Erzurum exported 280,000 head of sheep, about half of which came from "Persian Koordistan and Russia." His list of major export markets included Syria, Egypt, which had been hit by an epizootic a few years earlier, and Kayseri but not Istanbul.[42] In a report filed with the Grand Vizierate in May 1864, the Administrative Council of Erzurum also highlighted the role of this province as the hub of trade networks that connected Ottoman markets with each other and with Russia and Iran. Local merchants and those coming from Syrian provinces annually purchased about 100,000 sheep from the districts of Erzurum and

Van and about the same number from Iran and Russia. Most of these sheep were exported to the Aleppo and Damascus markets, and a minor portion was sold to Istanbul.[43] Likewise, according to another report by Consul Taylor, most of Erzurum's sheep exports, amounting to 300,000 heads, ended up in Syria and Egypt in 1872.[44]

One reason for the low level of exports to Istanbul might be that merchants were deterred by the long and expensive journey. Despite orders to the contrary, government officials and tax farmers along the route continued to impose burdensome taxes on them. In 1859, the government abolished tolls and other taxes levied on sheep and instead imposed a single tax in their place, amounting to 1.5 piasters in Anatolian provinces per head.[45] Yet, a petition by a merchant named Elhac Mehmed shows that this decision did not immediately change practices on the ground. According to his complaint, when Mehmed was driving a flock of 1,200 sheep from Erzurum to Istanbul in 1860, the director of the İpsile (today's Doğanşar) subdistrict in Sivas forcibly took eighteen of his animals as a toll.[46] It is, however, important to note here that merchants trading with Aleppo and Damascus encountered similar problems. In 1862, an Erzurum merchant named Yusuf filed a petition complaining that while passing through the district of Hama, the Mevali and Tırki tribes had raided his flock and stolen 600 sheep. Although 150 of these animals were returned to him after he paid 9,000 piasters to the heads of the two tribes, he could not recover the rest.[47] According to a British consular report for 1863, merchants headed to Aleppo and Damascus were giving presents to influential people along the road, apparently to prevent such incidents.[48]

Another, and perhaps greater, obstacle to the growth of exports to Istanbul consisted of the substantial losses suffered by some Erzurum merchants due to fraudulent practices by their Istanbul customers. One of these merchants was Süleyman Aga, who struck a deal with a certain İstavraki for the sale of 943 sheep at 76.5 piasters per head and received an advance payment of 100 liras in December 1863. However, it shortly became apparent that İstavraki was a swindler (*batakçı*). He sold eighty-one of the animals at twenty to forty piasters per head. Upon being informed about this, Süleyman had Istavraki arrested by the police and the unsold animals returned to him by the Istanbul Municipality. At around the same time, however, he was ordered by the judicial authorities to return the advance payment he had received on the grounds that the money in question belonged to another person named Rüstem Ağa. Moreover, because they had not been fed properly by İstavraki, Süleyman's remaining sheep had lost a considerable amount of weight. He could thus sell them only at around forty piasters per head.[49] Quite possibly, during the 1860s, the Erzurum merchants experienced more such events than their central Anatolian counterparts because they then did not have a head trader to oversee their interests in the capital. As news about Süleyman Ağa and people like him spread quickly through Erzurum, most of the other merchants there became reluctant to make shipments to Istanbul.

Unfavorable political and climatic conditions in the late 1870s constituted a further factor that curbed livestock exports to Istanbul and other markets. A major event in this period was the Ottoman-Russian War of 1877–78, which placed a heavy strain on meat supplies in Anatolia, forcing the government to temporarily ban the export of sheep from Anatolian ports to domestic and foreign markets.[50] The loss of the *sancak*s of Kars and Çıldır also caused a certain amount of damage to animal husbandry in Erzurum, as they accounted for about 20 percent of the total goat and sheep population in the province.[51] Yet, the damage was partially mitigated by the fact that thousands of refugees who came from these districts to Erzurum after the war brought their livestock with them.[52] The inflow was evidently so large that it occasioned relief among government officials. Hence, while the government issued an order in 1880 banning the export of livestock from Van and Diyarbekir provinces due to a disease, probably a cattle plague outbreak, in eastern Anatolia, Erzurum was excluded from this ban.[53]

However, this feeling of relief was not well-founded. In 1879, Erzurum province, particularly its eastern part, was hit by a long and harsh winter, decimating the cattle and sheep populations. According to a May 1880 report by British Colonel William Everett, the Passin district lost about half of its oxen and 70 percent of its sheep population. The mortality among the animals was also enormous in Eleşgirt, located in the Bayezid *sancak*.[54] About four months later, he wrote that "the collection of the sheep tax in [Erzurum] in the present year was a notoriously iniquitous proceeding. Enormous numbers of sheep perished in the spring owing to want of food, but no allowance was made for them."[55] Similar weather conditions prevailed in the following year, causing further livestock losses (see Figures 3.1 and 3.2).[56] As one response to this calamity, the government imposed a ban on the export of livestock from Erzurum province in 1882. Although the ban was lifted the following year, exports remained considerably low. According to British consular reports, while the district of Erzurum exported an average of 40,000 sheep annually in the late 1870s and early 1880s, shipments in 1883 amounted to only around 25,000 heads.[57]

It did not, however, take long for recovery to take hold. Although Figure 3.1 shows a sharp drop in the number of sheep and goats in the postwar period, this was partly a result of territorial losses and the administrative reorganization of the province. While after 1877, the figures did not include Muş and Van, Kars and Çıldır were also excluded from the figures for 1879 and later. If these four *sancak*s are not considered for the pre-war period, the recovery in the remaining ones (Erzurum, Bayezid, Erzincan, and Bayburt) becomes visible. As Figure 3.2 illustrates, the number of sheep and goats in these remaining *sancak*s began to increase after 1882 and came close to prewar levels by the early 1890s. In 1894, only a year after a drought-triggered famine hit the province, the population of these animals was reported to be 1.5 million, roughly the same figure as in 1877.[58] Meanwhile, Erzurum

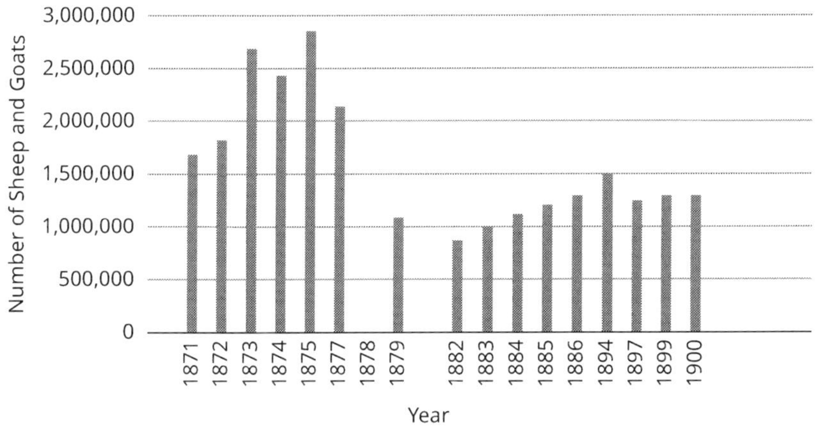

Figure 3.1 The Number of Sheep and Goats in Erzurum Province (1871–1900). Source: The data for the period between 1882-86 have been collected from *Trade and Commerce of Erzeroum Reports of the British Consulate*. The data for the other years have been taken from the provincial yearbooks and BOA, İ.MMS 65/3070, doc. 3.

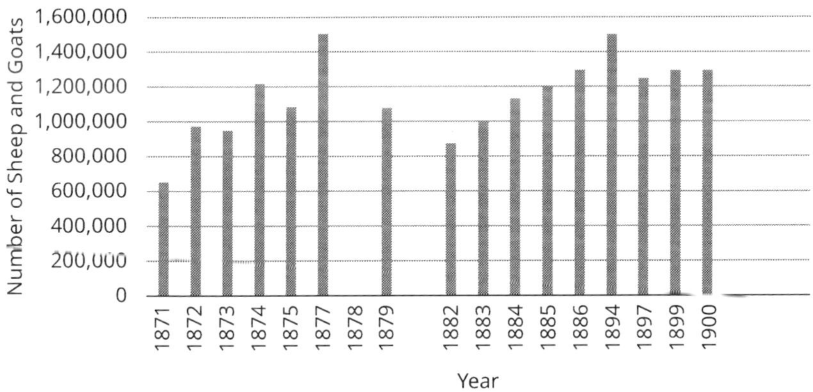

Figure 3.2 The Number of Sheep and Goats in the *Sancaks* of Erzurum, Erzincan, Bayburt, and Bayezid (1871–1900). Source: Data source for this figure is the same as Figure 3.1.

also continued in its role as a hub of inter-imperial trade. A British consular report from the mid-1880s highlighted its close relations with the new Russian province of Kars as follows: "It is usual for small proprietors of sheep [in Kars] to combine and send herds of from 600 to 1,000 head to Baiburt and Erzeroum, where they are bought by merchants from Damascus and Aleppo...A rich proprietor is mentioned as sending as many as ten such large herds to those towns, and the annual export from Kagizman alone is about 15,000 sheep."[59]

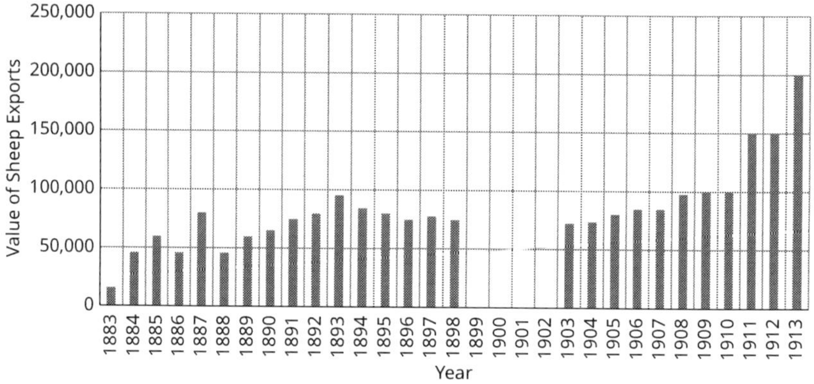

Figure 3.3 The Value of Sheep Exports from Erzurum (in British Pounds)

These developments were accompanied by a revival in export trade. Figure 3.3, based upon the data from the reports of British consular officials, indicates that between the mid-1880s and early 1910s, the value of sheep exports from Erzurum to other provinces followed an upward trend, albeit with some fluctuations.[60] It is important to note that a substantial portion of the wealth generated by increased exports was concentrated in the hands of the region's Kurdish tribal chiefs, especially those who joined the Hamidiye Light Cavalry in the 1890s. As Janet Klein underlines, the Hamidiye chiefs "used sundry means to acquire the land, animals, and possessions of their weaker neighbors and clients."[61] For example, during the massacres of the Armenians in 1894–96, they dispossessed many peasants of their animals. In 1901, the British vice-consul in Van reported that "since the disturbances in 1896 large numbers of sheep have passed into the hands of powerful Kurdish chiefs. The profits from their sale thus remain locked in a few hands, instead of being generally dispersed throughout the district."[62]

During the late nineteenth and early twentieth centuries, many tribal chiefs also purchased the right to collect tithes and sheep taxes from districts where they enjoyed a position of authority. This practice contributed to an increase in grievances among Armenian, Kurdish, and other (Muslim and non-Muslim) rural communities over taxation. At times, when peasants and tribal commoners failed to pay their taxes, one common response of tax farmers and government tax officials was to seize their animals and household items. This practice not only enabled tribal chiefs to increase the size of their flocks but also fostered a favorable business environment for sheep merchants, as some of the seized animals were sold at low prices in local markets.[63] Here is one example from the early 1890s: One of the subchiefs of the Hayderan tribe, in his capacity as the director of the Patnos district in the *sancak* of Bayezid, collected nearly 1,000 sheep from the villages round. According to an informed observer, "these animals appear to have been seized from Christians and Mussulmans alike, and [the director named] Hussein is already in treaty with a merchant in this town [Patnos] for their sale."[64]

Concurrently with these developments, an important shift occurred in the destinations of sheep exports from Erzurum. While Syrian provinces remained important markets, their significance began to wane in the 1900s. As both Ottoman and British officials observed, a large portion of Erzurum's sheep was directed toward the Istanbul and Egyptian markets.[65] According to a 1905 report by the Istanbul Municipality, merchants and tribes in Erzurum province had 150,000 sheep ready to be sold. Of these, 110,000 would be sent to Istanbul.[66] In the following several years, exports to Egypt exceeded those to Istanbul because meat prices there were much higher than in the capital.[67] By the early 1910s, however, Istanbul had once again become the major importer. The British Consul of Erzurum reported that in 1911 and 1912, the sheep exported from his consular district were worth 150,000 pounds annually. In both years, two thirds of this amount was derived from shipments to Istanbul.[68] The following section examines the variety of factors underlying this shift in trade flows.

Strengthened Links with the Imperial Capital

During the half-century preceding World War I, the Ottoman cities that received livestock from Erzurum experienced considerable population growth. The greatest numerical growth occurred in Istanbul. With a population of over a million people by the early 1900s, it saw an increased demand for meat, as highlighted in Chapter 1 and will be discussed further in Chapter 6. Meanwhile, supply shortages resulting from the Ottoman Empire's territorial losses in Rumelia, harsh winters and epizootics that killed large numbers of sheep, along with cholera outbreaks that impeded the flow of trade, led to occasional increases in the price of meat in the capital.[69] While these developments encouraged the Erzurum sheep merchants to increase their shipments to Istanbul, changes in trade routes and advances in transportation technologies made the city more easily accessible to them. From the early 1880s onward, they increasingly exported their animals to Istanbul by sea through the port of Trabzon rather than by land.

A key facilitator of this change was the rivalry between the Ottoman and Russian empires over the Iranian transit trade. The Russian efforts to divert this trade from Trabzon to their own ports culminated in the opening of two railroad lines, one running from the Black Sea port city of Poti to Tiflis, and the other running from Tiflis to Baku. As these lines lowered transportation costs, a larger amount of Iranian trade began to pass through Poti, resulting in a decline in Trabzon's

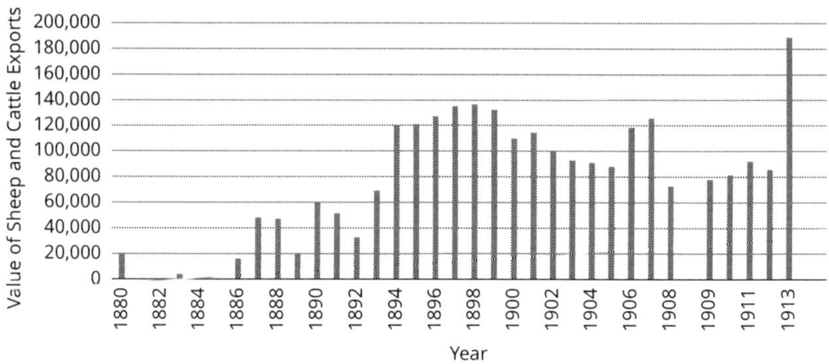

Figure 3.4 The Value of Sheep and Cattle Exports from the Trabzon Port to Istanbul (in British Pounds)

position as a transit port. The decline was, however, partially compensated by an 1883 decision of the Russian government to increase import duties in order to make its industries more competitive on the Iranian market. Thereafter, an increasing number of steamers laden with merchandise for Iran began to discharge their cargo in Trabzon. Yet, as the bulk of Iranian exports now moved through other ports, there was only a limited amount of freight available to these ships on their return trips from Trabzon.[70]

In order to avoid losses due to this situation, the Trabzon agents of steamship companies, such as the Austrian Llyod, French Messagerie Maritime and Paquet, and Ottoman Giurgiu, began to search for new customers who would provide them with return cargo. They approached and tried to convince the sheep merchants from Erzurum and nearby districts to use their ships to send animals to the capital. Available statistics show that their efforts proved successful in shifting the bulk of the trade to the Trabzon route. While, according to British consular reports, only about 1,000 head of sheep were exported from Trabzon in 1883, that number increased to 19,840 in 1886 and to 85,000 in 1891. Although the figures for the following two years were far lower, a strong recovery ensued, resulting in exports ranging between 80,000 and 110,000 heads in the first decade of the twentieth century. As Figure 3.4 shows, this increase in volume was accompanied by an increase in the value of exports after the mid-1880s, albeit a more moderate one.[71]

Merchants preferred the sea route to the land route mainly because it was faster. It took about ten days to drive their flocks from Erzurum to Trabzon, and from this port, Istanbul could be reached generally in four to six days by steamships, with a carrying capacity up to 5,000 head of sheep.[72] The travel time on alternative routes, including those partly served by rail, proved considerably longer. In 1892, most of the sheep bound for the capital were walked to Ankara instead of Trabzon

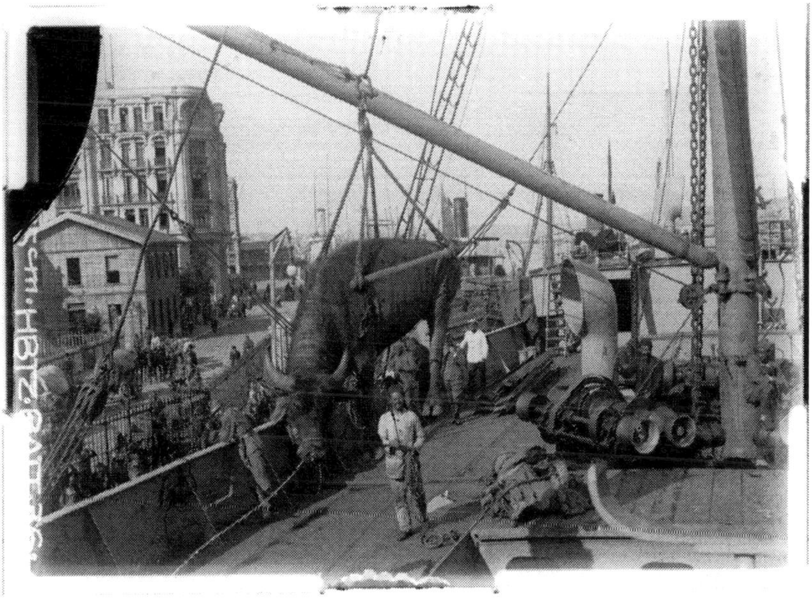

Photograph 3.1 Embarkation of Buffaloes in Istanbul in 1917. Source: Österreichische Nationalbibliothek.

and then transported over the newly opened railroad to Istanbul. However, within just one year, the Trabzon route regained its primacy. This was mainly because the Ankara route took about a month longer, and merchants soon realized that the long journey was injurious to the animals.[73] Moreover, those traveling overland from central and northeastern Anatolia to Istanbul still sometimes faced attacks by tribes and bandits, resulting in the loss of animals and money. Yet, once the sheep were loaded onto the ships at Trabzon, they were safe from such attacks.[74]

This, however, does not mean that the sea route was without its difficulties. To begin with, during their journey to Trabzon, merchants and animals sometimes suffered traumatic events such as robbery and accidents. In February 1900, for instance, the local press reported the collapse of the upper floor of an inn near Trabzon, which was hosting a Bayburt merchant destined for Istanbul along with his 450 sheep. Unfortunately, twelve of the animals were buried under the debris.[75] Upon arrival at the coast, new difficulties emerged. In Trabzon, steamers had to anchor offshore due to inadequate port facilities, and sheep flocks were ferried to them by boats. As iron cranes lifted the animals onto the ships' decks, many suffered broken legs, and some died from their injuries.[76] Moreover, in stormy weather, the voyage to Istanbul took longer than the average, up to ten days. During this time, animals were packed in congested depots, where fatal incidents were not uncommon. For example, in April 1894, when a Paque Company steamer laden with sheep was caught in a storm in the Black Sea, the crew confined the animals to the vessel's storage space. As a result, 743 sheep died from lack of oxygen. Those fortunate enough to survive such incidents suffered from serious problems, such as difficulty in walking. According to merchants, they often needed a ten-day period of rest and fattening before being sent to slaughter.[77]

The sea route also experienced occasional interruptions due to disease outbreaks. In 1892, during the Fifth Pandemic, cholera outbreaks occurred in both Erzurum and Trabzon. The latter was hit again a year later, leading to the port being closed to foreign shipping for several months. As pointed out in the preceding chapter, the government's principal response to such outbreaks was to establish a vast network of quarantine stations. The cargo, crews, and passengers of vessels voyaging from Trabzon to Istanbul had to undergo quarantine at the lazaretto of Sinop. Although sheep flocks were exempt from this regulation, they had no choice but to wait for the end of their shepherds' quarantine, unless their owners arranged for them to leave Sinop earlier on another ship under the care of new shepherds.[78] These developments, combined with famine in Erzurum, led to a substantial decline in trade volume. According to a report by the mayor of Istanbul, the number of sheep exported from the Black Sea coast to Istanbul decreased by about 68,000 heads from 1891 to 1892.[79]

In response to this difficult situation, sheep merchants adopted alternative routes, such as the one that passed through Ankara, to reach the capital. They also appealed to the government for modifications to quarantine regulations. In a petition presented to the governor of Erzurum, they demanded to be placed in quarantine in Kavak (Bosporus) rather than in Sinop. The rationale behind this preference was that while they were in the lazaretto of Kavak, their animals could be handed over to their Istanbul agents, who would take them to pastures in the city.[80] Although it evidently did not receive a positive response from the government,[81] this proposal shows that by the early 1890s some Erzurum merchants had access to networks that would help them to keep their business running smoothly, even when they were not physically present. Large Istanbul-based merchants, engaged in the business of importing live animals from Anatolia and other parts of the empire, played an important role in the establishment of such networks.

The late nineteenth century witnessed an important development in the organization of the livestock trade from northeastern Anatolia. For most of the century, livestock merchants' general tendency was to travel long distances between Erzurum and the consumer markets in the west and south in person, accompanied by their shepherds, servants, and associates. As the above-mentioned story of Süleyman Ağa demonstrates, some of those trading with Istanbul suffered heavy losses in the 1860s because they were not adequately informed about the status and soundness of their customers during their short stays in the capital. Although, as discussed in Chapter 6, the government made various efforts to address this situation, they appeared to have limited impact. In the 1870s and 1880s, merchants from Anatolia and Rumelia sent numerous petitions to central authorities, complaining that due to large debts owed to them by Istanbul butchers, they had run into serious financial difficulties. In their petitions, merchants also frequently highlighted their lack of price-negotiating power with butchers.[82] In response to these problems, and capitalizing on advancements in communication and transportation technologies, some wealthier merchants from Erzurum decided to settle in Istanbul and conduct their business from there, similar to their central Anatolian counterparts. They managed to do this through a network of agents and partners in the provinces, with whom they could communicate quickly by telegraph. As the aforementioned story of the Hayderan subchief shows, one way for these merchant networks to collect sheep from Erzurum and nearby provinces was to build up strong business relations with powerful tribal figures in possession of large flocks. Another way, and to some extent related, was to become involved in tax collection. One contemporary observer wrote that in the late 1870s, some tax farmers in Erzincan were visiting villages under their jurisdiction, together with sheep merchants, who purchased animals, probably at below-market prices, from villagers unable to pay their taxes.[83] By such means, Istanbul-based merchants managed to procure large supplies of sheep.

One of these merchants was Abdullah Efendi bin Said from Damascus. By the late 1880s, he was residing with his family in the Beylerbeyi district of Asian Istanbul and had an office in Sultan Odaları Han in Mahmutpaşa, a bustling commercial district located on the European side of the city. When a public prosecutor interrogated him in 1887 about a complaint he had filed against a municipal official, Abdullah provided an account of how he ran his business from Istanbul. According to this account, he owned flocks of sheep in Erzurum and Tripoli. When he decided to take some of them to the market, he sent a telegram to his agents in these places, ordering that the animals be brought to the capital by Kurdish drovers. Once they arrived in Istanbul, the sales were carried out by these drovers, to whom Abdullah Efendi probably disbursed generous payments.[84]

A few years after Abdullah Efendi's interrogation, two Erzurum merchants named Topçuzazde Ahmed and Şeyhzade Ahmed Efendi, who had been bringing sheep to Istanbul for some time, decided to establish a permanent residence there. Like Abdullah, Şeyhzade set up an office in an inn in Mahmutpaşa and began to order large shipments from northeastern Anatolia and other parts of the empire. In the second half of 1898, his agents brought nearly 30,000 sheep to the Istanbul market. About a third of these animals came from Aleppo and the rest likely from Erzurum. Although in later years Şeyhzade took on two partners, both

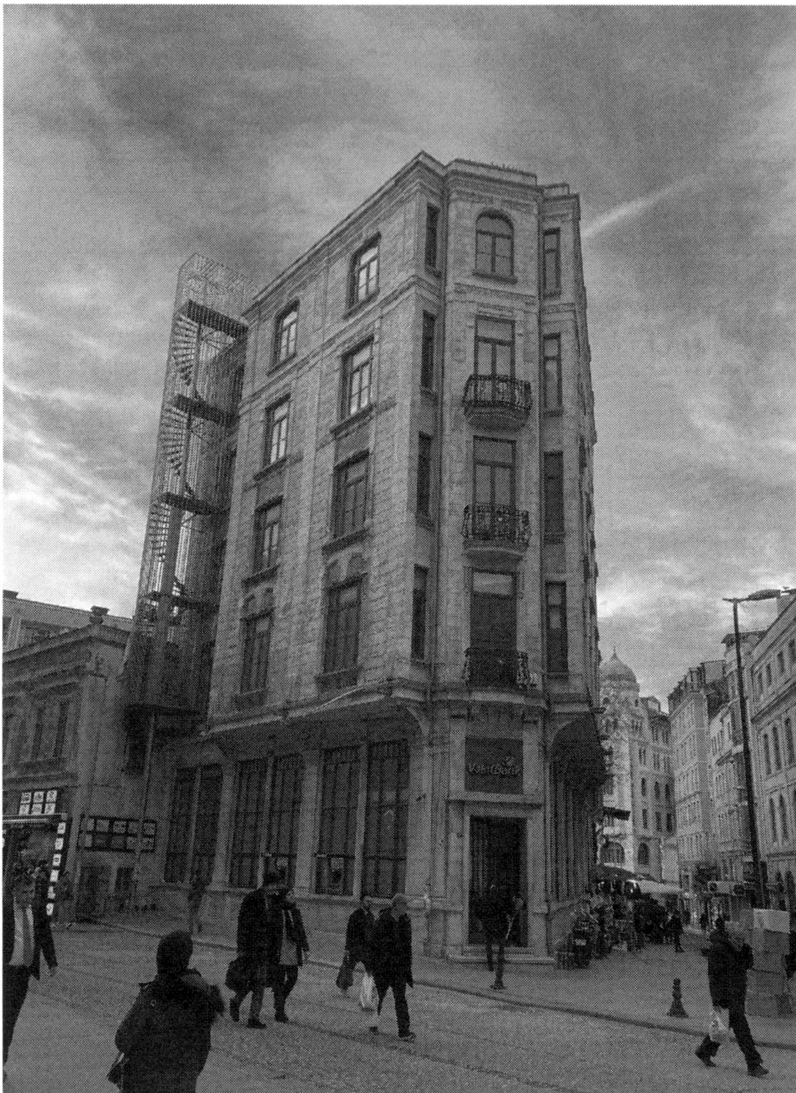

Photograph 3.2 Contemporary View of the Erzurum Han in Istanbul. Photo Credit: Muratcan Zorcu.

from Erzurum, the volume of his orders seemed to gradually decline. The three partners, however, remained in the business until 1903, when they switched to trading textiles. In comparison, Topçuzade carved out a longer career as a sheep merchant. Entering the business with the support of an Erzurum notable, he had established himself as a major supplier of meat to the capital by the late 1890s. Between January 1898 and December 1899, he imported nearly 55,000 sheep for the consumption of Istanbul residents. Despite some ups and downs in the following years, this venture continued until the outbreak of World War I, when a significant portion of eastern Anatolia became a war zone and subsequently fell under Russian occupation. The profits he earned during this period allowed Şeyhzade to purchase an inn, Erzurum Han, located near Mahmutpaşa.[85]

Conclusion

In the period from the eighteenth to the early twentieth century, northeastern Anatolia gained importance as a major exporter of sheep to different regions of the Ottoman Empire. The above paragraphs highlight the dynamic nature of these trade networks, reaching across the empire's borders, by demonstrating that their significance and organization changed over time. While sheep exports to Istanbul increased by the early twentieth century, there was some decline in shipments to the Syrian provinces. This shift was largely due to two factors. The first concerned improvements in transportation technologies. Steamships greatly shortened the voyage and reduced the risks involved in long-distance trade. As merchants began to increasingly prefer the sea route, Trabzon maintained its status as a major port, despite a considerable shift in the direction of the Iranian transit trade. Second, territorial losses suffered by the Ottomans in Rumelia and the subsequent population growth in the capital city increased the demand for Anatolian sheep in Istanbul. These changes had a significant impact on the lives of animals. Long sea voyages and arduous journeys on foot resulted in numerous casualties among the livestock. Severe weather conditions, disease quarantines, and incidents of animal theft further exacerbated the harsh conditions they faced.

A confluence of demographic, economic, environmental, political, and technological factors presented both obstacles and possibilities that led to changes in the organization of the sheep trade. Until the final decades of the nineteenth century, the Erzurum merchants driving their flocks to Istanbul stayed there only temporarily. Thereafter, akin to their central Anatolian counterparts, some began to settle in Istanbul and run their business through a network of agents and partners. This move allowed them to pursue their interests in Istanbul more effectively. It also evidently alleviated the difficulties that Erzurum-based merchants faced in the capital, as people like Şeyhzade and Topçuzade Ahmed provided them with useful information about market conditions and access to their networks. These, in turn, ensured the continuation of trade networks between Erzurum and Istanbul, even during challenging times. Thus, it comes as no surprise that in 1900, six Erzurum merchants, alongside Derviş and Haydar Beys mentioned in the previous chapter, received decorations from Abdülhamid II for their role in keeping meat prices low in the capital.[86] The sultan apparently knew these merchants well, as he also had large investments in livestock raising. His farms in the districts of Mihaliç, Kirmasti, and Karesi in northwestern Anatolia had large flocks of sheep, some of which were exported to the capital for slaughter. The following chapter focuses on Hüdavendigar province, where these farms were located, and explores its rise as a major supplier to the Istanbul meat market.

CHAPTER 4

Hüdavendigar: A 'Model' Province on the Passageways

Abstract

This chapter focuses on Hüdavendigar province, which stretched from northwestern to central Anatolia, and demonstrates how a combination of factors – geography, climate, demography, and state policies- interacted to shape its livestock production and trade. With its fertile pastures, the province not only remained an important livestock-raising center but also became a major passageway and stop-over for Anatolian and Rumelian sheep merchants and their flocks en route to the capital, İzmir, and Bursa. This mobility, on one hand, contributed to the growth of Hüdavendigar's sheep exports in the late nineteenth and early twentieth centuries. On the other hand, coupled with an influx of refugees from Crimea, the Caucasus, and Rumelia, and efforts by local notables to expand their holdings, it led to escalating land conflicts. The chapter argues that these developments triggered increased state intervention in the economy, ecosystems, and animal healthcare. From the 1840s onward, state investments in the province led to the establishment and expansion of an imperial farm and the conversion of some wetlands into farmlands. The period also saw a heightened focus on animal welfare, reflected in the introduction of quarantine regulations and increased vaccination efforts by the government to contain contagious diseases.

Keywords: Northwestern Anatolia; land conflicts; the Mihaliç Imperial Farms; animal welfare; migratory flows; trade networks

The province of Hüdavendigar, bordered by Ankara province to the east, the Aegean Sea to the west, Aydın and Konya provinces to the south, and the Marmara Sea to the north, was an important economic center in the Ottoman Empire. In the nineteenth and early twentieth centuries, it exported a variety of agricultural products, such as cereals, cotton, olives, and opium, to other parts of the empire and overseas.[1] The province also had a dynamic manufacturing industry, with silk weaving occupying a central position for centuries. Although the weaving industry had lost most of its markets by the mid-1850s, its decline was compensated by the rapid growth of export-oriented sericulture and silk-reeling. In the late 1890s, filatures, numbering close to 100, produced around 400,000 kilograms of raw silk annually, spun from cocoons of caterpillars raised predominantly in the region.[2]

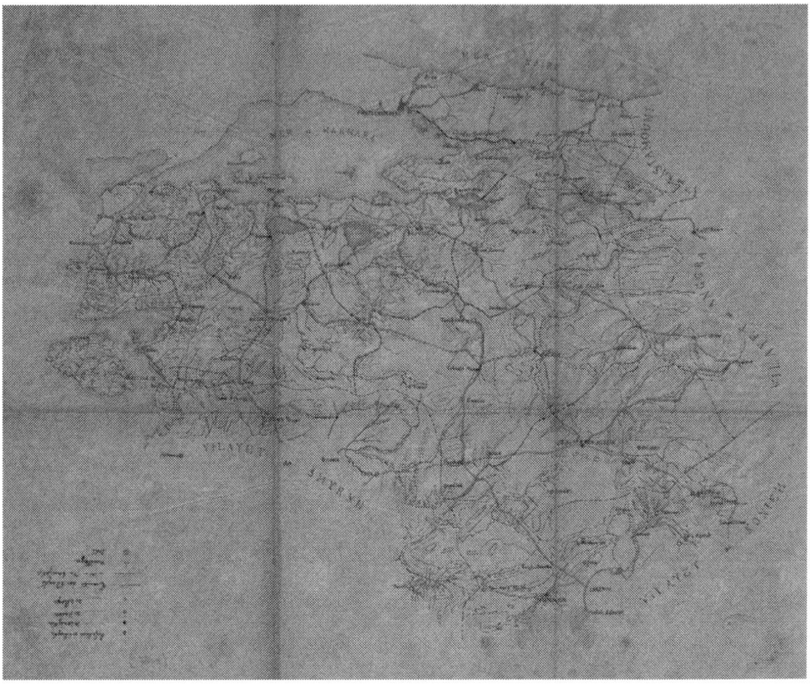

Map 4.1 The Map of Hüdavendigar Province
Source: BOA, HRT.h 959, 29 Zilhicce 1300 (31 October 1883)

While the literature has acknowledged the significance of silkworms in the provincial economy, this chapter seeks to contribute to it by discussing the role of another animal in generating substantial revenues and wealth: sheep. Raised in large numbers across the province, sheep not only provided wool as the primary material for the thriving carpet industry of western Anatolia but also served as a source of meat for urban markets.[3] From at least the 1840s onwards, consumers in Istanbul, Bursa, and İzmir heavily relied on flocks arriving from different parts of the province.

The chapter delves into this role of Hüdavendigar as a major supplier of sheep for slaughter, beginning with an examination of the province's diverse ecosystem. It highlights how the climate and landscape fostered conditions conducive to animal husbandry and then discusses how these conditions, combined with improvements in maritime transportation, underpinned the expansion of sheep exports, with a particular focus on the trade to Istanbul. However, this expansion was not without its challenges. The chapter reveals how the burgeoning export business, in interplay with environmental, demographic, and political dynamics (such as the prevalence of wetlands and the influx of refugees) sparked frequent land conflicts and escalated the risk of disease outbreaks for both humans and non-human animals. Finally, it explores initiatives undertaken by various governmental actors to mitigate these challenges and safeguard animal welfare, thus illustrating the extent to which the lives of sheep and other livestock became subject to state intervention during the last decades of the empire. In addition, while other sections of this book emphasize the state's regulatory efforts in animal husbandry and trade, this chapter underscores its engagement as a livestock producer. This involvement allowed at least one late Ottoman sultan, Abdülhamid II, to emerge as a notable sheep merchant.

Landscape, Climate, and the Major Centers of Livestock Raising

In contrast to other chapters that discuss regional economies encompassing areas larger than provincial units, the focus in this chapter shifts to the regional economy of northwestern Anatolia, which mainly intersected with the provincial boundaries of Hüdavendigar. This province, consisting of the *sancaks* of Bursa, Karesi, Kütahya, and Karahisar, featured two distinct ecosystems along the transit routes spanning from northwest to central Anatolia. While it had access to the Marmara and Aegean Seas through the former two *sancaks*, it was linked to the Aegean hinterland and central Anatolia through the latter two.[4] The province had an uneven landscape with highs and lows. While a large part of it was covered by mountains clothed with forests, such as Olympus (Uludağ) in Bursa and the Emir Mountains in Karahisar, vast plains in its northwestern part were dotted with streams, such as Nilüfer and Susurluk, and lakes, such as Apolyont (Uluabat) and Manyas. These geographic conditions, together with climate, had direct consequences on the lives of humans and non-human animals. One major climatic event that seemed to have a major impact on the region was the Little Ice Age, dated roughly from around 1350 to 1850.

Faruk Tabak argues that long wet seasons witnessed during this period resulted in frequent floods and inundations, facilitating wetland growth and causing damage to agricultural production in the lowlands of Anatolia. Faced with these challenges, many peasants altered their settlement patterns. They abandoned their villages in malaria-stricken plains and set up new lives at higher elevations.[5] Zeynep Küçükceran highlights the substantial effects of these conditions on the district of Mihaliç (today's Karacabey), surrounded by lakes and rivers. Increased rainfall, recurrent flooding, inundation of rivers, and expansion of wetlands contributed to a decline in croplands and the "gradual seizure of vast commons by sheep throughout the nineteenth century."[6] These developments, in turn, paved the way for the formation of large farms (*çiftliks*) that were mostly rented to sheep merchants.[7]

Mihaliç, along with the nearby districts of Kirmasti (today's Mustafakemalpaşa) and Atranos (today's Orhaneli), were among the major centers of livestock raising

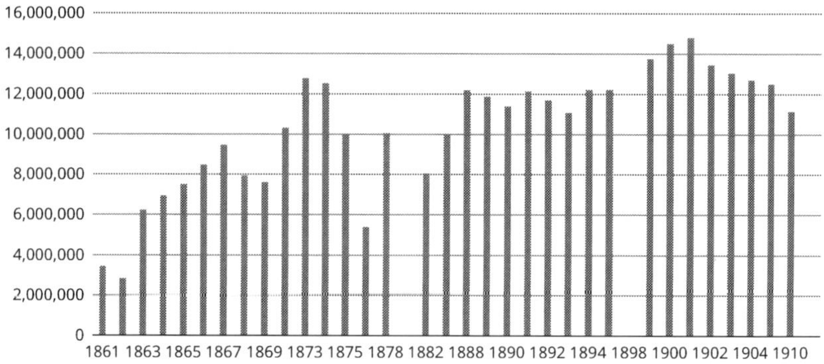

Figure 4.1 Sheep Taxes Collected in Hüdavendigar Province (in Ottoman Piasters)

in the *sancak* of Bursa. Although continuous data on the number of livestock in these and other parts of Hüdavendigar province are lacking, sheep tax revenue figures available for various years enable us to make informed guesses. In the Bursa *sancak* of 1873, the highest revenues for this tax imposed on sheep and goats were recorded in Karacaşehir (337,892 piasters), Mihaliç (275,832 piasters), Bursa and Kite (238,752 piasters), Atranos (201,140 piasters), and Kirmasti (113,752 piasters).[8] At that time, in Hüdavendigar province, the tax was fixed at four piasters per head of animal, meaning that Ottoman tax officials counted a total of about 147,700 sheep and goats in Mihaliç, Atranos, and Kirmasti. As Figure 4.1, compiled from Ottoman provincial yearbooks, shows that tax revenues underwent a substantial decline at the provincial level in 1875, probably because the famine that hit central Anatolia decimated livestock populations in the *sancaks* of Kütahya and Karahisar. However, the situation in Kirmasti, Mihaliç, and Atranos did not seem as dire. The revenue figures suggest that they had in total about 162,500 sheep and goats in 1876.[9] Despite frequent disease outbreaks during the following decades, the populations of these animals continued to increase in the three districts in question, reaching nearly 200,000 in 1905 according to official statistics.[10] It is important to note that these figures, derived from tax registers, were underrepresented. Because of its moderate climate, with warm autumns and relatively mild winters, and its plentiful meadows and pastures irrigated by the Nilüfer and Susurluk Rivers, Mihaliç and its neighboring areas became favored destinations for Rumelian merchants en route to Istanbul, who chose to winter their flocks there.[11] For instance, in November 1870, the *Levant Herald* reported that barges and small ships had recently carried about 100,000 sheep from Gelibolu (Gallipoli) to the piers on the other side of the Dardanelles.[12] Once landed, these animals were mostly driven to pastures in Karesi, Mihaliç, and Kirmasti. However, many of them did not make it into the official statistics for these districts because they headed to Istanbul before tax officials arrived in early spring.[13]

Sheep-raising was also widespread in the eastern and southeastern parts of the province. These areas housed sizeable semi-nomadic tribal populations, providing them with access to large meadows and pastures for grazing.[14] In 1873, the *sancak* of Kütahya paid 2,865,912 piasters as sheep tax, meaning that tax officials there counted about 700,000 head of sheep and goats.[15] Although the ensuing famine reduced this number to around 560,000, it had not taken so long for recovery to come.[16] In 1905, the official Ottoman statistics recorded the sheep and goat population in the *sancak* of Kütahya as 873,574. The same statistics also highlight the role of the neighboring Karahisar *sancak* as a major center of animal husbandry. Together, the two accounted for slightly over 60 percent of the province's total sheep population which was 1,362,500.[17] As the following section illustrates, some of these animals were eventually exported to Istanbul and other urban markets for slaughter.

Flourishing Trade Networks and Increasing Land Pressure

Karahisar occupied an important position in animal trade networks in Anatolia. As discussed in Chapter 2, merchants from Konya province used this district as a stop-over point en route to the livestock markets of Istanbul, Bursa, and İzmir. Furthermore, government correspondence and merchant petitions from the nineteenth century often mentioned it, along with Kütahya, as suppliers of sheep, especially to Bursa and İzmir.[18] For instance, reports from Bursa reveal that in late 1848 or early 1849, ten merchants from Karahisar, all affiliated with the Bozulus tribe's Karabağ branch, sold 3,882 sheep to the city's butchers. The merchants purchased about 80 percent of these animals from villages in Karahisar and the rest from the members of the Cihanbeyli tribe.[19] This figure was significant, considering that by the early 1900s, the annual consumption of sheep in Bursa was about 70,000 heads, amidst a population that had more than doubled in the preceding five decades.[20] Similar reports had also emerged from İzmir. In September 1864, the Administrative Council of İzmir noted the city's reliance on imports from Konya and Kütahya to meet its demand for meat.[21] This dependency was also emphasized in a 1906 report by provincial officials to the Council of State.[22]

Meanwhile, the northwestern districts of Hüdavendigar province established closer trade relations with Istanbul.[23] A sultanic order from 1825 underlined that Mihaliç, Bandırma, and Mudanya had for many years been supplying the capital with lambs for the feast of Khidir (*Ruz-ı Hızır*), celebrated in early May.[24] About three decades later, in 1856, the Grand Vizierate, in an order issued to the governor of Hüdavendigar province, mentioned Mihaliç as one of the major suppliers of sheep to

Istanbul during the winter months.[25] This observation was shared by British consular officials in Bursa. According to their reports, annual sheep exports from Bandırma, the chief port of Mihaliç and Kirmasti, to Istanbul ranged between 90,000 and 130,000 heads in the early 1860s.[26] As the capital grew in population during the following decades, leading to higher demand for meat products, exports from Bandırma surged to reach 300,000 heads per annum in the 1890s.[27] This means that the capital was then drawing about one-fifth of its supplies from the southern shores of the Marmara Sea.

An important factor behind this increase was the improvement in transportation facilities. As contemporary accounts reveal, barges pushed by towboats were widely used to transport live animals from Bandırma to Istanbul.[28] Moreover, since at least the 1860s, there were regular ferries operating between these ports, and their number increased over the years. For instance, the İdare-i Mahsusa, an Ottoman steamer company, was running a weekly Bandırma-Istanbul service in 1877, which increased to biweekly by the early 1890s.[29] Remarkably, on the eve of World War I, reports by sheep merchants in the capital highlighted a daily influx of two or three ships from Bandırma, each laden with several thousand animals.[30] However, it is important to note here that the sea journey lasting nine to ten hours was not without its dangers.[31] In mid-March 1872, the *Levant Herald* reported that an Aziziye Company steamer coming from Bandırma "with a heavy cargo of sheep and cattle ... went ashore in a dense fog ... near San Stefano [Yeşilköy]."[32] According to press accounts, this accident did not result in any loss of life, but there were others that did.[33] For example, in late May 1890, two steamers from İdare-i Mahsusa collided between Bandırma and Istanbul. One of them, named Beşiktaş, sank within a few minutes with its cargo of 600 sheep. According to the daily paper *Sabah*, none of these animals survived the accident.[34]

The increase in maritime traffic between Bandırma and Istanbul was closely associated with a growth in the volume of sheep shipments from Rumelia to Mihaliç and its environs for grazing. By the turn of the century, Gelibolu had become a bustling transfer port, prompting local authorities to discuss imposing a tax on livestock being transported from there and devoting the revenue collected to the renovation of its pier and wharf.[35] The arrival of large numbers of Rumelian merchants, in need of pastures for their flocks, also resulted in increased demand for land in Mihaliç and Kirmasti. Farm holders with lands to rent out emerged as major beneficiaries of this development. Most merchants were apparently willing to pay high rents because the region allowed them to send their animals to Istanbul in late winter or early spring, a time when meat prices there tended to rise due to reduced deliveries from both Rumelia and Anatolia. Their business was quite profitable, as indicated by the fact that over time, some managed to form their own farms.[36]

One such merchant was a certain Abdülcelil Ağa. In the latter half of the nineteenth century, together with his two brothers, this Albanian entrepreneur acquired two farms, Camandıra and Poyrazbahçe, in Mihaliç. Then, his son Galip, who was awarded the title of pasha during the Hamidian period, significantly expanded the family's landholdings by using his political influence at the central and local levels.[37] An official inspector's report highlighted that he was holding most of this land without a title-deed (*tapu*): "In fact we see everywhere a difference between the real amount of the land and the amount recorded on its *tapu*. But it is something very unprecedented and very rare to see a difference such as in this case, i.e. 1,700 *dönüms* [425 acres] on the *tapu* and 10,000 *dönüms* [2,500 acres] on the ground."[38] This situation caused bitter resentment among the residents of Mihaliç. Feeling empowered by the Young Turk Revolution, they took to the streets in large numbers in 1908 to protest against the pasha, compelling him to temporarily leave the district. However, it seems that, just like Çayırlızade Hilmi, whose story was recounted in Chapter 2, Galip soon managed to turn the tide in his favor by establishing connections with the new ruling elites. By the summer of 1909, a government decree reached local officials in Mihaliç, mandating police protection for his property rights.[39]

At the turn of the twentieth century such conflicts were rampant in Hüdavendigar province due to increased pressure on land available for farming and grazing. This pressure stemmed primarily from two factors: the growing importance of the sheep economy and the influx of large numbers of refugees to Anatolia. The latter was driven by military conflicts between the Ottoman Empire and Russia, especially the Crimean War and the Ottoman-Russian war of 1877–78, and the Russian expansion in Crimea and the Caucasus. According to official statistics, in the few years following the war of 1877–78, more than 40,000 refugees were settled in Hüdavendigar. By the early 1890s, the number had increased to 189,028, constituting about 11 percent of the province's population.[40] The settlement process, however, was far from straightforward. Extensive wetlands in the districts of Bursa, Mihaliç, and Kirmasti, covering a total area of 635,000 *dönüms* (158,750 acres), limited the availability of land for that endeavor.[41] In response to this situation, some of the pastures in the province were converted to farmlands. There were also frequent complaints that the immigrants established villages on lands owned by the locals.[42]

Conflicts arising in such situations were often mediated by local officials, some of whom viewed the increased land pressure as an opportunity to generate extra income. One prominent example was Ramazan Bey, who served as the *kaymakam* of the Yenişehir district near Bursa in the beginning of the 1880s. He faced trial for several charges, including the unauthorized rental of common pasture lands in villages without residents' approval. Allegations continued when he was appointed to Kirmasti in 1885. One accusation was that he rented out some pasture lands there to desperate immigrant communities and pocketed the rent money. However, he then incited locals to attack the pastures and destroy crops cultivated by the immigrants, leading to confrontations and fatalities between the two groups. Ramazan's interests seemed to extend beyond immovable properties. During his tenure as the *kaymakam* of Yenişehir, he reportedly engaged in sheep trade using the funds of the district's credit office (*menafi sandığı*) as starting capital without authorization. To make this venture profitable, he forced local inhabitants and policemen to make purchases from him. Additionally, Ramazan was charged with involvement in animal theft, a prevalent issue in Hüdavendigar province at the time. He allegedly collaborated with bands of bandits stealing livestock and extorted money from the Kirmasti villagers seeking the return of their animals.[43]

In the following years, complaints continued to be heard about the activities of local government officials. In 1893, for instance, the headmen and residents of Ormankadı and Kumkadı villages in Kirmasti filed a petition, claiming that Ali Haydar Bey, the *kaymakam* of the district, was selling the villages' pasture lands through auction to sheep merchants and disregarding their needs.[44] However, another petition from the same period suggests that Ali Haydar Bey held the auction not to sell, but to rent out the land in question. The two signatories of the latter document, who were apparently sheep merchants, complained that although they had rented out the pasture for seventy-one liras, the *kaymakam* later leased the land to another tenant for only twenty-six liras.[45] Complaints against Ali Haydar Bey continued unabated until the end of his tenure in Kirmasti in 1898. To cite one example: in 1895, a certain Ahmed from Tepecik village sent a telegram to the government, stating that the *kaymakam* had rented out the village pasture to an Albanian sheep merchant and thereby disrupted the villagers' husbandry activities.[46]

The cases from Yenişehir and Kirmasti illustrate how the struggle for land intensified in Hüdavendigar province with the influx of large refugee populations and profit-seeking sheep merchants. It is important to note that the government did not merely play the role of mediator in these conflicts. It also sought to assert environmental agency. The policy of opening new lands for settlement and cultivation by draining swamps emerged as a major initiative in the second half of the nineteenth century. This policy aimed to ease tensions between the locals, recently settled refugees, and merchants, as well as to contain the spread of infectious diseases. For the latter purpose, the government also initiated measures to regulate the mobility of livestock and increase their immunity. The following section will analyze how these initiatives worked in practice and assess their impact on the region's sheep economy.

State's Agency in Rural Development

Housing the foundation place, İznik, and the first capital of the empire, Bursa, the province of Hüdavendigar held considerable symbolic and strategic value for the Ottoman ruling elites. Its proximity to Istanbul not only facilitated closer oversight by state authorities but also established it as an important testing ground for new initiatives and policy implementations. As the initial venue for some of the Tanzimat reform projects, Hüdavendigar's prominence was further enhanced during the reign of Abdülhamid II.[47] This was partly due to the sultan's efforts to reinforce his legitimacy by, in the words of Selim Deringil, creating "a veritable cult of Ottomania ... around the historical heritage of the Ottoman dynasty."[48] In that spirit, he ordered the foundation of the Ertuğrul *sancak*, out of İznik and its surrounding area, and devoted special attention to rebuilding the tombs of Ertuğrul Gazi, the legendary founder of the Ottoman dynasty, Sultan Osman, and their wives.[49]

Furthermore, during both the Tanzimat and Hamidian periods, Hüdavendigar benefited from investments in infrastructural projects. Among these, the drainage of swamps had been on the agenda of the government since at least the early 1860s. For instance, during his tenure in Bursa in 1863 as the inspector of reforms in western Anatolia, the renowned Ottoman bureaucrat Ahmed Vefik Efendi (later Pasha) initiated projects aimed at reconstructing the city, improving its roads, and settling 400 immigrant households from Crimea in İznik.[50] The last project involved draining swamps around the İznik Lake and building houses for the newcomers. By securing forced donations for the state-run Circassian charity, Ahmed Vefik achieved considerable progress in housing construction. Within a short span of time, accommodation was provided for 200 immigrant households. However, the financial burden of completing the swamp drainage system was substantial. Lacking sufficient funds, the Circassian charity struggled to cover the costs of the project. To make matters worse, the local willingness to support the charity waned after Ahmed Vefik Efendi's departure. Ultimately, most of the settlers deserted the area, and some among the remaining ones died from infectious diseases.[51]

By the early 1860s, hundreds of immigrant households from Crimea had also settled in Kirmasti and Mıhaliç, supported by local inhabitants who contributed approximately 31,000 piasters to build homes for them. Central authorities promised recognition for their contributions in two newspapers, *Takvim-i Vekayi* and *Ceride-i Havadis*.[52] However, escalating refugee flows by the century's end began to lead to conflicts over scarce resources, particularly land, as immigrant populations surpassed 35,000.[53] The government responded by opening new lands for settlement and agriculture through the drainage of wetlands in Mihaliç, Kirmasti, and Karesi under the supervision of foreign engineers.[54] Despite some initial successes, state-led initiatives waned due to budgetary constraints, prompting concessions to private entrepreneurs for reclamation projects. However, these efforts proved largely ineffective. Complaints emerged in the early twentieth century regarding a certain Rauf Bey's failure to fulfill obligations for wetland drainage in Kirmasti and Mihaliç.[55] During this period, residents of these and nearby districts also attempted drainage works, but their efforts similarly resulted in limited success.[56] Thus, in the early years of the Turkish Republic, the region still harbored thousands of acres of wetlands.[57]

The continued prevalence of wetlands brought mixed outcomes. On one hand, it fueled ongoing land conflicts and contributed to malaria outbreaks by providing breeding grounds for mosquitos.[58] On the other hand, ephemeral wetlands rendered large areas suitable for grazing, bolstering the region's status as a major sheep exporter. The growth in export trade, alongside the influx of immigrants especially after the 1877–78 war, accelerated animal mobility and thus heightened the risk of disease spread among livestock populations.[59] In the late 1870s and early 1880s, Hüdavendigar, along with a number of other provinces such as Adana, Aydın, and Aleppo, faced an outbreak of epizootic disease, likely cattle plague. It decimated large numbers of farm and draught animals and forced the government to ban their export. The situation in Hüdavendigar was so dire that, in 1882, the ban was extended there for another three years.[60] Not long after the end of the ban, a new outbreak of cattle plague emerged in western Anatolia. According to official reports, it arrived in Kirmasti in 1890 and quickly spread to more than ten villages, killing about 200 animals. The disease continued its death march for several more years. By 1891, about 45,000 animals in Hüdavendigar and Aydın provinces had fallen victim to it. That same year, it also spread to Istanbul when a merchant from Manyas sold his infected livestock on the city's peripheries. Shortly afterwards, plague cases began to be reported in different parts of the capital.[61]

To prevent further outbreaks of cattle plague and other diseases, such as anthrax (*şarbon*), foot-and-mouth disease (*şap*), variola or cowpox (*çiçek*), clostridial myositis or black disease (*yanı kara*), and distomatosis (*kelebek*), the government took several precautions in the 1890s.[62] In 1891, checkpoints were set up to control and isolate animals that arrived from the cattle plague infected regions to Istanbul.[63] At around the same time, a commission formed under the Ministry of Forests, Mines, and Agriculture prepared a regulation to contain the spread of animal diseases. This document, titled "Regulation for the Protection of the Health of Animals" (*Zabıta-i Sıhhıye-i Hayvaniye Talimatnamesi*), was approved by the government in 1893 with the stipulation that it would initially be enforced in Hüdavendigar, which had been designated as a model province for public works and agriculture by a sultanic order, before being extended to other parts of the empire.[64]

The regulation, consisting of eighteen articles, sought to contain epizootics through mainly two measures: quarantine and isolation of infected animals.[65] It assigned most responsibility for combating diseases to state veterinarians. According to Articles 2 and 3, when a disease broke out in a *sancak*, its sub-governor was required to send a veterinary inspector to infected districts within twenty-four hours. The inspector was tasked with diagnosing the disease and, with the help of local officials, taking necessary scientific precautions against it. While Article 8 stated that no one was allowed to interfere with the inspector during these duties, the following one authorized only him to demand the lifting of quarantine measures. The regulation also assigned certain tasks to veterinarians who were on duty in uninfected regions. Article 11 required them to examine the animals entering their districts by sea or overland. Furthermore, they were granted a large degree of control over export trade. Article 12, for instance, noted that a person who wanted to move his livestock outside of his province had to present a letter of declaration assuring that the animals were healthy. Only after this letter was approved by a state veterinarian or a municipal doctor would he be given permission to export his flock.[66]

By placing the primary responsibility for handling animal diseases on veterinarians, the regulation aimed to prevent chaos in administrative cadres in times of epizootics. However, it was notably vague in terms of reducing the risks to the health of animals, lacking mention of preventive measures such as vaccination and limiting interactions between livestock and wild animals. Furthermore, it failed to provide veterinary inspectors with clear guidance on fulfilling their responsibilities. Compounding these issues, both Ottoman and foreign sources indicate that veterinarians often lacked enforcement power against herders seeking to take their animals outside disease-stricken areas, due to insufficient support from police and gendarmerie forces.[67] For instance, in 1907, reflecting on the cattle plague outbreak affecting Hüdavendigar and the neighboring provinces of Aydın and Konya over the preceding several years, a British consular official observed that "the measures taken by the Government proved both inadequate and ineffective. The isolation and surveillance of the infected localities were evaded by various means."[68]

The ineffectiveness of quarantine prompted efforts by the government to develop other measures against the spread of animal diseases. A major step was taken in 1898 when Dr. Maurice Nicolle, the director of the Imperial Bacteriology Laboratory (*Bakteriyolojihane-i Şahane*), established in 1893, identified the germ causing the cattle plague and began manufacturing serum against it.[69] This innovation became an important tool in combating the aforementioned outbreak in the early twentieth century.[70] According to press reports from the first months of 1906, a certain quantity of serum was dispatched from İstanbul to Kirmasti and various districts of Aydın province, where it helped mitigate the effects of the plague.[71] Shortly afterwards, in November 1906, Abdülhamid II issued a decree ordering the shipment of necessary serum doses to Bandırma and Mihaliç, upon being informed of the disease's high mortality rates in those areas.[72] It is noteworthy that by this time, the use of serums had expanded to include other diseases as well. For instance, in 1900, the Istanbul Municipality proposed the vaccination of about 25,000 sheep on farms around Mihaliç against anthrax, which was spreading in the district.[73]

The selection of Hüdavendigar as a pilot province for the implementation of the 1893 regulation, along with the concerted efforts by the sultan and his bureaucrats to enhance vaccination rates in Kirmasti and Mihaliç, was influenced mainly by two factors. Firstly, as noted earlier, Kirmasti and Mihaliç were among the principal suppliers of live animals for slaughter to Istanbul. Secondly, since the 1840s, these districts had been the site of an imperial endeavor, the Mihaliç Imperial Farms (*Mihaliç Çiftlikat-ı Hümayunu*), which became a major center for livestock raising.[74] The contribution of this enterprise to the region's sheep economy will be further explored in the following section.

The Mihaliç Imperial Farms

Although personal landholdings of the sultans had existed under the name of *havass-ı hümayun* (crown lands) in previous centuries, the formation of imperial farms was the novelty of the Tanzimat reforms.[75] While there was no distinction between state expenses and the personal expenses of the sultans in earlier periods, the reforms introduced a formal separation of the sultan's treasury from the central state treasury. This limited the political and financial powers of the sultans as most of the revenue sources of the Privy Purse (*Hazine-i Hassa*) were transferred to the central treasury. As compensation for this, the palace began to receive a specified annual allowance from the Ministry of Finance starting in 1840. Furthermore, the management of about six imperial farms, founded on crown and royal endowment lands, was entrusted to the Privy Purse. One of these was the Mihaliç farms, established to supply wool to state-run textile factories in İzmid and İslimye, and to develop agriculture and animal husbandry by employing scientific methods and techniques.[76]

In the mid-1840s, the Mihaliç Imperial Farms encompassed eleven individual farms across the districts of Mihaliç, Kirmasti, and Karesi, covering a total of 24,112 *dönüms* (6,028 acres) of croplands and 42,402 *dönüms* (10,600 acres) of pastures.[77] Over time, the enterprise significantly expanded its holdings through purchase and rental. For example, the Karayani farm in Mihaliç was acquired for 30,000 piasters in 1850. Around the same period, the farms managers' proposal for renting pastures on Mount Olympus was put into practice. In the subsequent years, the enterprise further extended its pastures through additional rentals.[78] Consequently, by the early 1880s, the area covered by it exceeded 85,000 *dönüms* (21,250 acres), allowing the maintenance of large numbers of livestock. Between 1855 and 1876, the cattle population on the farms more than doubled, increasing from 274 to 631. Concurrently, sheep farming emerged as a significant venture. In the 1840s, tens of merino sheep were imported from Crimea to produce smooth and fine quality wool for state-run textile factories.[79] Through natural increase, their numbers surged to about 4,000 by the end of the decade and to nearly 39,000 in 1876.[80] Moreover, around the mid-century, the farms began crossbreeding experiments to improve the wool quality of local sheep. By mixing the merino sheep with the indigenous varieties, a population of 6,096 mixed-breed sheep was achieved in 1864. Over the following years, such efforts continued, albeit on a smaller scale, leading to lower densities by the early 1880s.[81] This development likely stemmed from a decline in global wool prices, triggered by a drop in demand following the American Civil War, and decreased purchases by state-run factories.[82]

Managing thousands of sheep and cattle required a large labor force, initially sourced from temporary migrant workers from Bulgaria. In the late 1840s, the Mihaliç Imperial Farms employed between forty-five and sixty-two shepherds from Plovdiv (Filibe) and Pazarcık, offering them annual contracts that mostly began in October.[83] A primary responsibility of the shepherds was to ensure the well-being of animals spending at least part of the winter and early spring in barns, and to prepare them for reproduction. They were then tasked with taking the flocks assigned to them to the summer pastures of the imperial farms. It appears that retaining these shepherds was not an easy task. The managers of the farms complained that although they were paid almost half of their salary in advance before their arrival in Mihaliç, many of the shepherds deserted and went back to their homes.[84] Despite such problems, the practice of recruiting labor from Bulgaria continued well into the early 1880s. Then, it gradually disappeared as immigrants knowledgeable in the techniques of raising the merino and other sheep breeds settled in large numbers in villages around the farms. These villages, however, did not only serve as a source of labor for the Mihaliç Imperial Farms. Their rapid growth, fueled by the waves of immigration, brought increased land pressure and conflicts, some of which were quite long-lasting. For instance, a pasture conflict between the imperial farms and the Azadlı village in Kirmasti, whose population increased about tenfold at the turn of the twentieth century, persisted from the Hamidian period through the early decades of the Turkish Republic.[85]

In addition to such conflicts, in the late 1870s and early 1880s, the farms' managers had to contend with a series of environmental and economic challenges. As highlighted in the preceding chapters, in 1879–80, abnormal weather conditions struck many parts of Anatolia, including the northwest, and decimated livestock populations. According to a British officer's report from April 1880, during the lengthy and severe winter in Hüdavendigar, "450,000 cattle, sheep, and goats are said to have perished."[86] The Mihaliç Imperial Farms did not remain untouched by this calamity. In 1880, its merino sheep population was reported to be 16,000, representing a 59 percent decline from 1876. The decline in cattle numbers was even more dramatic, reaching its nadir in 1881 with only 123 remaining. The dire situation was further exacerbated by economic difficulties, particularly the decline in the profitability of merino raising due to decreased purchases of wool by state-run factories and falling prices.[87]

In the face of these challenges, those in charge of the Mihaliç Imperial Farms began to explore new sources of income. In 1880, they engaged in negotiations with at least two entrepreneurs willing to rent the farms along with all their buildings and livestock. One of them, named Mustafa Efendi, was a government meat contractor, while the other, named Giurgiu Pano, had investments in various fields. After serving as a grain, olive, and soap contractor to the army in the 1870s, Pano started in the early 1880s a steamer company named the Giurgiu, running ships between the Ottoman ports, and began operating mines in the Zonguldak coal field.[88] Although his bid of 400,000 piasters for annual rent was lower than that of Mustafa, Abdülhamid II ultimately chose to make a contract with him. This decision was based on two grounds. First, unlike Mustafa, he agreed to assume some of the debts of the Mihaliç Imperial Farms, and second, he named the prominent Galata banker George Zarifi as his guarantor.[89] Being also Abdülhamid II's banker and financial advisor, Zarifi's influence among Ottoman ruling circles increased in the late 1870s and early 1880s, thanks primarily to shifts in the political balance of power in the empire.[90]

During the Tanzimat period, as the bureaucracy gained an upper hand over the sultans, the management of most of the imperial farms was transferred from the Privy Purse to the Ministry of Finance. The Mihaliç Imperial Farms did not remain unaffected by this development, as its revenues began to flow into the central treasury by the mid-1860s. However, after Abdülhamid II's enthronement in 1876, the locus of power shifted to the Yıldız Palace, where the new sultan lived and worked. In line with this shift, Abdülhamid II aimed to expand his financial power at the expense of the Sublime Porte. Thus, he not only reclaimed the imperial farms and other properties that had been transferred to the Ministry of Finance but also expanded his landed possessions.[91] In taking these steps, the sultan was quite possibly in close contact with George Zarifi.

As his banker, Zarifi also helped Abdülhamid II handle a major family problem in the early years of his reign. The problem dated to 1876, when the empire went through political turmoil. In May of that year, Sultan Abdülaziz (r. 1861–76) was deposed in a coup, and his nephew, Murad V, was installed as his successor. Shortly after his enthronement, it emerged that the new sultan had accumulated large debts with Christaki Zografos, another prominent Galata banker, during his princedom. When Zografos demanded repayment, several pieces of jewelry belonging to the deposed sultan's family were handed over to him. Only a few months after this transaction, in August 1876, Murad V was deposed on the grounds that he was mentally unfit. One of the first actions of his successor, Abdülhamid II, was to negotiate with Zografos for the return of the jewels, which were both materially valuable and symbolically important as royal possessions. In these negotiations, George Zarifi played a key role by promising to cover the debts of Murad V, upon which Zografos agreed to return the jewels.[92] It was likely in return for this service that Abdülhamid II awarded Zarifi and Pano a contract for the rental of the Mihaliç Imperial Farms for a term of three years, with a possible extension to ten years.[93]

While the documents consulted do not specify the exact duration that the contract remained in force, they indicate that the option to extend was not exercised. By the latter half of the 1880s, the management of the farms had reverted to the Ministry of Privy Purse. Concurrently, as the demand for wool diminished, animal husbandry for meat gained impetus, leading to a change in the breed composition of the farms' sheep flocks. According to Necmettin Odabaşı, between 1880 and 1904, the merino population nearly disappeared, while the number of local *Dağlıç* and *Kıvırcık* sheep, known for their higher quality meat, fluctuated between about 19,000 and 23,000.[94] This shift enabled Abdülhamid II to become one of the principal suppliers to the Istanbul meat market. From the 1880s to the early 1900s, the volume of sheep and lamb exports from the Mihaliç Imperial Farms often exceeded several thousand heads annually. For example, between mid-April and late May 1886, about 4,000 sheep, mostly old or infertile, were transported from the farms to be auctioned in Istanbul.[95] This number was subsequently reported as about 2,000 in March 1888, 4,600 between January and April 1896, and 4,000 from March 1906 to February 1907.[96]

Sheep from the Mihaliç Imperial Farms were in high demand in Istanbul for two main reasons. First, a considerable number of them were shipped to the city in late winter and early spring, a period when slaughter animals were in low supply. Second, the farms' administration offered them for sale at relatively low prices, especially the aged female ones, known as *marya*. For instance, meat derived from the Mihaliç *marya* was auctioned at six to eight piasters in the winter of 1889, while sheep merchants sold a *kıyye* of mutton to Istanbul butchers at nine to ten piasters.[97] During this and other periods, the primary buyers of the farms' sheep in the capital included government meat contractors and wholesale butchers. One notable contractor was Yeorgios Hrisovergis, who made a considerable fortune in this business, as will be discussed in Chapter 6. In December 1881, he sent one of his agents to Mihaliç to negotiate for the purchase of 3,200 sheep from the farms.[98] About five years later, in April and May of 1886, another contractor named Anastas purchased more than 1,000 sheep and lambs at auctions organized by the farms' officials.[99] Meanwhile, two wholesale butchers in the Bahçekapı and Fındıklı districts of the capital won bids at three auctions for the sale of 900 sheep.[100]

Conclusion

This chapter has demonstrated how a combination of factors – geography, climate, demography, and state policies – interacted to shape livestock production and trade in Hüdavendigar province. With fertile pastures covering both its eastern and western parts, the province became a major passageway and stop-over for Anatolian and Rumelian sheep merchants and their flocks, en route to the capital and other consumer markets. This mobility, further compounded by the influx of tens of thousands of refugees from the 1850s onward, led to escalating conflicts over land, particularly over common village pastures. In such conflicts, notably in Kirmasti and Mihaliç, the interplay between environmental factors, such as the presence of large wetlands, and political dynamics often enabled powerful figures like Galip Pasha to expand their landholdings at the expense of small peasants. As the pace of wetland reclamation efforts remained slow because of economic difficulties faced by the empire, and perhaps also due to the resistance of merchants and large landholders who had a stake in the sheep economy, livestock trade from Hüdavendigar to Istanbul experienced a significant growth from the 1860s to early 1900s.

Abdülhamid II was the highest in rank and most well-known among the large landholders in Hüdavendigar. As his political fortunes rose, the sultan consolidated and significantly enhanced his economic position. Within the first decade of his reign, he had already emerged as a prominent livestock merchant, a status achieved through state investments in establishing and expanding the Mihaliç Imperial Farms. Despite its control changing hands several times with the fluctuating power dynamics among Ottoman ruling elites, this enterprise remained agile, adapting to market conditions. Initially established to raise merino and crossbreed sheep for wool for state-run textile factories, the farms shifted toward livestock husbandry for meat production during the Hamidian period, as the factories' demand for wool waned. While this shift likely persisted into the Young Turk period, following Abdülhamid II's loss of control over the imperial farms, a resurgence in merino sheep raising occurred in the 1930s with the establishment of a large wool factory in Bursa as part of the republican Turkish state's first industrial plan.[101]

Along with these developments, the late nineteenth and early twentieth centuries also saw increased efforts by the Ottoman government to safeguard animal welfare by containing the spread of contagious diseases in Hüdavendigar and other parts of the empire. In addition to mobility-restricting measures to combat outbreaks among cattle and sheep populations, serums against various diseases became available, thanks to the work of a state institution, the Imperial Bacteriology Laboratory. These measures, especially the quarantine regulations, did not always yield the anticipated outcomes, as highlighted in the preceding paragraphs.

Nevertheless, they apparently had a considerable role in Hüdavendigar's continued prominence as a center for sheep export, despite a cattle plague outbreak that persisted throughout much of the first decade of the 1900s.

This chapter has also demonstrated how sheep as a commodity in high demand in Istanbul contributed to the emergence of Bandırma as an economically dynamic port on the southern coast of the Marmara Sea. The following chapter moves to explore other important livestock ports in Anatolia, namely İzmir, İskenderun, Antalya, and Mersin, thus drawing attention to the major consumer markets for meat beyond the imperial capital. Istanbul's large and growing population made it an attractive site for sheep and cattle merchants, but many of these individuals also kept an eye on alternative markets. As the following discussion will detail, Egypt, with its strong trade links to different parts of Anatolia, constituted such an alternative at the turn of the twentieth century.

CHAPTER 5

Eastern Mediterranean Ports and Livestock Trade

Abstract

Focusing on four ports -İzmir, İskenderun, Mersin, and Antalya- on the western and southern coasts of Anatolia, this chapter demonstrates how calamities catalyzed the establishment and expansion of livestock trade networks. Recurrent disease outbreaks and climate-related hazards not only compelled livestock raisers in Anatolian and Syrian provinces to convert their emaciated animals into cash but also helped them, along with merchants, secure flourishing export markets. By the early twentieth century, numerous ships laden with cattle and sheep were navigating from these ports to Alexandria, Port Said, and Crete among other eastern Mediterranean locations. However, this booming trade raised concerns among some Ottoman officials about the provisioning of cities, leading to export bans for cattle and the continuation of municipal price controls on meat in İzmir until the empire's end. The boom also contributed to the commercialization of pasture lands in western Anatolia, which restricted locally raised flocks' access to customary grazing areas, threatening their subsistence. Additionally, the chapter reveals that after arriving at the ports for shipment, many animals continued to face dire welfare challenges; some drowned on the open shores of the Mediterranean due to inadequate port facilities, while others perished from the rigors of the sea voyage.

Keywords: Eastern Mediterranean; İzmir; İskenderun; Mersin; Antalya; Egypt; disease; urban provisioning; trade networks

The preceding two chapters have revealed the importance of sea routes in establishing and maintaining trade networks that connected livestock producing regions of northeastern and northwestern Anatolia with Istanbul. This chapter shifts the discussion to the export of animals from the western and southern coasts of the peninsula, tracing the movements of cattle and sheep from the ports of İzmir, İskenderun, Mersin, and Antalya. It demonstrates that shipments from these ports were oriented towards varied destinations, the most prominent of which included Alexandria, Port Said, Crete, Malta, and Piraeus. Thus, while not questioning the role of Istanbul as the empire's chief importer of livestock for slaughter, this analysis shows that the capital was not without its rivals. By the early twentieth century, competition, especially from the Egyptian ports, had intensified to such a degree that the imposition of restrictions on shipments there became a frequently debated issue in government circles. Although certain steps were taken in that direction, export trade from İskenderun, İzmir, and Mersin followed an upward trend during the period in question. As the following lines will highlight, in all three ports, this upswing was largely due to animal disease outbreaks across the eastern Mediterranean.

Although the upward trend in exports was a common feature across these ports, major differences were still evident among them. While İskenderun and İzmir led in terms of shipment volume, Mersin, though not matching their numbers, outperformed Antalya. Focusing on each of the four ports individually, the chapter explores the underlying economic, environmental, and geographic factors contributing to this variation. It argues that the scope and intensity of the connections they established with interior regions, which had large supplies of cattle and sheep, played a particularly important role in setting İskenderun and İzmir apart from the others. Additionally, it highlights that the rise of these ports as major livestock trade hubs in western and southern Anatolia was accompanied by tensions and conflicts, involving a broad range of actors including animals, their raisers, merchants, and government officials. These conflicts were particularly pronounced in İzmir, driven by the city's increased demand for meat and the accelerated pace of agricultural commercialization in its hinterlands. As the following account will show, they had major consequences for the welfare of animals, in terms of their access to food, and for the organization of the meat trade in İzmir.

İzmir

Mapping the Terrain

In the late nineteenth and early twentieth centuries, İzmir served as the administrative capital and chief port of Aydın province, encompassing the *sancaks* of Aydın, Denizli, İzmir, Menteşe, and Saruhan (Manisa) in western Anatolia.[1] The province generally enjoyed a temperate climate, characterized by mild winters and humid springs and autumns, and was endowed with rich water sources. The rivers Bakırçay, Gediz, Little Meander, and Great Meander were particularly important, irrigating large tracts of farmland, meadows, and pastures. Consequently, the province was renowned for its advanced agricultural production, featuring major cash crops such as figs, raisins, olives, tobacco, and citrus fruits. It also supported considerable animal populations. Although some archival documents offer insights into sheep tax revenues for the 1860s, the lack of specific data on taxation rates restricts our ability to accurately estimate the livestock numbers. For example, in

1861, the sheep tax totaled 3,400,000 piasters for the entire province, resulting in an estimated count of 2.2 million sheep and goats.[2] Ottoman official statistics for 1879 and 1883-84, based on tax registers, recorded the number of these animals as 2,611,299 and 2,820,239, respectively.[3]

Although their populations underwent a decline in the late 1880s and early 1890s due to deaths caused by a prolonged drought and a concurrent cattle plague outbreak, recovery came quickly.[4] In 1895, Ottoman tax officials in Aydın counted a total of 1,224,396 sheep and 1,726,925 goats.[5] However, as highlighted in the preceding chapter, the new century began with another, more serious outbreak of cattle plague. In a 1906 report, the British consulate-general of İzmir described the situation in Aydın province as follows:

> Cattle plague, which has been decimating the animals of this district for the last three years, got, in the course of 1906, beyond all control, and spread to all parts of the vilayet. On the other hand, the unusually severe and prolonged winter (1906–07) caused more than an average mortality among the small cattle. No exact figures are available; it is, however, generally admitted that the loss, both in bovines and ovines, must have been heavy. The consequence was that prices of meat and dairy produce have advanced considerably, and farmers found themselves short of teams for ploughing purposes, donkeys having to be utilized in certain districts.[6]

According to a later consular report from 1911, although the situation was improving likely because of increased rates of vaccination, the disease still prevailed in the province. Over the last two years, it had killed slightly over a million goats, 776,000 sheep, and 440,000 cattle.[7] The ravages of the outbreak and the subsequent recovery were also recognized in Ottoman official statistics for 1913, which reported the sheep population of the province to be around one million, a figure about 20 percent lower than that of 1895, and the cattle population as slightly over 310,000.[8]

One major cause for the prevalence of cattle plague, as discussed in the preceding chapter, was the increased migratory movements toward western Anatolia from the mid-nineteenth century onwards. Between 1877 and 1891, more than 70,000 refugees from Rumelia settled in Aydın.[9] Furthermore, like Hüdavendigar, this province – particularly the districts of Bergama in the Bakırçay basin, Bayındır, Tire, and Ödemiş in the Little Meander basin, and Söke in the Great Meander basin – was favored by both local breeders and Anatolian and Rumelian merchants seeking suitable locations for wintering their sheep flocks.[10] Although many of these flocks eluded official statistics due to their departure before tax officials arrived in the spring, their presence contributed not only to disease outbreaks but also to Aydın's development as a significant center for livestock husbandry and export. As the following section will demonstrate, shipments from its districts were primarily directed towards the rapidly growing city of İzmir, as well as to Istanbul and Egypt, through İzmir and other nearby ports.

A City with Dual Roles: Consumption Center and Export Port

The emergence of İzmir as a major port city started in the seventeenth century when a confluence of factors, including the Celali uprisings, wars with the Safavids in Iran, and climatic changes, led to the rerouting of the Anatolian trade routes toward the southwest. Over the following periods, İzmir became closely integrated with the capitalist world economy, notably through its exports of agricultural products and raw materials, such as figs, opium, raisins, and natural dyes to overseas markets. By the last quarter of the nineteenth century, it had established itself as the leading export port of the Ottoman Empire and was second only to Istanbul in imports.[11] This economic vibrancy generated population growth, with the number of inhabitants increasing from around 110,000 in the 1830s to 200,000 by 1890 and reaching 300,000 in the 1910s.[12] Within this context of growth, İzmir evolved into a major center of consumption aligning with Robert Mantran's characterization of a 'stomach city.'[13] In the early twentieth century, its butchers annually slaughtered about 145,000 animals – 90,000 sheep and lambs, 35,000–40,000 cattle, and 18,000 goats – effectively doubling the figures in Bursa.[14]

İzmir sourced its cattle and sheep for slaughter both from within Aydın province and from outside regions, particularly the neighboring provinces of Konya and Hüdavendigar. While these animals were mostly herded to the city on foot, the advent of two railroad lines in western Anatolia during the latter half of the nineteenth century introduced a new transportation alternative. As Chapter 2 has noted, by the early 1900s, merchants increasingly utilized Salihli, a station on the İzmir-Kasaba line, as an assembly point for sheep driven on foot from Hüdavendigar and Konya. After a brief rest period in this town, the flocks were loaded onto trains to complete their journey to İzmir.[15] Concurrently, the other line, which ran from İzmir to Aydın, also saw growing utilization among merchants. According to a British consular report, the number of livestock transported on it increased from about 40,000 in 1908 to 53,000 in 1910.[16] Quite possibly, most of these animals were headed from the interior districts of Aydın province to İzmir, for slaughter or export.

From at least the early nineteenth century onward, one important export market for this region was Istanbul. In October 1802, Sultan Selim III (r. 1789-1807) issued a decree ordering the purchase of 9,000 sheep from the districts of Aydın, Saruhan, and Suğla (today's Kuşadası) to offset a decline in shipments from Rumelia. This was aimed at provisioning the imperial palace and army units in the capital.[17] About three years later, in January 1806, a subsequent sultanic decree addressed to the governors of these three districts required the organization of the purchase and transport of 7,500 sheep to Istanbul for the troops.[18] While such provisionist practices were phased out over the following decades, shipments from Aydın province seemed to continue and even grow in volume. An 1891 report of the Istanbul Municipality highlighted the province as one of the primary suppliers of sheep to Istanbul, not only during the summer but also throughout the winter.[19] In 1905, despite the cattle plague outbreak affecting western Anatolia, Istanbul municipal officials noted that the number of sheep and lambs arriving from İzmir and its environs reached 30,000 within the first five months of the year.[20] Likewise, reports by the governor of Aydın indicated that sheep and goat exports from İzmir, Bergama, and Dikili to the capital exceeded 7,000 heads in March-April 1908.[21]

Egypt emerged as another major export market for İzmir and nearby ports, as frequent disease outbreaks from the 1840s onward depleted its livestock supplies.[22] One such outbreak in 1842 decimated many plough animals, severely hampering agricultural production. To address this problem, the governor of Egypt, Mehmed Ali Pasha, requested permission from the imperial center to import livestock from various districts in Anatolia and Rumelia, including Plovdiv, Silistra (Silistre), Aydın, Karahisar-ı Sahib, Kayseri, Kütahya, and Saruhan. The Ottoman government responded positively, granting authorization to a merchant named Bahadıroğlu Bedros to make plough animal purchases for Egypt in Aydın and Saruhan.[23] Egyptian authorities again resorted to imports from Anatolia and Rumelia when the country was hit by another, seemingly more serious outbreak in 1863–64, which resulted in the deaths of hundreds of thousands of animals.[24] In response to their demand, the Ottoman government authorized the shipment of 150,000 sheep to Egyptian ports by the summer of 1864.[25]

The central authorities determined this number of sheep and the specific ports of shipment through negotiations with local governments. In August 1864, the Grand Vizierate sent a telegram to the Administrative Council of İzmir, inquiring whether it would consent to the collection and export of 92,500 sheep from İzmir and Kuşadası. The council responded negatively, arguing that the province's livestock supplies were insufficient to meet the local demand for meat, necessitating imports from Konya and Kütahya. When a shipment of 10,000 sheep from Kuşadası to Egypt took place in May of that year, mutton prices in İzmir increased by more than a third. To curb further price rises, the council imposed a temporary export ban from İzmir and its neighboring ports. Taking this feedback into account, the office of the Grand Vizierate ultimately authorized the shipment of only 20,000 sheep from İzmir, noting that these animals had been collected from the Anatolian interior by a merchant named Fotiadis before the ban went into effect. Thus, their absence would not precipitate a meat shortage in İzmir.[26]

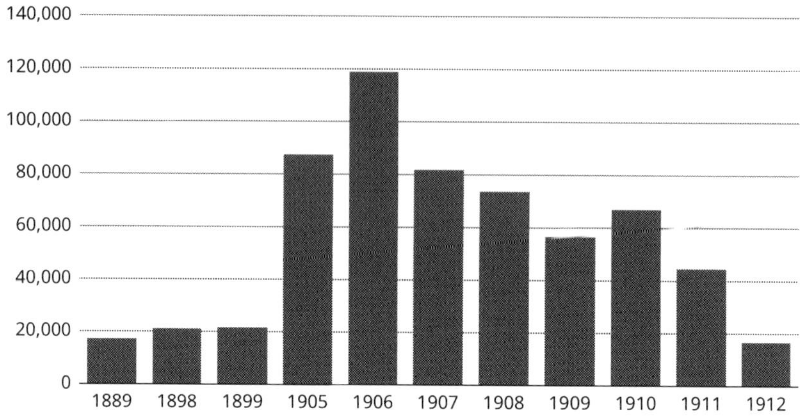

Figure 5.1 Livestock Exports from İzmir, Ayvalık, and Dikili (Head). Note: The table is compiled from British consular reports on the trade of İzmir (Smyrna). The figures for 1889, 1898, and 1899 represent cattle exports from Ayvalık and Dikili, while those from 1905 to 1910 cover exports of cattle, goat, and sheep from İzmir. The 1911 data pertains to goat and sheep exports from İzmir, and the 1912 data to only sheep exports from this port.

After the containment of this epizootic, Egypt continued to be an attractive market for Anatolian livestock, with meat prices rising due to increased demand from urban growth and subsequent disease outbreaks.[27] This became particularly evident following the Egyptian government's 1904 prohibition on slaughtering local cattle for food, a measure taken in response to the cattle plague that had been afflicting the country for several years.[28] According to Ottoman official statistics, the number of cattle shipped from the port of İzmir to Egypt and Crete was only 1,201 in 1903, but rose to 5,640 in 1904 and exceeded 12,000 in 1905.[29] The figures for ovine exports were similarly significant: in early November 1904, customs officials in İzmir recorded 11,783 sheep shipped to Alexandria since March of that year.[30] In the following year, British consular officials reported that sheep exports amounted to 67,000 heads, with a large portion destined for Egyptian ports, and exceeded 100,000 heads in 1906. Although there was a subsequent decline as the cattle plague waned in Egypt, the export figures remained substantial, fluctuating between 53,000 and 75,000 heads annually from 1907 to 1910 (See Figure 5.1).[31]

The increased volume of exports to Egypt, combined with the presence of cattle plague in central and western Anatolia, raised concerns among Ottoman officials that scarcities of plough animals and meat would soon ensue. Consequently, in 1905, the Sublime Porte enacted a ban on the export of plough animals from the ports of Beirut, İskenderun, İzmir, and Salonica.[32] This measure, which remained in force for several years, proved effective. Between 1905 and 1908, cattle exports from

İzmir declined by more than 90 percent, as noted by the French company operating the quay in the city.[33] During this period, the Administrative Council of Aydın had been advocating for the extension of the ban to include shipments of non-ploughing cattle and ovine. In a telegram addressed to the Ministry of Interior in October 1905, the council members claimed that the high volume of sheep exports to Egypt would lead to exorbitant meat prices in both İzmir and Istanbul.[34] Despite these concerns, when the Council of State reviewed a subsequent telegram from the Administrative Council of Aydın in July 1906, it decided against extending the ban for two reasons. First, the increase in meat prices was attributed not only to the expansion of export trade but also, and more importantly, to animal diseases that swept through Aydın province and other parts of the empire. Second, extending the ban would harm merchants from Hüdavendigar and Konya, as most of the animals exported from the port of İzmir came from these provinces.[35]

Although promptly approved by the Council of Ministers and the sultan, the decision by the Council of State failed to resolve the issue conclusively. In October 1906, the Administrative Council of Aydın, undeterred, issued an announcement to halt sheep exports abroad after a fifteen-day notice period. While this measure remained unimplemented due to a lack of approval from the higher echelons of the government, local officials in İzmir and Istanbul, driven by the ongoing cattle plague epizootic and severe winter conditions in central and western Anatolia, persistently pushed for a ban on sheep exports in 1907 and 1908.[36] In mid-September 1907, the mayor of Istanbul highlighted that approximately 50,000 sheep had been transported to İzmir from Konya in the preceding forty days, predominantly for shipment to Alexandria. He warned that without a temporary prohibition on such exports, meat prices in the capital would inevitably surge.[37] Likewise, in early 1908, the governor of Aydın asked his superiors in Istanbul to disallow the export of sheep and cattle outside the province for two months.[38] These pleas, however, did not lead to a policy shift, as both the Council of State and Council of Ministers were wary that imposing a wide-scale ban would disaffect livestock raisers and merchants.[39] Faced with inaction by the central government, it seems that some provincial officials in Aydın took the initiative themselves to curb the export of livestock and keep meat prices in İzmir and nearby towns moderate. For example, in March 1908, a merchant named Mustafa filed a petition complaining that local officials in the port town of Dikili refused to allow the shipment of his flock, comprising 1,000 sheep, to Istanbul.[40]

In addition to such temporary initiatives, provincial officials had a well-established policy tool at their disposal to mitigate spikes in meat prices due to İzmir's dual role as a major consumption center and an exit port for western and central Anatolian livestock. Unlike the situation in many Ottoman cities, the practice of setting a fixed price for meat remained intact in İzmir throughout most of the period between the 1850s and World War I.[41] According to a report by the governor of İzmir, a commission had been established in the city to enforce this policy by 1856.[42] Approximately three decades later, in early 1884, a cattle butcher named Hristo Dimaki filed a petition to the Sublime Porte, complaining about the imposition of a price ceiling on meat by the İzmir Municipality. In response, the governor of Aydın noted that setting a fixed price for meat was a longstanding practice in İzmir, although it had ceased to be enforced over the last several years. During this time, butchers like Hristo found ample ground for profiteering. They pushed the cost of meat for the city's residents up to fifteen piasters per *kıyye*, triggering widespread complaints among them. Thus, the governor concluded, the municipality decided to resume its policy of setting fixed prices for beef and mutton.[43]

A dispute over the *gabela* tax on kosher meat within the Jewish community of İzmir highlights the enforcement of this policy also in the early 1890s, a period when quarantines established to prevent the spread of the ongoing cholera outbreak in the empire threatened supply shortages.[44] The dispute started in August 1892, when the Chief Rabbinate of İzmir issued a decree preventing Jewish butchers from adding the *gabela* fee, amounting to one piaster per *kıyye* of meat, to the municipality's fixed sales price – an established practice in the city – and requiring them to pay the tax themselves. Faced with strong protests from community butchers, numbering around thirty, this decision soon came before the Administrative Council of Aydın for review. In November 1892, the council members suggested two potential resolutions to the rabbinate: either it could rescind the August decree and restore the old practice, or the decree could be maintained with a reduced *gabela* fee while granting the butchers the offal of slaughtered animals free of charge.[45] The sources we consulted do not detail the rabbinate's response to these suggestions or the ultimate outcome of the dispute. However, they confirm that the practice of price fixing persisted into the early twentieth century, with the involvement of not only municipal officials but also butchers and livestock merchants. For instance, on the eve of World War I, journalist Hüseyin Rıfat noted that over the previous five to six years, butchers had increased their influence over the İzmir Municipality and gained a greater say in meat pricing decisions.[46]

Before concluding this section, it is important to note that the emergence of İzmir and nearby ports in western Anatolia as livestock export hubs affected not only urban but also rural dynamics. During the late nineteenth and early twentieth centuries, districts favored by non-local merchants for winter pasturing became hotspots for escalated conflicts over grazing lands. One such conflict centered on the Hasbucak pasture in Bergama.[47] The fact that its owner, Zahide Hanım from the notable Karaosmanzade family, was an absentee landlord living in Istanbul allowed peasants from nearby villages to have a virtually free rein to use parts of this land for grazing their animals and threshing crops. However, the situation changed in the early 1890s when Zahide Hanım leased the pasture to an Albanian livestock merchant named Tahir Ağa, who denied access to the villagers. Following investigations by local officials in Bergama to address the ensuing conflict, the Administrative Council of Aydın ruled in 1895 that the villagers, despite lacking title deeds to the disputed land, should be allowed to continue utilizing it to maintain their subsistence.[48] Yet, this decision did not resolve the dispute, as it resurfaced about a decade later when Zahide Hanım leased the pasture to another Albanian merchant, Mustafa Ağa, for sheep farming. In 1911, it ultimately escalated into an armed clash between Mustafa's guards and villagers, resulting in one death and one injury.[49]

Along with the growing demand from merchants like Tahir and Mustafa, a primary driver of such conflicts was the increased use of land for cash crop cultivation, as western Anatolia became integrated into the capitalist market economy. In 1911, a British consular official on duty in the districts of Ayvalık and Bergama observed that there was great enthusiasm among landowners to break up new lands for cultivation, mainly to extend olive and vine plantations. This led to the shrinkage of grazing lands and, consequently, a decrease in cattle, sheep, and goat populations.[50] The situation was similar in other parts of Aydın province, where Onur İnal notes that, over the last decades of the nineteenth century, a large area of pasture and forest had been transformed into fig orchards.[51]

İskenderun

The town of İskenderun, situated at the eastern end of Anatolia's Mediterranean coastline and at the foot of the Amanus Mountains, had emerged as an important livestock export port by the end of the nineteenth century. This prominence was partly attributable to the extensive grazing lands in the surrounding areas, particularly within Aleppo province – of which İskenderun was a part – and the neighboring Adana province. A 1906 report by Henry Zohrab Longworth, the British Consul of Aleppo, noted the abundance of "vast plains and rich pastures ... east on the Euphrates, west on the Orontes, and north on the Jehan [Ceyhan]." The consul further observed that "large grazing grounds ... border the lakes of Antioch and Mudick... Buffaloes in herds are mostly to be seen wallowing in the mire of the Antioch swamps."[52] These lands, utilized mostly by pastoralist nomads for seasonal pasturing, sustained large numbers of livestock.[53] In the early 1890s, US consular agents estimated that tribal groups pastured around 2 million sheep across Aleppo province from the spring to autumn.[54]

By that time, İskenderun had forged strong commercial ties with most districts of Aleppo, as well as with various provinces to its north and east, further contributing

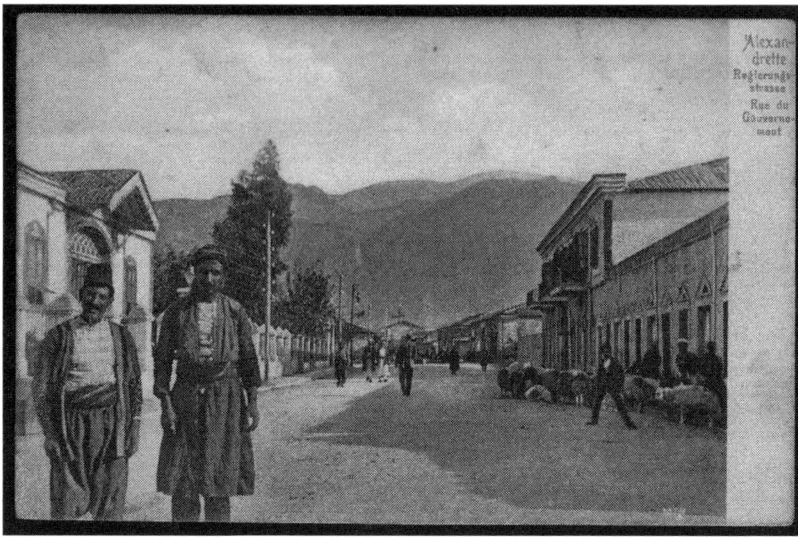

Photo 5.1 Sheep on the Streets of İskenderun in the Early Twentieth Century.
Source: The Istanbul Municipality Atatürk Library Collection

to its rise as a major export port. For example, in 1899, the British vice-consul in Van reported an improvement in trade with Aleppo, pointing out merchants' growing preference for the route from İskenderun.[55] About a decade later, his counterparts in Aleppo observed that goods being imported to and exported from districts like Kilis, Maraş, Aintab, Urfa, and Diyarbekir were all "passing through Alexandretta."[56] Since at least the late 1860s, cattle and sheep had been prominent in these trade flows, largely due to the increased demand from Egypt.[57] In 1871, a foreign observer remarked that eastern Anatolian livestock were a significant component of the cargo on nearly every steamer heading downward from Syrian ports.[58] By 1875, this trend had persisted, with annual shipments of cattle and sheep from İskenderun to the Egyptian coasts reaching 5,473 and 59,161 heads, respectively.[59] These figures experienced a downturn in the latter half of the decade, which was attributable to a government-imposed ban on the exports of ploughing cattle from İskenderun in response to a previously discussed animal disease outbreak affecting Aleppo and several Anatolian provinces.[60] Yet, a notable recovery and growth ensued in the 1880s and early 1890s. According to an 1894 report by the Administrative Council of Aleppo, the port was annually exporting about 80,000 sheep and 12,000 cattle, with these livestock originating from a broad region that extended as far as Baghdad.[61]

This growth in export trade soon triggered complaints from merchants and local officials about the insufficiency of facilities at the port of İskenderun, which

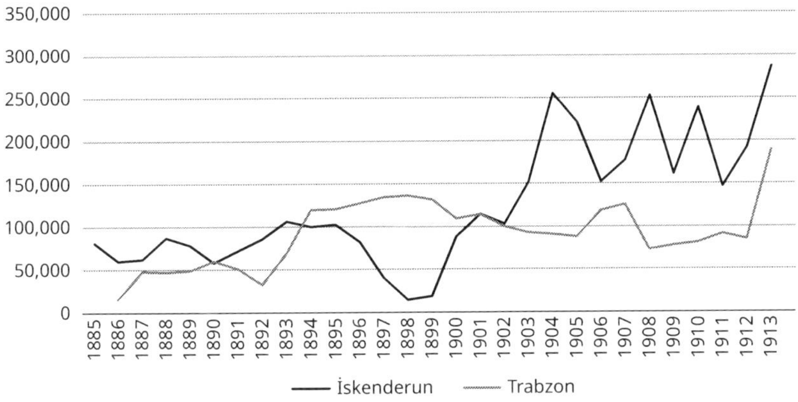

Figure 5.2 Comparison of Livestock Exports from the Ports of İskenderun and Trabzon (in British Pounds)

accommodated hundreds of ships annually.[62] By the mid-1890s, the town, with a population of around 6,000 people, lacked a pier for boats ferrying cattle and sheep to steamers anchored offshore. Consequently, merchants were compelled to embark their flocks from an open shore, leading to the drowning of some animals. Moreover, some cattle and sheep managed to escape their human guardians and wreaked havoc in the town. In response, the Administrative Council of Aleppo proposed the construction of a pier, to be financed through a new tax on cattle (one piaster per head) and sheep (five *paras* per head) exported from İskenderun. Shortly after central authorities approved this proposal with halved tax rates in late 1894, provincial officials began to voice another significant concern: the shortage of veterinarians and lack of facilities for examining animals destined for Egypt.[63]

This concern was raised at a time when cattle plague began to spread in the Syrian provinces of the empire. Identified in Damascus in 1893, the disease reached Aleppo province within a few years, resulting in the deaths of thousands of cows, oxen, and sheep. This devastation not only impaired agricultural production but also caused meat prices to surge. The situation worsened in 1897 when the Egyptian government enacted a ban on the import of cattle and sheep from Syria, leading to a significant downturn in the region's livestock export trade and revenues (See Figure 5.2). According to British consular reports, cattle shipments from the port of İskenderun fell from 14,680 heads in 1895 to approximately 5,900 in 1897, plummeting further to just 2,050 in 1899. Meanwhile, sheep exports also saw a dramatic reduction, declining more than 80 percent to 11,500 heads in 1899. However, with the lifting of the ban by the Egyptian authorities in the subsequent year as the disease abated, the situation quickly reversed. The 1900 figures indicated that 14,445 cattle and 41,300 sheep were exported from İskenderun.[64]

The upward trend continued over the next several years, driven by a major cattle plague outbreak affecting primarily Egypt, as well as the northern parts of the eastern Mediterranean. As discussed in the previous section, the Egyptian government's response to this "terrible scourge" by prohibiting the slaughter of local cattle for food created "an unusual demand" for imports.[65] Henry Barnham, the British Consul of Aleppo, observed that cattle and sheep raisers in Syria, whose flocks were also threatened with the plague, saw this as an opportunity. "Having lost part of their stock by disease," he wrote, "they were eager to find a good price for the remainder lest they should lose it in the same way."[66] This situation enticed Ottoman and foreign export merchants, drawn by the prospects of lucrative profits from livestock sales to Egypt, to make large-scale purchases in and around Aleppo province, extending as far as Mosul, Baghdad, and Amarah.[67] A significant portion of the animals acquired by these merchants subsequently ended up in İskenderun for shipment to Egypt. In December 1904, a veterinary official there reported that, from March of that year until then, 31,500 cattle and 77,700 sheep were sent to Port Said and Alexandria. By the end of the year, cattle exports came close to 37,000 heads, while ovine shipments exceeded 100,000, allowing İskenderun to outstrip Trabzon, the chief outlet for northeastern Anatolian sheep, in the value of livestock exports (see Figure 5.2).[68] This encouraged some steamer companies to initiate special regular services from İskenderun to the Egyptian coast for livestock transport.[69]

While 1904 marked a peak for İskenderun's export trade, the following decade saw the port facing occasional setbacks. The 1905 ban by the Ottoman government on exporting animals suitable for ploughing resulted in a 46 percent reduction in the volume of cattle shipments in its first year.[70] Then, in 1909, violence targeting Armenian populations in Adana and surrounding districts – including İskenderun, Osmaniye, Maraş, and Antioch – precipitated another downturn. Compared to the previous year, the value of cattle and sheep exports fell by about one-third.[71] 1911 was also challenging, as a series of environmental and financial calamities befell Aleppo. During the winter of that year, described by Raphael Fontana, the British Consul of Aleppo, as "without precedent in the memory of man," about four-fifths of the sheep in the province died due to cold and hunger. This crisis was further exacerbated by the withdrawal of credit by banks following the Italian declaration of war against the Ottoman Empire in Tripoli in the autumn, leading to the bankruptcy of many sheep merchants.[72] Consequently, by the end of the year, the value of livestock exports from İskenderun reached its nadir for the period between 1903 and 1913. However, as Figure 5.2 indicates, neither this crisis nor the two preceding downturns lasted long. Instead, they were followed by a strong recovery, which owed much to the robust trade links with Egypt.

The fact that Egypt established itself as the major customer for İskenderun's exports does not, however, mean that Alexandria and Port Said enjoyed a monopoly on shipments from there. In 1897, when the Egyptian market was closed, about 90 percent of İskenderun's cattle exports, amounting to 5,900 heads, were directed to Istanbul and Crete, with the remainder sent to Malta.[73] These destinations were, nonetheless, more than temporary alternatives to Egypt during times of hardship. In the periods both before the imposition and after the lifting of the ban, they maintained ongoing contacts with İskenderun. For example, in mid-June 1908, the daily paper *Sabah* reported the arrival of a steamer from there to Istanbul, laden with sheep belonging to a notable government meat contractor.[74] A court case brought against the Ministry of Health by a merchant named Osman Eyüp Ağa not only provides an earlier example of such contacts but also reveals that animals could be exposed to serious suffering during their sea journeys. According to Ottoman official correspondence, Osman Eyüp embarked his 2,000 sheep at İskenderun onto an Istanbul-bound ship operated by the Hacı David Company in May 1895. Upon arrival in the Dardanelles, public health officials in Kale-i Sultaniye (Çanakkale) subjected the vessel to a quarantine of five days on the grounds that it had en route stopped at a port infected with cholera. During the quarantine period, some of Osman Eyüp's sheep, already weakened by days at sea, died, leading him to sue the Ministry of Health and obtain ultimately a compensation payment of 2,000 liras.[75] Sheep densely packed in ships with limited food had little chance of survival during these long voyages.

Mersin

Mersin, a small village to the west of İskenderun with about 100 residents in the early 1850s, emerged as the major port of Adana province in the following decades. At the turn of the twentieth century, it not only served as an outlet for cotton, cereals, and other agricultural products grown in the fertile lands of the Çukurova plain but also fed the trade of interior districts such as Niğde, Kayseri, Yozgat, and Sivas.[76] These developments, leading to the growth of its population to over 20,000, were largely enabled by improvements in transportation networks and infrastructure. Notably, the opening of the sixty-seven-kilometer-long railway line between Mersin and Adana in 1886 linked the former to one of the most important cotton-producing sub-regions of Çukurova. By that time, investments by the local government and capitalist entrepreneurs had also considerably enhanced the functioning of Mersin port. While, in the early 1870s, it had four piers, two of which were made of wood and the other two of stone, by the late 1890s, this number had increased to seven, considerably facilitating anchoring and hauling works.[77]

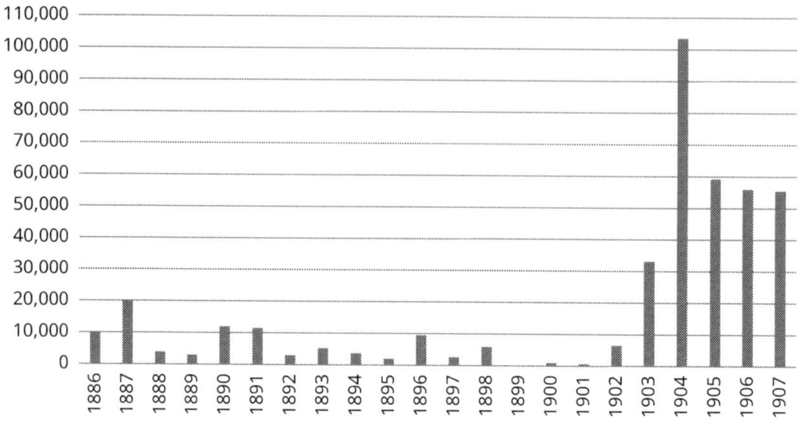

Figure 5.3 The Value of Livestock Exports from Mersin (in British Pounds)

From these piers to sailing vessels and steamers anchored offshore, local boatmen ferried a wide variety of export goods, including live animals for slaughter, albeit at modest levels from the mid-1880s to the late 1890s. According to British consular reports from this period, the value of annual cattle exports – including both cattle and sheep – exceeded 10,000 pounds only three times, indicating that their volume often amounted to several thousand heads. Although this trend saw occasional upward movements, it was short-lived. When, for example, Adana, along with central Anatolian provinces, was hit by a drought in 1887, thousands of animals were sold at low prices by their raisers before they died of hunger. However, the resultant growth in exports was quickly undone in 1888, as the ongoing adverse weather conditions, coupled with the hasty sales of the previous year, considerably reduced the livestock population available for trade.[78] With the subsequent improvement in weather conditions, leading to at least a partial recovery of the population, export activity regained some momentum. In 1891, shipments of cattle and sheep climbed to 7,650 heads, but this uptick was also swiftly reversed due to ensuing challenges, including cattle plague and cholera outbreaks in 1892 and 1895, respectively (see Figure 5.3).[79]

The low volume of exports recorded by consular officials is striking, given the large livestock numbers in Adana province, despite the decimating consequences of government-enforced tribal sedentarization in the 1860s and 1870s. While tax officials counted 1,096,667 sheep and goats there in 1879, a figure slightly above the one for Erzurum, by the eve of World War I, Ottoman official statistics reported their population as approximately 1.7 million. According to the same statistics, there were also about 360,000 cattle, used mainly for ploughing the fertile lands of Çukurova.[80] As the British Vice-Consul in Adana reported in 1903, the trade of these animals was an important component of the provincial economy, with Mersin being only one of the various outlets for them.[81] Merchants in the eastern part of the province, which remained as the latest settled area of Çukurova, apparently favored the closer port of İskenderun for their shipments to Egypt and other markets.[82] In contrast, major livestock-raising centers in the west, such as Silifke and Gülnar, had long-established networks with the northern interior that extended to Konya province, serving as wintering grounds for sheep flocks from there.[83] It is plausible that, rather than being exported from Mersin, some of these animals were directed to northern and western markets after returning to their summer pastures, while some others catered to the growing demand for meat in the two nearby flourishing urban centers, Mersin and Adana.[84]

Despite these restraining factors, and although still lagging far behind İskenderun, Mersin's export trade witnessed considerable growth in the early years of the twentieth century (see Figure 5.3). According to both Ottoman and foreign sources, a significant driver of this development was the increasing demand from Egypt.[85] The aforementioned British consular report for 1903 identified Alexandria and Jaffa as the principal destinations of livestock shipments from Mersin.[86] In November 1904, a veterinary official in Mersin sent a telegram to his counterparts in the capital, revealing that from March of that year until then, a total of 9,537 sheep and 3,480 cattle had been dispatched to Alexandria, Malta, and Piraeus. In the days and weeks that followed, these numbers continued to rise due to two factors: first, the ongoing cattle plague outbreak in Egypt, and second, the fact that most livestock shipments from Mersin took place during the six-month period from September to March. Consequently, the value of exports reached a peak level by the end of 1904 (see Figure 5.3). About a year later, the Istanbul Municipality reported that the primary market for livestock trade from Mersin, handled by both Ottoman and foreign merchants, was Alexandria, followed by Piraeus, Beirut, and Jaffa.[87] Likewise, a US government document from the 1910s noted cattle, goat, and sheep exports to Egypt among the major trade activities in Mersin.[88] As the links with Alexandria strengthened, steamer companies, seeking to capitalize on the growing market demand, began to offer improved services to livestock merchants. For instance, the Khedivial Company, which made weekly stops at Mersin, was reportedly renowned for its facilities, enabling safe and rapid transport of cattle and sheep to Egypt.[89]

Although Istanbul was not mentioned in any of the above documents, this does not indicate a complete absence of contact with Mersin. In fact, during periods when the capital's established supply lines faced shortages, shipments from this southern port appeared to reach noticeable levels. For instance, in May or June 1878, amidst a meat scarcity triggered by the recently concluded 1877–78 war against Russia, a British-flagged ship from Mersin anchored off Istanbul's Marmara Sea coast and unloaded 4,000 head of sheep at the Haydarpaşa pier.[90] In 1892, the capital may have received similar shipments from the south when its sheep supply from the Black Sea coast was significantly constrained due to government-imposed cholera quarantines. According to tax-farmers authorized to collect the tax on slaughter animals in Istanbul, many Anatolian merchants responded to this constraint by directing their flocks to southern markets and ports, including Aleppo, Damascus, and Mersin. From the latter, some of these merchants likely made their way back to the capital via the sea route along the Mediterranean and Aegean coasts, aiming to take advantage of rising meat prices there.[91]

Antalya

The district of Antalya, located on the southwest coast of Anatolia, was characterized by its mountainous terrain, abundant fertile lands for cultivation, and extensive forests. Livestock raising constituted a major economic activity, particularly among its tribal populations who engaged in seasonal migrations between the lowlands in Antalya and highland summer pastures in Beyşehir, Seydişehir, and Hamidabad, all within Konya province. In 1898, Gustave Keun, the British Vice-Consul in Antalya, used Ottoman tax registers to report the district's goat, sheep, and camel populations as 580,000, 60,000, and 28,000, respectively. He also provided estimates – likely overstated – of there being 150,000 milk cows and 100,000 ploughing oxen. Fifteen years later, Ottoman official statistics showed that the combined populations of sheep and goats remained at roughly the same levels, with the total for oxen and cows nearing 165,000. Despite these relatively large numbers, livestock trade from Antalya stayed limited, often lagging behind Mersin.[92] As indicated by Figure 5.4, compiled from British consular reports, the volume of annual shipments did not seem to exceed 10,000 heads during the late 1890s and early 1900s.

One major reason for this limited volume was that, unlike İskenderun and Mersin, Antalya did not have strong animal trade networks with Egypt.[93] Exports from there were mostly, if not exclusively, oriented towards the nearby Aegean islands, which had smaller consumer markets where cattle were in higher demand than sheep or goats. The figures showed an upward movement at times when merchants could also undertake shipments to other destinations. A notable instance was in 1907, when about half of the goat and sheep exports ended up going to Egypt.[94] Similarly, Gustave Keun noted that the more than two-fold increase in cattle exports between 1909 and 1911 was partly due to a "brisker trade" with Egyptian ports, facilitated in transit through the island of Rhodes. According to the vice-consul, another driving force behind this development was a recent outbreak of cattle plague in Antalya. Coupled with the severe winter of 1910, the disease decimated

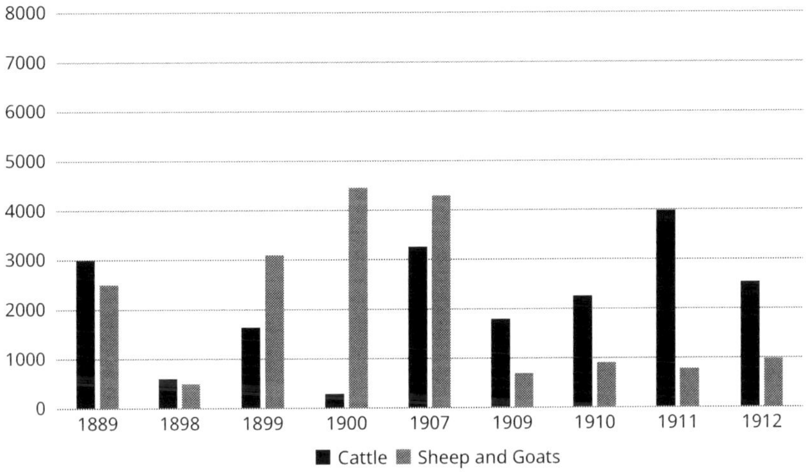

Figure 5.4 Livestock Exports from Antalya (Head)

a significant number of cattle and goats. Fearing further losses, cultivators and livestock raisers were prompted to dispose of their surviving animals.[95]

Rural populations in Antalya responded to earlier calamities threatening their flocks in a seemingly similar way. When the district was hit by a drought in 1899, which dried up the grazing lands and caused significant animal losses, sales of livestock showed a considerable increase compared to the previous year (see Figure 5.4).[96] In 1905, pastures were again damaged severely, this time by excessive wet weather during the winter months. With most peasants lacking sufficient stocks of fodder, their flocks suffered losses from malnutrition, totaling more than 5,000. Meanwhile, outbreaks of pleuropneumonia, particularly severe in the northern parts of the district, and of foot-and-mouth disease in the south, led to considerable mortalities among emaciated camels, cattle, goats, and sheep. One immediate consequence of these combined challenges was an expansion in livestock trade, as noted by Gustave Keun: "The general trade for 1905, compared with that of 1904, showed an increase of 10,000 [pounds] in exports. ... The surplus in exports was most noticeable in cattle, silk, and cocoons."[97] It is, however, important to note that such calamity-induced upsurges did not often last long. The expansion observed in 1899 was swiftly followed by a sharp decline in cattle exports the following year, directly attributable to a reduction in their population due to the drought. Likewise, when the cattle plague prevalent in the district was contained in 1912, cultivators and livestock raisers felt relieved and thus, cattle exports fell by more than a third compared to the previous year.[98]

Conclusion

This chapter has demonstrated the role of calamities in the establishment and expansion of livestock trade networks. Recurrent disease outbreaks and climate-related hazards compelled rural communities in Anatolian and Syrian provinces to quickly sell their emaciated animals for cash, while also enabling them to access flourishing export markets. By the early twentieth century, numerous ships laden with cattle and sheep were navigating from İzmir, İskenderun, Mersin, and Antalya to Alexandria, Port Said, and various other eastern Mediterranean ports. The trade with Egypt, in particular, proved so profitable that it attracted not only Ottoman but also a significant number of foreign merchants, notably those based in İskenderun and Mersin. However, this boom was not without its challenges and disputes. Provincial officials in İzmir called for regulations to curtail the city's role as a livestock export center, aiming to cater to the growing local demand for beef and mutton. Yet, despite pressure from them and their counterparts in the Istanbul Municipality, the government, concerned not to alienate mercantile interests in central and western Anatolia, refused to impose a ban on sheep exports from İzmir and other ports. This decision, in turn, induced the İzmir Municipality to maintain the practice of setting a fixed price for meat until the end of the empire, showing the importance of local dynamics in setting the pace for the adoption of liberal economic policies.

The chapter also sheds some light on the question of how the lives of cattle, sheep, and goats were affected by the increased demand on them for slaughter. The commercialization of pasture lands in western Anatolia, triggered by this increased demand, enabled large landholders, such as Zahide Hanım from the Karaosmanzade family, to secure lucrative lease contracts with non-local sheep merchants. However, it also resulted in restricted access for locally raised flocks to customary grazing areas, threatening their subsistence and provoking tense land conflicts. The situation was further aggravated by the integration of İzmir's hinterlands into the world capitalist economy as a supplier of various cash crops, leading to the accelerated conversion of pastures into farmlands. Welfare challenges continued for the animals after they arrived in port towns and cities for shipment to Egypt and other markets. While many of them drowned on the open shores of the Mediterranean due to poor port facilities, some, just like their counterparts that had been embarked at Trabzon and Bandırma, could not cope with the rigors of sea voyage and died on the decks of ships.

The loss of animals in transport and restrictions imposed on their movement during disease outbreaks not only placed individual merchants in a difficult position but also caused serious setbacks in exports, particularly from İskenderun and İzmir. Despite these challenges, both ports, along with Trabzon and Bandırma, remained pivotal livestock trade hubs in Ottoman Anatolia until the end of the empire. This resilience was largely attributable to their diversification beyond a single market. As the above account reveals, even during the late 1890s when its primary market, Egypt, faced a temporary closure, İskenderun's export figures remained at noteworthy levels, thanks to its ongoing contacts with Crete, Malta, and Istanbul. Growing demand from the imperial capital also played a key role in the vibrancy of İzmir and Dikili. According to merchants' accounts, on the eve of World War I, İzmir's daily exports of cattle and sheep to Istanbul amounted to thousands of heads.[99] The following chapter will explore how the trade of these animals, along with those coming from other parts of the empire by land or sea, was organized once they arrived in Istanbul, the largest 'stomach city' of the Ottomans.

CHAPTER 6

Feeding the Imperial Capital

Abstract

This chapter examines the organization of sheep and fresh meat trade in Istanbul, the largest consumer market of the Ottoman Empire. It discusses the evolution of provisionist policies from the late eighteenth to the mid-nineteenth century, highlighting how the demand for a steady meat supply for the imperial palace, army, and other state institutions enabled meat contracting to become a viable business. Concurrently, state efforts to keep meat prices affordable for Istanbulites influenced market dynamics through price controls and shipment quotas, directing the flow of sheep from provinces to Istanbul. Then, in response to surging meat prices driven by wars, famines, and disease outbreaks, the government abolished such measures by the early 1860s and introduced liberal economic policies. This, however, did not result in a completely free market. Instead, the government took various steps to establish a public health-oriented regulatory regime to ensure the wholesomeness of meat supplies. Moreover, in times of supply shortages, old protective measures were often revisited, and some were temporarily reintroduced. Finally, this chapter reveals that while Istanbul's sheep and meat markets were prone to breakdowns, challenging small-scale butchers and merchants, they also provided opportunities for more established ones to expand their fortunes.

Keywords: Istanbul; provisionism; liberal economic policies; public health; abattoir

While Bursa, İzmir, Cairo, and Alexandria were important consumption markets, Istanbul ranked first among them, thanks to its status as the capital and the largest center of population in the empire. Ensuring a steady supply of provisions for its residents was a major concern for the Ottoman state from at least the sixteenth century onwards. Meat, particularly mutton, ranked second to grain in importance among foodstuff imports to Istanbul.[1] As Anthony Greenwood notes, "the authorities involved in regulating the city's mutton supply looked first to the Balkans,"[2] yet we have shown that the Anatolian supply increased in importance from the late eighteenth to the early twentieth centuries. This chapter focuses on how this transformation influenced the livestock trade in Istanbul. First, we discuss how provisionist policies worked in the first half of the nineteenth century. On one hand, the need to provide a steady meat supply for the imperial palace, army, and other state institutions led to the rise of sheep merchants, particularly government meat contractors, as important economic actors. On the other hand, state efforts to keep meat prices affordable for Istanbul residents pressured market dynamics with price controls and shipment quotas that required the orientation of sheep from Anatolia to Istanbul.

Then, the chapter discusses the effects of the adoption of liberal policies, such as the abolition of the *ondalık ağnam* tax, shipment quotas, and price controls. While this change took place in the context of severe conditions of wars, famines, epidemics, epizootics, and financial difficulties, it did not allow market forces free rein. In times of crisis, state interventionism revived in different forms. Old protective mechanisms, such as the regeneration of guilds and reintroduction of price controls, were accompanied by new practices, including the redefinition of the role of the head trader and commercialization of the Uzunçayır meadow as the first entrance point of the Anatolian sheep to the city. The chapter argues that this fragile environment posed not only challenges but also opportunities for sheep merchants and butchers. As the following lines will demonstrate, some among them ended up accumulating substantial economic capital.

Finally, after explaining the trade dynamics and its management, the chapter focuses on livestock as an active part of urban life. Upon arrival by land or sea, they moved, grazed, and were sold and slaughtered in the capital. Each of these activities became a sanitation and regulation concern for state authorities. An orderly march of animals from their arrival ports to inner-city pastures, the maintenance of forage and meadows, and the absence of a central abattoir exemplified these concerns. Moreover, the densely populated and disease-prone city environment necessitated additional sanitation measures. State attempts to address these issues and ensure a regular supply of livestock continued throughout the period under investigation.

A Regulatory Regime of Provisioning

As discussed in the introduction chapter, to ensure a steady flow of slaughter animals to Istanbul, the government set up a complex provisioning system in which a variety of actors played a considerable role. A major concern of the state was to supply meat to the palace, government officials, troops, and state dependents. For this purpose, it employed meat contractors, who were awarded contracts through an auction process where candidates offering the lowest price for meat to be delivered won the bid. During the early nineteenth century, most of the *Kıvırcık* sheep collected as *ondalık ağnam* by tax farmers were handed over to these contractors, while some were sold to butchers in Istanbul to be slaughtered and retailed to ordinary consumers. However, after this tax was converted to cash in some districts of Rumelia in the late 1840s, the contractors were compelled to undertake large-scale purchases from livestock raisers to fulfill their obligations, which now included delivering 5,000 head of sheep per month to butchers.[3] The latter number could be increased in times of potential difficulty. For example, to prevent a shortage of meat in the winter of 1856–57, the Council on Financial Accounting under the Ministry of Finance called the meat contractors, Hacı Hüseyin and Dimitraki, to a meeting. There, the two entrepreneurs signed a document promising that in the four-month period between mid-December and mid-April, they would deliver 32,000 head of sheep to the Istanbul butchers.[4]

Besides establishing a robust and flexible network of supply, another major goal of the Ottoman state authorities was to prevent lamb, mutton, and beef from becoming largely unaffordable for the population. To achieve this, they sought to effectively regulate market transactions. As part of this effort, they required livestock merchants and other suppliers destined for Istanbul not to sell their flocks en route but to drive them to designated places in the city. For example, dairy owners in the capital's nearby districts of Çatalca, Çekmece, and Silivri, who provisioned the city with thousands of lambs for the feast of Khidir, were often required to ensure that they would deliver their animals to slaughterhouses in Yedikule. Upon arrival in Istanbul, they also did not have the right to select their customers at will. In Yedikule and other designated markets, such as the çiftlik of Kara Ahmetli in Eyüp and Uzunçayır, authorities allowed sales only to the city's guild butchers.[5] However, exceptions were made during times of scarcity, granting lamb owners the right of 'sale on foot' (*ayaktan satış*), allowing them to sell directly to any customers without such restrictions.[6]

To keep costs from rising in transactions between merchants and butchers, as well as between butchers and consumers, the government sought to enforce price controls through the *narh*. While setting the *narh*, an important factor that the officials in charge had to consider was seasonal fluctuations in supplies. The decline in livestock shipments to Istanbul during winter and early spring had generally led to higher prices for meat and sometimes even to the temporary closure of butcher shops.[7] Furthermore, the arrival of spring did not always bring an easing of the inflationary pressures. For instance, because of scarcities caused by the Ottoman-Russian war on the Danube, the consumer price of a *kıyye* of mutton reached slightly over forty *paras* by the summer of 1808. This elicited a strong response from the government. With the direct intervention of Grand Vizier Alemdar Mustafa Pasha, the new *narh* was set at twenty-five *paras*.[8] In making this move, the chief motive of the pasha was a political one. He had witnessed how popular unrest, fueled by scarcities and soaring food prices, contributed to the fall of Sultan Selim III's New Order (*Nizam-ı Cedid*) just a year earlier.[9] He thus knew that to maintain its position of power, his government should take immediate measures to curb inflation. Yet, like other Ottoman ruling elites of his period, Alemdar Mustafa was also aware that such measures should not alienate livestock suppliers. Otherwise, lamb, sheep and cattle shipments to Istanbul would further decline. Because of this concern, suppliers were often granted a say in pricing decisions. Especially during the feast of Khidir, when plenty of meat was a crucial part of celebrations, the government authorities were willing to accommodate their demands for increased lamb prices to ensure shipments to Istanbul.[10]

However, the *narh* system and other aforementioned regulatory measures were by no means fully effective. During the eighteenth and early nineteenth centuries, there were frequent complaints that some butchers and speculators met livestock merchants en route to the capital and purchased their cattle or sheep illicitly. Then these animals were sold in Istanbul at prices above the *narh*. Likewise, there were occasional reports that meat contractors did not fulfill their responsibility to provide a certain number of sheep for the city's butchers.[11] Yet, despite such challenges, the Ottoman state did not relinquish its regulatory control over livestock and meat markets until the 1850s. At this point, a shift occurred from regulation to a greater reliance on free market forces. The following section examines developments that undermined the Ottoman provisioning system, followed by analysis of how liberalization proceeded.

From a Provisionist to a Liberal Economy

From the 1830s onwards, the Ottomans embarked on a set of liberal economic reforms aimed at easing the flow of merchandise across the country.[12] These reforms were partly a response to the sharp upward movement of the prices during the previous decades. The Istanbul meat market did not remain unaffected by this inflationary trend, fueled to a great degree by the frequent debasement of silver coinage in circulation, interruption of supplies because of recurring wars and territorial losses in Rumelia, and nearly continuous outbreaks of famine, animal disease, and other calamities.[13] Over the fifty year period between September 1779 and September 1830, the official price of a *kıyye* of meat increased more than sevenfold, reaching over 1.5 piasters (sixty *paras*), and had climbed to ninety *paras* by the very end of the 1830s (See Figure 6.1). The upward trend continued during the following decades. In the early 1840s, both the residents and visitors to Istanbul were complaining that mutton was rarely sold under three piasters per kıyye.[14] The scarcities imposed by the Crimean War later drove prices to more than double this level.[15] As shown in Figure 6.2, which was compiled from Ottoman state documents and newspaper reports, the end of the war did not halt this upward movement. On the contrary, as sheep and cattle populations were decimated by a harsh winter, meat prices reached a new high of fifteen–sixteen piasters per *kıyye* in late 1857 and

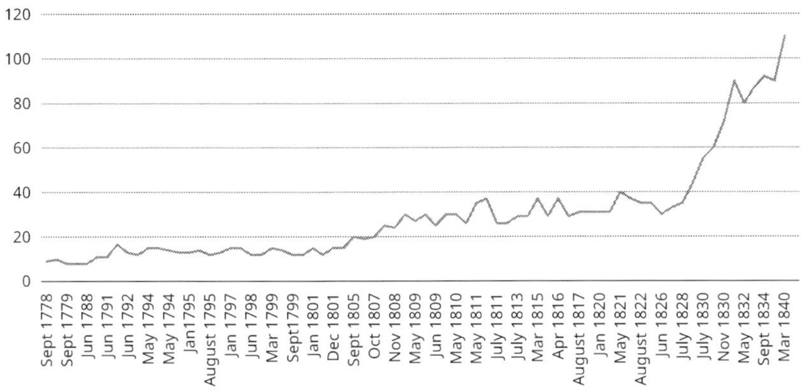

Figure 6.1 Narh Prices for Mutton in Istanbul, 1778–1840 (in *paras* per *kıyye*). Source: Çakmak, "Narh ve Nizâm Kayıtlarına Göre İstanbul'da Koyun Eti Fiyatları," pp. 80-84.

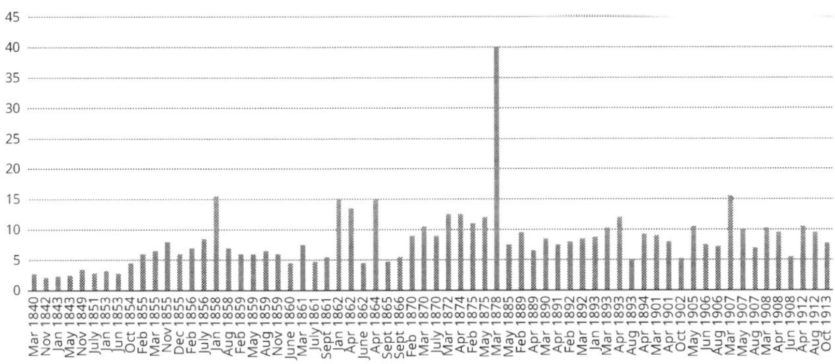

Figure 6.2 Mutton Prices in Istanbul, 1840–1913 (In piasters per *kıyye*)

early 1858.[16] The next year saw a discernible decline from this high point, thanks mainly to a mild winter, and then came a period of relative calm. Things, however, turned upside down once again in the early 1860s when the vast amount of paper money issued by the government to address the empire's growing financial problems caused a major wave of inflation. The inflationary environment deterred merchants from engaging in business, leading to a substantial reduction in live sheep exports from both Anatolia and Rumelia to the capital. As a result, mutton prices reached fifteen piasters in the winter of 1861–62.[17]

It was in this context of high inflation that the Ottoman ruling elites began to question the efficacy of their urban provisioning policies for meat. By the mid-nineteenth century, they predominantly held a view of economic rationality that presumed markets operated more efficiently when left to their own devices.[18] Hence, like their counterparts in Europe and the Americas, they embarked on a set of liberal economic reforms that undermined the state's regulatory control over livestock and meat markets in Istanbul. In a report addressed to the Grand Vizierate in March 1855, the Supreme Council of Judicial Ordinance argued that it was the butchers' monopoly on meat that caused the recent surge in meat prices and proposed its abolishment. After being examined by an expert committee composed of representatives from the Ministries of Finance, the Marketplace, and Trade, Sultan Abdülmecid (r. 1839–61) approved this proposal and put it into effect in early 1856.[19] Shortly afterward, the practice of setting *narh* for meat came under heavy attack in government circles for discouraging shipments to Istanbul. Hence, around the late 1850s or 1860, the Municipality of the Sixth District announced that the pricing controls would no longer be continued in districts under its jurisdiction, namely Galata, Pera, and Tophane. This decision was then extended to other parts of the city in the spring of 1862.[20]

The era of liberalization also witnessed the dismantling of regulations that sought to ensure a steady supply of livestock to the imperial capital. As discussed in the preceding chapters, in 1857, in response to a treasury crisis, the government eliminated the *ondalık ağnam* tax and instead levied a monetary tax on each head of sheep. Another major blow to meat provisioning occurred just over a decade later with the abolishment of the practice of imposing annual quotas on certain tribes and provinces in Anatolia. Thereafter, Istanbul, whose population including the environs grew from approximately 500,000 in the late 1850s to 895,000 in 1884, and exceeded a million by the early twentieth century, mainly relied on free market mechanisms for meat supply, with demand rising considerably alongside the population.[21] The annual consumption of sheep increased from between 600,000 and 800,000 in the 1840s to slightly over one million in the early 1870s and to 1.5 million three decades later, remaining around this level until the outbreak of World War I.[22]

As the rising demand could often be met through increased imports, especially from Anatolia, major inflation in meat prices rarely occurred during this new era. Prices generally followed an established seasonal pattern. They moved upward to between seven and ten piasters in the winter and the early spring months when livestock shipments to Istanbul dropped by about half. As supplies increased from mid-spring to fall, they fell and remained in a range between five and 7.5 piasters. However, at times when wars, climate disruptions, and disease outbreaks resulted in a shortage of sheep and other livestock in the capital, this pattern was broken. For example, in the famine year of 1875 in central Anatolia, winter prices for mutton hovered around twelve piasters per *kıyye*. Likewise, the decimation of livestock populations in this region and other major supply centers for the capital, caused by the long and cold winter of 1906–07 and the cattle plague, drove prices up to sixteen piasters per *kıyye* in March 1907.[23]

A more vigorous surge took place during the Ottoman-Russian war of 1877–78. As discussed in Chapter 2, the government issued large sums of *kaime* to cover wartime expenses, causing its value to drop by more than 300 percent. Consequently, livestock merchants rapidly lost confidence in paper currency and demonstrated a strong reluctance to bring their animals to the market.[24] The situation further deteriorated as supplies were increasingly diverted to troops in Rumelia. In early March 1878, the daily paper *Basiret* noted that the price of a *kıyye* of meat had more than tripled from its February 1875 level.[25] While the period between the mid-1880s and World War I did not witness such an upward movement in prices, Istanbul still faced occasional shortages, which resulted in inflationary pressure on the meat market. In the early 1890s, a major cause of this was epidemic and epizootic outbreaks. For instance, the government temporarily banned livestock shipments from İzmid in late 1889 and early 1890, as the district, located along the route connecting central and northeastern Anatolia to the capital, was hit by cattle plague.[26] Only a few years later, in 1892, quarantine restrictions imposed to prevent the spread of cholera significantly decreased the number of sheep exported from the Black Sea coast to the capital, as discussed in Chapter 3. Thus, by the end of March 1893, the price of meat had reached twelve piasters.[27]

The Old Within the New

The wave of liberal reforms did not entirely sweep away the institutions and practices of the old order, largely due to concerns about such upward price movements. When a cholera epidemic that appeared in Hijaz in 1865 spread to Istanbul in the summer of that year, sheep merchants en route to the capital became frightened and refused to drive their flocks beyond Çorlu in Rumelia and İzmid in Anatolia. This soon resulted in meat scarcity, prompting the government to dispatch several officials to these districts to pressure the merchants to change their decision. This move seemed to bear fruit quite quickly. According to the merchants' accounts, by late September, about 20,000 head of sheep had arrived from İzmid to Üsküdar. Around the same time, the government took another important step and temporarily reinstated the practice of setting *narh* prices for meat.[28]

About thirty years later, during another cholera outbreak, price fixing once again came to the agenda of the government. Upon receiving reports that the retail price of meat rose to thirteen–fifteen piasters per *kıyye*, the secretariat of the Yıldız Palace issued a directive in mid-March 1893 to the Istanbul Municipality to resume *narh* imposition. However, Rıdvan Pasha, the mayor of Istanbul, immediately responded with a letter opposing this measure on the grounds that once the municipality began to set a price for meat, sheep merchants would curtail their shipments to Istanbul.[29] This argument proved effective, as the order from the palace was consequently not put into practice. In the following decades, the position represented by Rıdvan Pasha remained dominant in government circles, even during food supply shortages occasioned by World War I. In a parliamentary speech delivered in March 1917, Grand Vizier Talat Pasha stated that his government would not establish fixed prices for meat and other essentials because such measures would discourage merchants from bringing outside merchandise for sale in Istanbul and thereby exacerbate scarcities. Yet, as prices continued to rise, he changed his stance a few months later. From then on, until the end of the war, meat prices remained subjected to the *narh*. However, this did not curb the inflationary spiral. In early 1918, the residents of Istanbul had to pay more than 100, and by some accounts up to 200 piasters, for a *kıyye* of mutton.[30]

Another important component of the old order that persisted in the new one was the post of head trader. As discussed in Chapter 2, while duties assigned to this post underwent several important changes following the abolishment of the regulations concerning the shipment quotas of the Cihanbeyli and affiliated tribes, there were still continuities between the old order and the new one. In both, the head trader's major task was to oversee and facilitate the sheep trade from central Anatolia to Istanbul. When the quota system was in force, the post holder's major responsibility was to first ensure the collection of the required number of sheep and later their delivery to the Istanbul market. After this system was abolished, head traders began to function primarily as intermediaries for the Cihanbeyli and other tribal merchants who brought their flocks to Uzunçayır, helping them find customers and actively taking part in the negotiation of prices.

By the early 1870s, head traders expanded the scope of their activities to include all Anatolian merchants who drove their flocks to Uzunçayır.[31] This move was apparently made to compensate for losses caused by the famine that prevailed in central Anatolia in 1873–75, resulting in a decline in live sheep exports from the region to Istanbul and consequently a decrease in head trader revenues. The government consented to it mainly because, at that time, there was a steady stream of petitions and newspaper reports drawing attention to abuses suffered by sheep merchants at the hands of fraudulent butchers. For example, in 1872, a group of Istanbul butchers filed a petition complaining that some of their counterparts refrained from paying their debts to merchants, which led to two problems: a decline in shipments to the capital and an increase in prices there.[32] Another widespread form of abuse by the butchers was manipulating the *çaşni* system to their advantage. *Çaşni*, an old and well-established custom, required that once a preliminary sales agreement was reached, the selling merchant would drive his sheep to a pen, where a sample of one in fifteen was selected to be slaughtered to determine the average weight of all animals in the flock. Newspaper reports indicate that some butchers deliberately selected lower-weight animals for this initial slaughter group, thereby reducing their purchasing costs.[33]

Upon reviewing such reports and petitions, authorities in Istanbul likely concluded that head traders, being thoroughly familiar with market conditions, could protect the interests of merchants by providing them with accurate information about the reputations of butchers. However, this positive perception changed dramatically in the late 1870s and early 1880s, when the imperial capital suffered frequent meat shortages due to the 1877–78 war against Russia, harsh winters, and animal disease outbreaks affecting various Anatolian provinces. Municipal officials mostly blamed profiteering Istanbul butchers for these shortages and concurrent price rises. According to their reports, these butchers met Anatolian merchants en route to Istanbul, purchased their flocks in advance, and then engaged in the speculative practice of sheep passing from hand to hand, with prices increasing each time. To make matters worse, instead of curbing such activities, the head traders cooperated with and even directed the profiteers. As mentioned in Chapter 2, these reports found a receptive audience within the higher echelons of the government, ultimately leading to the abolition of the post of head trader by the Council of State in December 1882, with its responsibilities delegated to municipal inspectors.[34]

The years leading up to the government's abolition decision saw another important development in the Istanbul livestock market, driven by the active role of head merchants: the commodification of land-use rights at the Uzunçayır meadow. One early initiative in this direction came from a certain Hacı Süleyman Ağa, who submitted a petition in January 1871 proposing to lease the meadow, then in the possession of the Privy Purse, for five years at an annual rent of 10,000 piasters. During this period, he would serve as head trader and, like his predecessors, take one sheep from every flock of 200, without charging an extra fee for granting grazing permits to merchants.[35] The government responded negatively to this proposal. Yet, when a similar one was put forth in the latter half of the decade, its outcome turned out to be different, mainly due to a severe financial crisis that led to a default on loan payments by the Ottoman Empire in 1875.[36]

This difficult financial situation required the government to find new revenue sources. Hence, the administration of the Privy Purse reversed its previous stance in 1879 and agreed to lease the Uzunçayır meadow to the incumbent head trader, also named Süleyman Ağa, who was a member of the Cihanbeyli tribe, for two years at fifteen liras per annum. Until then sheep merchants and itinerant butchers could freely graze their sheep in Uzunçayır to recover from the days-long journey to the capital. However, now Süleyman Ağa required them to pay a grazing fee of between five and twenty piasters per flock, in addition to the head trader's fee. After the expiration of his two-year tenancy term, neither Süleyman nor the two succeeding head traders, both from the Cihanbeyli tribe, were able to secure another contract. That was because the venture had become increasingly profitable, with shipments from Anatolia rising after the early 1880s, leading other entrepreneurs to offer higher rents for the meadow.[37] In 1884, Hacı Ali Rıza Efendi from Eğin, previously discussed in Chapter 2, won a five-year contract by offering 255 liras annually.[38] Then, in 1889, he secured another contract, extending his term for another five years. During this decade-long lease period, he earned considerable revenues by increasing the grazing fee per sheep by about sixfold and by providing intermediary services as a de-facto head trader for some Anatolian merchants in their transactions in Istanbul.[39]

However, over time, a variety of obstacles made it difficult for Ali Rıza Efendi to expand and even maintain his customer base. A major one was that some Anatolian merchants began to establish themselves in Istanbul, while another stemmed from changes in trade routes. As discussed in Chapter 3, from the mid-1880s onward, merchants from northeastern Anatolia increasingly chose to export their flocks to Istanbul by sea through the port of Trabzon rather than by land. When steamers laden with sheep from this region arrived in the capital, they either anchored offshore near the Kabataş pier or were moored at the Galata dock, which opened in the mid-1890s. After being unloaded, these animals were driven through the busy streets of Galata, the commercial and financial center of the city, which was also home to a moderately large sheep and goat population in the backyards of houses and butcher shops. From there, most of them were taken to meadows in Feriköy, Okmeydanı, and surrounding areas near the Kağıthane stream, where they were grazed and sold.[40] The growing importance of these meadows, which lay outside Ali Rıza's sphere of authority, threatened to cause a decline in his grazing revenues. To make matters worse for him, concurrently with this development, rival actors began to emerge, providing intermediary services to provincial merchants for their transactions in Istanbul. A notable example was the guild of livestock merchants from Rumelia and Anatolia.[41]

The Guild and Its Demand for a Regulated Market

As key institutions of the provisionist period, some guilds survived or were regenerated in the liberal era, playing a role in state attempts to control the livestock trade. Among them was the guild of livestock merchants, established in the mid-1880s and closely controlled by the Hamidian government. The sultan seemed to play a pivotal role in the appointment of its leaders.[42] The longest-serving person in the post of steward was one of his confidential chamberlains, Faik Bey. He began his tenure in March 1892 and remained in the post for more than sixteen years, until the Young Turk Revolution, shortly after which the organization was dissolved.[43]

This position ensured a steady and comfortable income for Faik Bey and his predecessors, as merchants were required to pay a stewardship fee of six *paras* per head of sheep brought to Istanbul for sale.[44] However, Ottoman ruling elites did not merely use the merchants' guild to provide economic benefits to their loyalists. Particularly during periods of decline in provincial exports to Istanbul, they sought to monitor merchants' activities and intervene in the market through guild leadership. One such time was in 1906 when a combination of factors discussed in the preceding chapters – including the rise in cattle and sheep shipments from various Anatolian ports to Egypt and the outbreak of animal diseases in different parts of the empire – pushed meat prices up.[45] To reverse this upward trend, the Istanbul Municipality authorized the deputy steward of the guild, Osman Bey, along with two notable sheep merchants, to establish open markets in various localities where merchants would undertake retail sales to the public at prices below those charged by butchers.[46]

The guild was, however, more than just a tool in the hands of the government. Sheep merchants from Anatolia and Rumelia pressured its leadership to voice their complaints and offer proposals for improvement, particularly in the 1880s. A common complaint was that butchers defaulted on the payment of their debts, leading to several petitions being submitted to the Council of State and the Grand Vizierate. One of these, penned in November 1887 by the incumbent guild steward, Abdullah Mahir Efendi, included detailed information about how business was conducted in the Istanbul livestock market. According to Abdullah Mahir, most of the sheep arriving in the capital were purchased wholesale by butchers who operated with more capital than their smaller counterparts. These wholesalers typically did not act individually but instead banded together in companies (*kumpanya*), which grew in number from twelve in the earlier years to twenty at the time of the petition. Yet, because they still could not afford to pay for all their purchases at once, the relationship between them and the sheep merchants was based on credit and trust. Following the delivery of the animals to a wholesaler-buyer, the selling merchant allowed him three weeks to pay the purchase money in cash. If the payment was made within this period, the wholesaler was entitled to a 4 percent discount on the purchase price, a practice that remained in use until at least the late 1910s.[47]

Abdullah Mahir claimed that this credit sale system worked to the great disadvantage of merchants, as some wholesalers defaulted on their payments. The resulting unpaid debts, amounting to over 60,000 liras at the time of the petition, had already driven a considerable number of merchants to financial ruin. According to another petition submitted by twenty-two sheep merchants to the Grand Vizierate in January 1888, butchers not only delayed payments but also manipulated the exchange rate between the gold Ottoman lira and silver piasters. Even though one lira was worth 108 piasters in daily use in Istanbul, the wholesalers counted it as between 116 and 120 piasters when making payments to their suppliers, thereby reducing their liabilities.[48] According to the guild leaders, these grievances could only be redressed by returning to a more regulated market order. For this purpose, they filed a series of petitions in the mid-1880s, demanding the government fix the value of the lira at 108 piasters in transactions between sheep merchants and Istanbul butchers. A few years later, they also came forward with a proposal to deal with the problem of unpaid debts: when a merchant reached an agreement with a wholesaler for the sale of his animals, the guild officials would issue a stamped certificate from the Istanbul Municipality. The animals would not be handed over until the wholesaler signed this certificate, which specified the number of sheep to be delivered to the purchaser, the price agreed upon between the parties, and the date of redemption. The adoption of this proposal, the guild officials argued, would be a notable step toward protecting merchants, who could then sue their defaulting customers with sealed and stamped documents in hand.[49]

As these demands were formulated in consultation with the merchant community, the guild was able to mobilize considerable support from them. Between 1887 and 1889, at least three collective merchant petitions were presented to the government, demanding the approval of the proposal concerning the use of stamped certificates. Such efforts did not remain fruitless. Before the end of the decade, the Council of State passed a decision ruling that wholesaler butchers should count the lira at 108 piasters in their transactions. Similarly, after lengthy deliberations on the issue of defaulted debts, the Istanbul Municipality issued a report to the Council of State, noting that the use of the guild's stamped certificates would make transactions between merchants and wholesalers more secure.[50] These moves, however, had little practical effect. Despite the Council of State's decision, the Ottoman lira continued to be valued above its market value throughout the late nineteenth and early twentieth centuries.[51] Furthermore, in disregard of the Istanbul Municipality's favorable report, the Council of State rejected the guild's proposal on the grounds that requiring purchasing butchers to sign certificates would make trade more difficult. Shortly afterwards, this decision was approved by the Council of Ministers and the sultan, noting that it was the merchants' responsibility to ensure that receipts given to them by wholesale butchers were properly stamped and sealed, so they could be used as evidence in a court case.[52]

As the efforts of the guild officials and merchants seeking a more regulated market failed, defaulted or delayed payments by wholesale butchers continued to be a problem until the end of the empire.[53] Consequently, for many merchants, it became difficult or even impossible to keep their businesses running.[54] It is important to underline here that although the merchants primarily attributed the problem of defaults to the dishonesty of Istanbul butchers, the issue had a broader context. Transactions between the merchants and wholesale butchers, who were the most prominent members of their profession, as well as between the wholesalers and retail butchers, numbering in the thousands, and between the retailers and their customers, were all based on credit.[55] Yet, the credit chain was highly vulnerable to breakdown, mainly because the government and many private entrepreneurs, including large-scale industrial enterprises, were often short of cash and unable to meet salary and other payments on time.[56] This situation had dire consequences for all of the aforementioned actors. First, government employees and other working-class people, hard hit by the arrears of salaries and wages, had to delay their payments to retail butchers, most of whom operated with a small capital base. As many of these butchers eventually went bankrupt or suspended payments, their suppliers – wholesalers – began to face difficulties in meeting their financial obligations. Second, as the largest customer for mutton in Istanbul, the Ottoman state at times accumulated unpaid bills to its meat contractors, who operated both as merchants and butchers. For example, a certain İsmail Hakkı Efendi, contracted to supply regular army troops in Istanbul with about 5 million kilograms of meat – the equivalent of more than 300,000 head of sheep – between July 1907 and June 1908, complained in early 1908 that the government owed him a considerable sum of 60,000 liras.[57]

Sheep and Meat Trade as a Profitable Business

Although he occasionally voiced such grievances, İsmail Hakkı had a long career as a meat contractor. He worked for the Privy Purse at least twice, first in 1897 and again in 1903. Then, in 1905, he was contracted by the Ministry of War to supply regular army troops in Istanbul, a position he held until the Young Turk Revolution. After the revolution, he continued his work with the government. According to a petition he addressed to the Council of State in 1911, he was then serving as the meat contractor for the dervish lodges (*tekke*) and hospitals in the capital.[58] İsmail Hakkı's story was neither unique nor very unusual in the late Ottoman Empire. There were at least several other prominent Muslim and non-Muslim entrepreneurs who stayed involved in the contracting business for years. In 1857, and again between 1859 and 1863, the sultan's palace and army in Istanbul were supplied with meat by Christaki Zografos, a prominent Galata banker mentioned in Chapter 4, and his partner Mustafa Ağa.[59] The 1880s saw the rise of another Greek entrepreneur, Yeorgios Hrisovergis. Between 1885 and 1891, he secured at least four contracts from the Ministry of War, three from the Privy Purse, and two from the Ministry of Navy. During this period, he used his financial resources not only to procure a large number of cattle and sheep but also to invest in increasing their meat productivity. For instance, he purchased a farm complex near Istanbul to fatten animals for slaughter by feeding them barley and beetroot. This venture seemed to be quite successful.[60] In a memorial poem published in an Istanbul Greek newspaper in August 1898, after his death, Hrisovergis was referred to as a "big merchant" who owned oil fields in the Caucasus and supplied meat to the sultan's palace.[61] As indicated in the preceding chapters, similar to contractors, some sheep merchants were also able to sustain their businesses for years, and sometimes even across generations. A notable example of the latter was Mühürdarzade İsmail from Erzurum, who likely began his business career in the late 1880s or 1890s. In 1900, upon the recommendation of the guild of livestock merchants, he was awarded a decoration by Sultan Abdülhamid II for his efforts to keep meat prices down in the capital. He continued to make large-scale shipments to Istanbul and other markets for some more years before passing the business to his son, Asım Vasfi, who would become a deputy in the Grand National Assembly in 1920.[62]

The long careers of these individuals as meat contractors and sheep merchants suggest that they were able to sustain their businesses on a profitable basis. One probable reason for this success was that they, along with other established entrepreneurs, had relatively large amounts of capital at their disposal, which allowed them to accommodate failures and delays in payments by the government and butchers. As indicated in the previous chapters, over time some of them moved their headquarters from their Anatolian bases to Istanbul, where they developed networks of agents and partners that extended to the principal sheep export centers and trade routes, ensuring access to a steady supply of sheep, even at times of shortage. For example, despite regulations prohibiting such actions, wholesale butchers complained that during the decimating winter of 1906–07, İsmail Hakkı Efendi made large-scale sheep purchases through his agents in the environs of Istanbul.[63] While İsmail Hakkı ordered most of these animals to be slaughtered to fulfill his contract with the Ministry of War, he also sold some to retail butchers.[64] Such sales promised big profits primarily for two reasons. First, meat scarcity drove prices in the capital to high levels. Second, like many sheep merchants in Anatolia and Rumelia, İsmail Hakkı likely took an active part in tax collection by purchasing sheep at below-market prices from villagers who were unable to pay their taxes.[65] Moreover, even if İsmail Hakkı or other merchants billed the Istanbul butchers at cost prices, they could still make a profit due to exchange rate differences between the capital and some provinces, such as Konya.[66]

Although the credit chain they were involved in was vulnerable to breakdowns, some butchers were also able to make large profits from their operations. This was particularly true for wholesalers purchasing several hundred head of sheep outright. They secured revenues mainly in two ways: first, they benefited from the customary right to take one sheep from each purchased flock free of charge; and second, they charged their customers a specific price – two piasters in the late 1880s

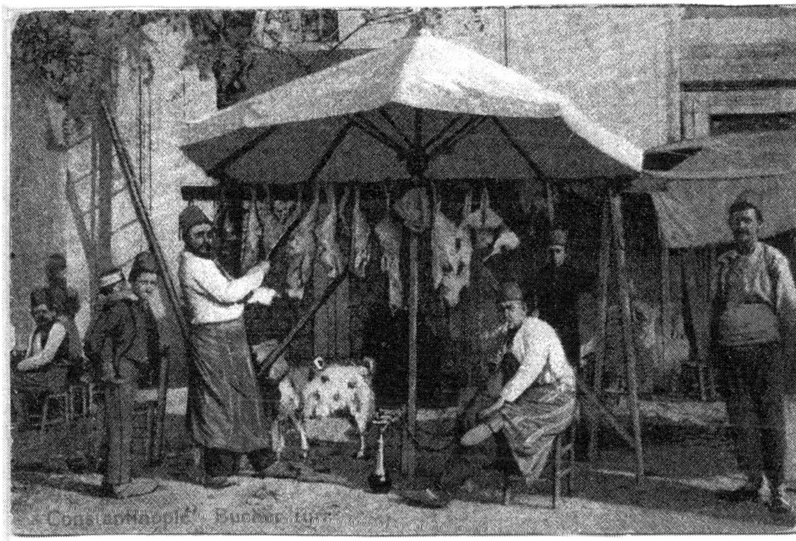

Photo 6.1 An Itinerant Butcher in Istanbul. Source: The Istanbul Municipality Atatürk Library Collection

and five piasters in the 1900s – for each head of animal transacted.[67] Moreover, the aforementioned speculative practice of sheep passing from hand to hand at increasing prices allowed those engaged in it to realize high profit margins. In May 1891, the daily paper *Sabah* complained about butchers who sold a *kıyye* of meat, which cost them three piasters, for seven piasters.[68] Such practices seemed to accelerate during the scarcities of World War I, provoking discontent among the residents of Istanbul as prices skyrocketed.[69] Butchers who wanted to take further advantage of wartime scarcities also increasingly resorted to selling goat meat as mutton and horse meat as beef at exorbitant prices. For example, in his memoirs, Haris Spataris, living in the Fener district of the capital, noted that one day shortly after paying 120 piasters for a *kıyye* of boneless beef, he discovered that what was sold to him was actually horse meat.[70]

Revenues accumulated from these various means enabled some Istanbul butchers to expand the scope of their business. For instance, a certain İsmail Ağa, who was based in the Tavukpazarı district, became the meat contractor for the dervish lodges and hospitals in Istanbul in 1892.[71] A later example is detailed in a book published by the Istanbul Chamber of Commerce in 1923, which states that the organization had more than 1,500 members divided into four classes according to their economic status and power. Among the thirty-six members designated as first-class merchants and financial intermediaries – such as bankers and banks

– was a butcher enterprise in Galata run by a certain Hacı Şakirzade Hacı Mustafa and his partners. Furthermore, nine butchers were enrolled in the organization as third and fourth-class merchants.[72] The next and final section of the chapter will focus on a major site of importance for these butchers and all the other constituent actors – both human and non-human – of the Istanbul livestock and meat markets: the slaughterhouses.

Slaughterhouses: Focal Points for Sanitation and Market Regulation

During the provisionist period, Yedikule was the primary district housing slaughterhouses for Rumelian livestock, while numerous others were spread throughout the cityscape. Inside the city walls, these establishments were mainly concentrated around Yedikule and Eğrikapı, with additional ones located in Hasköy, Balat, Ortaköy, Tophane, Galata, and Üsküdar.[73] Facilities like those in Yedikule catered to both Muslim and non-Muslim communities, whereas those in Ortaköy, Hasköy, and Balat served specific religious or ethnic groups, particularly the Jews.[74] Regulating the entry of animals into the city became challenging, especially with the adoption of liberal policies in the latter half of the nineteenth century. This period also saw a surge in the number of slaughterhouses, which reached approximately 150 by the early 1900s.[75] Additionally, many butcher shops slaughtered animals on-site, raising concerns over sanitation, hygiene, and the spread of epidemics and epizootics. These developments presented significant challenges for both the residents of the city and state authorities as they grappled with public health and safety issues.

To address these issues, in the 1880s, the Istanbul Municipality began employing veterinarians to inspect the sanitation of slaughterhouses and prevent the butchering of pregnant and diseased animals.[76] To pursue a more comprehensive solution, municipal officials also initiated plans for constructing a central abattoir. This sparked prolonged discussions and debates among various actors, including state authorities, butchers, and livestock merchants. The push for a central abattoir was driven by multiple factors: the city's burgeoning population, frequent outbreaks of epidemics and epizootics, and the demands of European residents for cleaner streets, all of which made hygiene a pressing concern. The popularity of the miasma theory, which attributed the spread of diseases like cholera and plague to foul odors, also underscored concerns about the improper disposal of bones and offal from butcher shops onto the streets. Although the municipality's efforts to establish garbage collection units diminished the need for stray dogs to scavenge waste, remains of slaughtered animals continued to be thrown into the sea, particularly off the coast of Eminönü and Kadıköy.[77] The prevailing winds from these areas often carried the stench inland, exacerbating health concerns among the populace.[78]

Public health risks escalated when butcher waste mingled with water sources, a common occurrence in areas like Kağıthane, where large flocks were grazed. Remains from slaughtered animals or those succumbing to disease were often inadequately buried or dispersed by stray dogs or winds.[79] Even smaller slaughterhouses were culpable, contaminating residential water sources through their negligence.[80] Alongside health concerns, state authorities viewed a central abattoir as crucial for regulating the meat market. Both the Istanbul Municipality and the Ministry of Interior argued that the dispersed slaughterhouses led to a lack of state oversight, which caused inflated meat prices and fostered unscrupulous practices, including the slaughter of underage lambs and calves, pregnant cattle, and sick animals, especially during times of scarcity. The construction of a central abattoir would allow for increased state control and intervention, helping to prevent such practices and facilitate rigorous checks on transactions between butchers and merchants, thereby ensuring better price controls.[81]

Under these considerations, in 1911, the Istanbul Municipality launched a public competition, ultimately selecting the proposal put forth by a French entrepreneur named Emil Camus.[82] He envisioned constructing a large-scale slaughterhouse in the district of Langa, strategically positioned near the Marmara Sea coast and the railroad line that connected the capital to Rumelia.[83] The facility would comprise distinct units for the reception and slaughter of animals, as well as for the preservation and distribution of their meat. Upon arrival via rail or ship, animals would be segregated by type and undergo veterinary inspection before being admitted to the abattoir. While awaiting slaughter, they would be housed in separate pens and provided with hay for sustenance. After being slaughtered, the meat would be stored in ventilated cold rooms, awaiting sale and distribution to customers. Adjacent to the abattoir, a livestock market would be established.[84]

Though modeled after modern centralized slaughterhouses in Europe and approved by municipal authorities, the plan encountered several objections, reflecting disparities between Ottoman and European husbandry and livestock trade practices. A petition lodged by the association of livestock merchants, the successor to the above-discussed guild organization, contested the concession granted to a foreign entrepreneur, citing the principle of national economy espoused during the Young Turk era. They contended that the concession gave Camus extensive control over a significant geographic area, spanning from Ayastefanos (today's Yeşiköy) and Pendik across the Marmara Sea coast to the Anatolian and Rumelian Kavaks in the Bosphorus, where he would have the authority to regulate the entry and slaughter of animals. Even meat contractors serving state institutions would fall under the jurisdiction of his facility, posing a challenge to Ottoman sovereignty by placing the meat provision for the military and other state entities in foreign hands.

Another objection raised by the petition highlighted the unique characteristics of the Ottoman livestock trade. The association argued that a single centralized abattoir would not adequately meet Istanbul's needs. The necessity for animals to wait several days before slaughter, combined with increased transportation costs due to the city's expansive geography, would inflate merchants' expenses and consequently drive meat prices up. Additionally, sheep and cattle accustomed to grazing on fresh pastures and meadows in Anatolia and Rumelia would suffer from being confined and fed dry hay, resulting in weight loss and a reduced meat supply to the city. Unlike densely populated European cities with limited grazing areas, Istanbul boasted extensive pastures and meadows like Uzunçayır and Okmeydanı, obviating the need for enclosed units. There was also no imperative for a centralized animal market, as these grazing lands already facilitated transactions between butchers and merchants. Overall, these objections likely served as a pretext to evade stringent control over purchases by butchers and the potential imposition of new taxes on merchants.[85]

Meanwhile, the concession granted to Camus also sparked a protracted debate between the Istanbul Municipality and the city's governorship, with each claiming the authority to grant concessions. Camus lodged a legal protest over the delays in contract negotiations and sought compensation for losses incurred during the extended waiting period. The outbreak of World War I severed communications between Camus and the Istanbul authorities, as France and the Ottoman Empire were in opposing alliances. As a result, Camus's concessions never received approval from the higher echelons of the government, and he did not receive any reimbursement for his expenses. Istanbul finally gained a central abattoir in 1923, located in Sütlüce near the Okmeydanı meadow, after an approximately four-year construction process undertaken by the municipality with state funding.[86] The failure to establish such a facility throughout the Ottoman era underscores two crucial points. First, despite state efforts to regulate and modernize livestock trade through a centralized abattoir, resistance from various groups, including merchants and some state actors, persisted. Second, the unique characteristics of the capital city, with its sprawling residential areas along two seafronts and abundant grazing lands, enabled merchants and butchers to challenge state control. Animals became integral to urban life, parading through the main streets, grazing in expansive meadows, and even residing in the backyards of homes and butcher shops.

Conclusion

This chapter has highlighted the dynamic nature of Istanbul's livestock and meat markets, arguing that seemingly contradictory trends could coexist within them. On one hand, in response to surging meat prices, the government introduced a series of liberal economic reforms. Unlike the case in İzmir, it abolished most regulations aimed at ensuring sufficient supplies at affordable prices for the residents of Istanbul. On the other hand, akin to its counterparts in the US, Mexico, and France, it began to establish a public health-oriented regulatory regime. This initiative led to attempts to introduce new actors, such as veterinary officials, and new spaces, such as a central abattoir, to ensure the wholesomeness of meat supplies. Moreover, regulatory efforts did not remain limited to sanitation and hygiene issues. Over time, different state actors actively sought new strategies, such as abolishing the head trader position and proposing the reintroduction of price controls, to mitigate meat prices during times of scarcity.

As indicated in the above paragraphs, defenders of regulation were not limited to government ranks. In the late nineteenth century, livestock merchants from Anatolia and Rumelia collectively pressed for closer oversight by the government and their guild on transactions with Istanbul butchers. This push for regulation stemmed mainly from the fact that, to build up and maintain their clientele, they had to operate in credit chains, which were vulnerable to uncertainties and breakdowns. Hence, bankruptcies were common, especially among small-scale merchants. However, for those who were well-organized through a network of agents and partners, and financially robust, the story turned out differently. The trade of live sheep, lambs, and cattle, commonly seen on the city streets, and their carcasses allowed figures like Christaki Zografos, Yeorgios Hrisovergis, and İsmail Hakkı Efendi to build and increase their fortunes.

CHAPTER 7

Conclusion

Abstract

This concluding chapter provides an overview of the book's findings, highlighting the unique approach of organizing the study based on regional economies. It discusses how the detailed analysis of central, northeastern, and northwestern Anatolia, four eastern Mediterranean ports (İzmir, İskenderun, Mersin, and Antalya), and Istanbul allows for a comprehensive examination of ecosystems, environmental factors, and the agency of human and non-human actors in the livestock trade. The chapter argues for an overall increase in livestock trade in Anatolia, particularly in the late nineteenth and early twentieth centuries, and identifies the winners and losers among human actors in this development. It also emphasizes the interconnectedness of regional markets and livestock economies and questions the perception of Istanbul as the central hub for Anatolian livestock trade, notably by pointing out the emergence of Egypt as a major competitor. Additionally, the chapter addresses the absence of a centralized large-scale red meat industry in the Ottoman Empire, discussing challenges such as the trade's vulnerability to environmental conditions, reliance on credit rather than cash flow, and the lack of necessary technologies and scientific developments for industrialized meat production.

Keywords: regional economies; red meat industry; trade hubs; livestock trade

The livestock trade thrived in Anatolia during the nineteenth and early twentieth centuries. Sheep and cattle were increasingly exported from different parts of the peninsula to Istanbul, Egypt, and major Anatolian and Syrian urban centers such as İzmir, Bursa, and Aleppo, as well as to Malta and Greece. This book has meticulously analyzed the ascent of the Anatolian livestock trade during a period marked by significant changes in state policies and societal and environmental dynamics. It has traced and documented the evolution of trade routes and networks over time, while also studying the environmental, social, and economic impacts of these changes on both human and non-human actors. By doing so, the book contributes to the recent scholarship that challenges the earlier studies, which overemphasize international trade and focus primarily on port cities as nodes connecting the empire to the capitalist world economy.[1] It has examined the growth of the domestic trade of animals and its implication for a diversity of actors involved in it under the given environmental, social, political, and economic conditions.

Studies that pay attention to regional differences often either use Ottoman provinces, contemporary nation-state borders, or broad generalizations of regions such as the Balkans, Anatolia, and Arab provinces.[2] This book has adopted a novel approach in Ottoman history by focusing on regional economies and ecosystems, a rarely explored unit of analysis. Ecosystems are characterized by the continuous interaction between organisms and their environment, influenced by both internal and external factors such as decomposition and climate. These ecosystems offer a diverse array of goods and services for human benefit, yet they are also subject to the influence of human communities. Regional economies emerge from the intricate interplay of goods, services, and human intervention within ecosystems. They are shaped by the advantages of geographical locations and the activities of human populations, leading to economic growth. Put simply, regional economies are the outcomes of various factors, including geography, ecosystems, and human endeavors working in tandem.

When ecosystems are taken into account, regional economies correspond to smaller units than Anatolia as a whole. The Anatolian landscape has different geographies from east to west and north to south. In livestock breeding and trade, a few regional economies emerged as successful combinations of landscape, climate, plants, animals, and humans, which led to large concentrations of livestock trade. The book has identified three regions (central, northeastern, and northwestern Anatolia) and four eastern Mediterranean ports (İzmir, İskenderun, Mersin, and Antalya) as the major centers of sheep and cattle trade. Except for northwestern Anatolia covered by Hüdavendigar province, these regions included areas larger than provincial and sometimes imperial boundaries. Central Anatolia encompassed the provinces of Ankara and Konya, while northeastern Anatolia included Erzurum province and the transborder region with Russia and Iran in the Caucasus. Meanwhile, the eastern Mediterranean ports, particularly İskenderun and İzmir, had strong trade connections not only with their immediate hinterlands but also with a broad region extending from central Anatolia and Syria to Egypt. The capital city, Istanbul, had its own regional economy as the central location where most Anatolian livestock trade was oriented.

The regions covered in this book had a combination of environmental, economic, social, and political constraints that shaped their involvement in livestock breeding and trade. Northeastern Anatolia's ecosystem had wet seasons and harsh winters in the highlands, providing fertile ground for sheep and cattle husbandry, especially in spring and summer pastures. Among the human actors of the trade were semi-nomadic tribes that practiced seasonal migration across the Ottoman, Russian, and Persian border areas. Their transhumance pattern facilitated herding large flocks and provided animals for neighboring regions as well as distant areas, such as Syrian provinces and Istanbul. There were both challenges and incentives that affected livestock trade in the region: the 1877–78 Ottoman-Russian war and the harsh winters following it were a major intervention in the lives of both animals and humans, leading to a sharp decline in sheep exports until the mid-1880s. The 1892–94 cholera outbreak, which led to quarantines all over Anatolia, similarly interrupted trade flows but ironically also proved beneficial for the region. The limitations on animal sales meant an increase in livestock capacity in the region. When the quarantines ended, sheep exports from northeastern Anatolia increased sharply. Naval transportation from the Trabzon port played a crucial role in this development.

Central Anatolia, which had enduring sheep trade connections to İstanbul, İzmir, and Bursa, was adversely affected by two major famines in 1845 and 1873–75. During the latter, the livestock populations sharply declined, adversely impacting shipments from the region to Istanbul and other markets. Some recovery of trade was visible in the 1880s, only to be challenged by cholera quarantines in 1892–94. Limited spring precipitation, along with the movement between winter and summer pastures around rivers and mountains were crucial for tribal livestock, which was the main source of sheep supply to Istanbul from the region. During the Tanzimat period, efforts to permanently settle semi-nomadic tribes led to some changes in livestock herding and its human actors. Although sheep merchants continued to define themselves with tribal identities, the dominant role of the tribal chiefs came to an end, especially after the sedentarization of the Cihanbeylis. A centralized trade network under the control of the tribal chief as the head trader evolved into a more decentralized and individualized trade system involving both tribal and non-tribal merchants in the 1880s. Yet, the volume of sheep trade to Istanbul and other cities remained substantial. The construction of railroads connecting the region to Istanbul and İzmir had limited influence on this, as merchants continued to move their flocks to market mostly on foot.

The province of Hüdavendigar, with its variety of climate and geography, was an important region for livestock breeding and trade. The inner part of the province, in addition to housing large numbers of sheep, served as a waypoint for tribal livestock of central Anatolia. Meanwhile, the coastal regions around the Marmara and Aegean Seas provided fertile ground for sheep and cattle herding with wetlands, rainy seasons, and large pastures. Hüdavendigar province was an intriguing example of state involvement in livestock breeding and trade. The Mihaliç Imperial Farms became a major center for the development of agriculture and animal husbandry, with state investments aimed at improving crossbreeding, nutrition, and healthcare of animals. These attempts led to the introduction of merino sheep and an increase in the number of local breeds on the imperial farms. Hüdavendigar region was not free of environmental, political, and social challenges. The Central Anatolian famine of 1873-75 had a considerable impact, reducing the number of tribal livestock raised and traded in the province. Animal diseases, especially cattle plague and anthrax, hit the region hard in different periods. The spread of the diseases among cattle and sheep populations in this province, and subsequently to most parts of western Anatolia and Istanbul, caught the attention of the Ottoman state. As a result, a wide-scale regulation of animal healthcare was prepared and implemented first in Hüdavendigar before being applied in other parts of the empire. Hüdavendigar's ecosystem changed with the arrival of new human actors in the second half of the nineteenth century. The inflow of large numbers of refugees from Rumelia, Crimea, and the Caucasus intensified the struggle over land among the newcomers, local villagers, and sheep merchants, especially in the western part of the province. With the expansion of the livestock trade, sheep merchants increasingly rented pastures in the districts of Mihaliç, Kirmasti, and Karesi to graze their sheep brought from Rumelia in late autumn and early winter. Then they waited for prices to rise in Istanbul during the winter and the early spring months to send them there by steamers departing from the port of Bandırma. Some of these sheep, together with local ones, were also likely consumed in Bursa.

Like Bursa, İzmir was a major destination for animals for slaughter. Green pastures in the northern and southern hinterlands of İzmir stocked large numbers of sheep and cattle, some of which ended up in the city's livestock market. Animals were also brought there from central Anatolia and Rumelia to be both consumed in the city and exported abroad. Other important eastern Mediterranean export ports were İskenderun, Mersin, and Antalya. İskenderun was the largest in terms of livestock trade volume, maintaining a regular supply of sheep and cattle from southern and eastern Anatolia, Aleppo, and Mosul to Alexandria, Port Said, Malta, Crete, and Istanbul. The popularity of this port was the result of the relatively easy geography for transportation from these regions. İskenderun and other ports were prone to the effects of epizootics too. The widespread cattle plague from 1904 to 1910, for instance, significantly increased shipments to the Egyptian ports, prompting the Ottoman government to temporarily ban the export of plough animals from the ports of Beirut, İskenderun, İzmir, and Salonica.

Istanbul was the major hub of livestock trade, where most of the trade networks discussed in the book were oriented. It was a center for state policies aimed at regulating meat supply and livestock trade. With a rapidly growing population that reached over a million at the turn of the twentieth century, the need to supply sufficient meat at affordable prices for its residents remained a major concern for state authorities until the end of the empire. While they imposed shipment quotas and special taxes such as *ondalık ağnam* to direct their trade to Istanbul at low prices during the provisionist era, the end of provisionism in the 1860s led to the adoption of free trade policies, allowing merchants to sell their animals anywhere at fluctuating prices. Yet, in practice Istanbul authorities, especially the municipality, remained adamant about securing a sufficient meat supply. In times of crisis such as wars, epizootics, and epidemics, some provisionist policies returned.

Although Istanbul was an urban consumption center, its ecosystem was not devoid of animal husbandry. Districts around both the European and Anatolian sides of the city housed considerable livestock populations. The European districts, in particular, were a major source of lamb brought to Istanbul during the feast of Khidir, in addition to supplying dairy products to the city. Even the butchers in Istanbul kept a few animals in their backyards or closed barns in the city neighborhoods. This intertwined life of animals and humans created health and sanitation problems, facilitating the spread of diseases like cattle plague. In response, the municipal authorities initiated measures to regulate slaughter, burial, and disposal of livestock, especially during epidemics and epizootics, and developed plans to construct a central abattoir.

Complex networks brought several actors of the livestock trade together in Istanbul, including butchers (both wholesaler and retailer), livestock merchants, meat contractors, the Istanbul Municipality, and other state offices, such as the Ministry of Interior and the Council of State. While state actors mainly wanted to have regular supplies at affordable prices, butchers, meat contractors, and merchants competed and conflicted with each other for access to a greater share of revenues generated from the livestock and meat trade. The analysis in this book provides valuable information about capital accumulation and trade networks both in the capital city and beyond.

Interconnected Regional Markets and Livestock Economies

The livestock trade expanded all over Anatolia, but its development followed different trajectories based on the dynamics of regional markets and ecosystems. This book has disassembled the Anatolian livestock economy into regions and thus challenged the viewpoint that sees the Ottoman economy as a single unit or an aggregation of the Rumelian, Anatolian, and Arab provinces. This dismantling into smaller regional units pays attention to local dynamics and gives an opportunity to make a comparative study of livestock trade and its human and non-human actors. It has shown that the overall expansion of the Anatolian livestock trade had common causes, including population increase in urban centers and territorial losses in Rumelia. There were also, however, diverse dynamics in each region that contributed to the expansion of trade.

While in northeastern Anatolia, technological developments such as steamships and telegraph lines contributed to the expansion of livestock trade to Istanbul and diminished the importance of the Syrian market, improvements in transportation networks did not much affect the development of trade in central Anatolia. The Istanbul-Ankara railroad was not a popular option for transporting sheep until the end of the empire. However, as in northeastern Anatolia, improvements in naval transportation expanded the volume and orientation of livestock trade from the eastern Mediterranean ports, particularly İskenderun and İzmir. In northwestern Anatolia, the port of Bandırma also became a major channel for increasing the volume of livestock trade by steamers to Istanbul.

While disassembling Anatolia into smaller regions, the book has also emphasized the interconnectedness of these regional economies. Animals and their human guardians from different regions did not only interact in their destination markets, such as Istanbul, Alexandria, Cairo, İzmir, and Bursa, but they also got in touch during their long marches in Anatolia. When they took the land route to Istanbul, northeastern Anatolian sheep and merchants passed through central Anatolia. As seen in several examples in the earlier chapters, this meant continuous interaction, cooperation, and sometimes conflict between central Anatolian tribal chiefs and northeastern Anatolian merchants. Likewise, as discussed above, large flocks of sheep seasonally arrived from Rumelia to Hüdavendigar and Aydın, resulting in the firm integration of merchants from the former region into the economic and political lives of these provinces.

With the expansion of the volume of trade, increasing contacts among human and animal actors from various regions led to the spread of epidemics and epizootics. Cholera was an integral part of the late nineteenth-century world. The 1892–94 outbreak, which spread through the Hijaz, the Syrian provinces, various parts of Anatolia, and Istanbul, disrupted the livestock trade, as quarantines prevented the movement of animals and their human guardians. At the turn of the twentieth century, Anatolia was also repeatedly hit by animal diseases, primarily cattle plague, spreading quickly from one region to another due to increased trade and migratory movements. While cattle plague outbreaks led to a massive number of deaths, they also expanded livestock trade networks by pressuring herders to sell their animals before the disease decimated them. This pressure, in turn, had the potential to put herders and merchants into conflict with state officials seeking to limit mobility to contain the outbreaks.

Overall, the examples provided in this book highlight vibrant interregional livestock trade networks that interconnected animals, merchants, tribes, shepherds, and butchers across various regions. While emphasizing the importance of these networks, this study shows that they were oriented toward diverse markets.

Decentralizing Provisionism: Was Istanbul a Hub of the Meat Trade?

The Ottoman state's provisionist policies, which aimed at maintaining the food supply of major urban centers, prioritized Istanbul. Satisfying the civilian residents of the city with their living conditions as well as feeding the army, palace, and bureaucracy were major concerns, that led the state authorities to orient major trade networks to Istanbul. Literature on provisionism heavily emphasizes the priority of Istanbul as a major destination for most of the empire's grain and meat trade.[3] In this literature, Istanbul emerged as a hub where a complex web of trade routes from Rumelia and Anatolia converged. As discussed in earlier chapters of this book, there were both incentives and enforcements for orienting livestock trade to Istanbul. This policy continued even after the provisioning system came to an end in the mid-nineteenth century. Mostly incentives, but also some enforcement, made merchants direct their flocks to Istanbul, especially in times of meat supply shortages. When shortages reached a dangerous extent, imposing export bans on cattle abroad and issuing orders to provincial merchants to send more animals to Istanbul were the most commonly used mechanisms. Therefore, scholars who study grain and meat provisioning tend to focus on Istanbul with a top-down perspective that starts in the capital city and considers provincial trade only in the context of its needs.

While arguing that Istanbul, with its growing population, was the major hub for livestock trade networks, the book has also highlighted that it was not free of competition. During the late eighteenth and early nineteenth centuries, lower *narh* prices in the capital sometimes oriented Anatolian sheep to other cities, such as İzmir, Bursa, Aleppo, and Damascus, where prices were higher. After the adoption of liberal economic policies, merchants and herders continued to carefully monitor the prices in Istanbul and other cities and oriented their animals accordingly. The development of transportation and communication networks made them much more knowledgeable about market dynamics in big cities. The analysis of the ports of İskenderun, İzmir, Mersin, and Antalya has shown that a major rival to Istanbul was Egypt. The decline in the number of local livestock due to epizootics, combined with growing demand for meat, drove prices up in Alexandria and Cairo. For many merchants in Anatolian provinces, boarding sheep at the ports of İzmir and İskenderun and sending them to Alexandria and Port Said became a profitable option.

Until the British occupation in the early 1880s, the Ottoman state was quite concerned with sending livestock supplies to Egypt in times of need. When, for example, epizootics hit the Egyptian countryside in 1842 and 1863–64, orders were issued to several Anatolian and Rumelian provinces requiring them to send a certain number of cattle and sheep to Egypt. As Chapter 5 explains in detail, such orders caused anxiety among local authorities in İzmir, who feared that meat prices would increase sharply. This fear was revived in the early 1900s, during the infamous cattle outbreak, which forced the Ottoman state to ban the export of plough animals. While local officials in both Istanbul and İzmir asked for stricter measures, such as extending the ban to sheep, their position did not find support from the upper echelons of the government, which were concerned about not alienating mercantile interests in central and western Anatolia. This, in turn, forced meat prices up in Istanbul.

Capital Accumulation and the Red Meat Industry

While increased livestock trade led to capital accumulation and the rise of a red meat industry in the Western world,[4] a similar development was not observed in the Ottoman Empire. There were some prominent Ottoman livestock raisers and merchants, meat contractors, and wholesale butchers who traded thousands of animals. Although they occasionally complained about the low profit of the business in their petitions to the state, some of these actors accumulated considerable capital and emerged among the wealthiest entrepreneurs of the Ottoman realm. Chapters of this book provide several examples of them: Christaki Zografos and Yeorgios Hrisovergis, who had long careers as meat contractors, were among the richest members of Istanbul's Greek community in the nineteenth century. Likewise, some provincial merchants, such as Mühürdarzade İsmail and his son Asım Vasfi, who brought sheep to the capital from various Anatolian provinces, and large landholders, such as Çayırlızade Hilmi and Zahide Hanım from the Karaosmanzade family, who raised significant numbers of livestock or leased their lands for pasture, accumulated not only economic but also political power over time. Yet, these developments did not lead to the rise of a large-scale red meat industry.

What were the reasons for this lack of industrialization? Why did the capital accumulated in the hands of merchants and livestock raisers not evolve into a large, mechanized business as happened in the Western world? Answers to these questions should consider the nature of trade and its human and non-human actors in the Ottoman realm. First, the livestock trade was sensitive to many factors, such as climate conditions, epidemics, epizootics, and famines. Most animals were kept in the open air or loosely constructed barns where extreme weather conditions could lead to casualties. Moreover, animals marching long distances on foot were vulnerable to extreme weather, theft, and lack of forage. Although improvements in rail and naval transportation reduced some risks, trains and steamships had their own difficulties for animals: while sea accidents could result in considerable casualties, stocking many animals in small wagons made feeding them difficult. Animal diseases could easily spread under these conditions as well. Thus, even the big merchants who traded thousands of animals were vulnerable to considerable losses depending on environmental and physical conditions. Profit gained one year could be lost in subsequent years when circumstances were not suitable for animal herding and transportation. Consequently, stable long durée accumulation of profit was quite limited.

Second, the livestock trade shared a common vulnerability with the other major sectors of the Ottoman economy: limited cash flow and increased indebtedness.[5] Although the volume of livestock trade was quite high, reaching over a million animals in the Istanbul market alone, direct cash payments were limited, as discussed in Chapter 6. Istanbul butchers often made payments months after their purchases, mainly because transactions between them and their customers were also based on credit. To make matters worse, the credit chain they were involved in was highly vulnerable to breakdown, which had dire consequences for even companies that brought together well-established wholesale butchers of the city. The situation was not very different for meat contractors doing business with the Ottoman state, the largest customer for meat in Istanbul. Prominent contractors like İsmail Hakkı Efendi often complained about arrears in their pay.

Third, the Ottoman state was a major player in the livestock trade during and after the provisionist period. State authorities used both incentives and force to orient animals to Istanbul. They tried to keep livestock prices low in order to provide an adequate meat supply at affordable prices in Istanbul. Price controls limited the profit margin of merchants and prevented capital accumulation during the provisionist era. The adoption of free trade policies created new opportunities and increased the volume of livestock trade in the second half of the nineteenth century. However, some provisionist measures were occasionally on the state's agenda in this period. While in Istanbul, price controls returned in times of extreme shortages, such as during the cholera outbreak in the mid-1860s and the last years of World War I, in İzmir, the mechanism of *narh* remained in force until the end of the empire. These measures had the potential to constitute another barrier to profit accumulation in the hands of sheep merchants.

Last but not least, scientific and technological developments in the fields of livestock breeding and butchering, as well as in preserving and transporting meat, remained limited in the Ottoman Empire. Maintaining the healthcare of livestock had already become a source of concern for the Ottoman state by the late nineteenth century. While some students were sent to Europe to be trained as veterinarians, a military and then a civilian veterinary school were founded in Istanbul.[6] Meanwhile, as discussed in Chapter 4, various measures (isolation, quarantine, and vaccination) were adopted to contain epizootic outbreaks. However, these efforts remained limited, partly because of the acute financial problems of the empire. Introducing new breeding techniques to increase meat output and implementing widespread sanitation and healthcare measures for tribal and other livestock raisers would necessitate appointing veterinarians to all districts and undertaking significant educational efforts—tasks that exceeded the capacity of the Ottoman state.

Moreover, while refrigerated train cars and steamers were put into use in the late nineteenth century and revolutionized the meat industry by carrying frozen meat in large quantities over long distances, this technology did not arrive in the Ottoman Empire until its demise. One probable reason for this was that the empire's railroad network was not dense and well-integrated. A similar situation was observed in the butchering industry. Although the construction of a centralized abattoir was on the agenda of Istanbul's municipal authorities for a long time, the project did not materialize until the early 1920s. This 'failure' stemmed from a variety of factors. While one was the municipality's lack of financial resources, another was the strong resistance of private slaughterhouse owners, who did not want to lose their revenues, and livestock merchants, who wanted to avoid increased costs.[7]

Winners and Losers of the Livestock Trade

While tracing the expansion of the Anatolian livestock trade, this book has drawn attention to both human and non-human agencies and identified big merchants, wholesale butchers, meat contractors, landlords raising livestock and renting pastures, and tribal leaders as the beneficiaries of the trade. Although, as discussed in the above section and chapters throughout the book, they acted under environmental, economic, social, and political stress, big merchants managed to profit and continue their trade in several ways. They were often able to purchase sheep and other animals for slaughter at cheap prices, thanks to their strong relations with local powerholders and state authorities. In northeastern Anatolia, tribal chiefs seized large numbers of livestock from both settled communities and tribal commoners and sold them to merchants at affordable prices. Merchants in this region and other parts of the empire also found opportunities to make cheap purchases when they accompanied tax officials and farmers during their tax collection tours. Likewise, wholesale butchers in Istanbul could earn lucrative profits by taking one sheep from each purchased flock free of charge, manipulating the exchange rate between the gold Ottoman lira and silver piaster, and engaging in various speculative practices.

This book has emphasized the role of both human and non-human agencies in the regional economies of the livestock trade. Thus, in addition to beneficiaries of the trade, we have also identified actors that carried the burden of it. Chief among them were sheep, cattle, and other livestock. Animals as commodities were transported and traded over long distances. The development of the livestock trade meant higher mobility for them both on foot and by train and steamers. The long journeys led to weight loss, illnesses, deaths, and the spread of diseases. During times of drought and famine, hundreds of thousands of them died because of lack of forage. At other times, quality nutrition, vaccinations, and preventive medicine were not available to many of them. Moreover, due to the rapid commercialization of pasture lands, especially in northwestern and western Anatolia, the access of local sheep to their customary grazing areas began to be increasingly restricted, threatening their subsistence.

Livestock raisers were inevitably negatively affected by these conditions. To make matters worse, they were often under pressure from state authorities and local powerholders. In the first half of the nineteenth century, state-imposed quotas squeezed the livelihood of many tribal herders in central Anatolia. Moreover, starting from the 1840s, tribes in this region were subjected to a campaign of sedentarization, which ultimately aimed to end their seasonal movements between winter and summer pastures. Many tribal members lost their animals in this process and became wage laborers and shepherds for local landholders and sheep merchants. However, as discussed in Chapter 2, tribal populations did not remain completely powerless in the face of this challenge. Using their position as major suppliers of sheep to Istanbul, some among them successfully negotiated with state authorities and continued their (long- and short-distance) seasonal movements, together with their flocks, for a long time.

Small-scale merchants and retail butchers in Istanbul and other major consumer markets also had to deal with some serious hardships. Merchants unfamiliar with business practices in Istanbul were frequently defrauded by wholesale butchers and meat contractors. Although they vocally demanded the establishment of a more regulated livestock market, especially in the 1880s, their efforts mostly failed. Defaulted or delayed payments by wholesale butchers continued to be a problem for them until the end of the empire. Meanwhile, as mentioned above, retail butchers operated their business on a credit system, which was vulnerable to breakdown, partly due to arrears in salary and wage payments to government employees and other working-class people. Moreover, butchers at times faced the threat of losing their established customers to new rivals. For example, when the price of meat increased significantly with the addition of the *gabela* tax in the late nineteenth century, Jews in Istanbul and İzmir began to make purchases from butchers operating outside the officially sanctioned system of the Jewish community.[8]

In conclusion, this book has traced the livestock trade in various regions of Anatolia throughout the nineteenth and early twentieth centuries. By tracing the long journeys of animals from the distant eastern borders of the empire, as well as from central and western Anatolia, and their passages through eastern

Mediterranean ports on their way to Istanbul, Bursa, Damascus, Alexandria, and other cities, we have analyzed human and animal actors involved in this trade, region-specific dynamics, and changing environmental, political, social and economic conditions over time. This book has demonstrated the existence of a lively domestic trade network that connected different regions to each other and to the imperial center, allowing for capital accumulation. It is a contribution to the economic, environmental, and social history of the late Ottoman Empire and Anatolia, which are fields still in need of further research.

Notes

Chapter 1: Introduction

1 White, *Three Years in Constantinople*, pp.105 and 107.
2 Genç, *XIX. Yüzyıl İstanbulu*.
3 See, for instance, Uzun, *İstanbul'un İaşesinde*; Greenwood, "Istanbul's Meat Provisioning."
4 Cora, "Transforming Erzurum/Karin," pp. 234–235.
5 An ecosystem is a complex of living organisms, their physical environment, and all their interrelationships in a particular unit of space. For the definition of the Ottoman Empire as an ecosystem, see Mikhail, *Under Osman's Tree*, p. 199; İnal and Köse, "The Ottoman Environments Revisited," p. 6.
6 Esslen, "On the High Price of Meat in the German Empire," p. 135; Horowitz, *Putting Meat on the American Table*, pp. 11–13; Woods, "Breed, Culture, and Economy," p. 295, Thelle, "The Meat City," p. 237; Guardia, Oyon, Garriga, and Fava, "Meat Consumption and Nutrition Transition in Barcelona," pp. 198 and 202.
7 Stanziani, *Rules of Exchange*, pp. 69–70; Horowitz, Pilcher, and Watts, "Meat for the Multitudes," pp. 1055–1083; Baics, *Feeding Gotham*, pp. 1–15.
8 Baics and Thelle, "Introduction: Meat and the Nineteenth-Century City," p. 185.
9 Olson, "Development of the National Cattle Trade," pp. 3–6; Specht, *Red Meat Republic*, pp. 152–161 and 191–201. Likewise, following the advent of railroads, sheep and cattle shipments from Scotland to England increased considerably. See Perren, "The Meat and Livestock Trade in Britain," pp. 385–400.
10 Woods, "Breed, Culture, and Economy," pp. 290–291; Barak, *Powering Empire*, pp. 58–59.
11 See, for example, Horowitz, Pilcher, and Watts, "Meat for the Multitudes," p. 1074; Mazanik, "Shiny Shoes," pp. 214–232.
12 Clark, "Livestock Trade Between Kentucky and the South," p. 580; Connor, "A Brief History of the Sheep Industry in the US," pp. 91, 93–165, 167–197; Bell, *Trends in the Sheep Industry of the United States*.
13 Woods, "Breed, Culture, and Economy," p. 300.
14 Karpat, *Studies on Ottoman Social and Political History*, pp. 282–284; Quataert, "The Age of Reforms," pp. 781–782; Wishnitzer, *Reading Clock, Alla Turca*, p. 229.
15 Grehan, *Everyday Life and Consumer Culture*, pp. 99–100.
16 Quataert, "The Age of Reforms," pp. 804–808.
17 In the early 1880s, half of the cattle destined for Moscow went there on foot. See Mazanik, "Shiny Shoes," p. 218.
18 Quataert, "The Age of Reforms," p. 800.
19 Tignor, *Modernization and British Colonial Rule in Egypt*, p. 337; Barak, *Powering Empire*, p. 68. According to Barak, annual meat consumption in Egypt "reached over 750,000 heads of cattle, goats, and sheep" by the mid-1910s. See Ibid., p. 71
20 Bilgin, "Osmanlı Sarayının İaşesi," p. 210.

21 This was part of provisionist economic policies aiming to ensure food supplies for the capital and other major urban centers of the empire and thus to keep their populations content. See Genç, *Osmanlı İmparatorluğu'nda Devlet ve Ekonomi*, pp. 39–67.

22 Greenwood, "Istanbul's Meat Provisioning," pp. 62–154.

23 Works analyzing the effects of this long-lasting crisis on the Ottoman Empire include Goldstone, "East and West in the Seventeenth Century," pp. 103–142; Tabak, *The Waning of the Mediterranean*; White, *The Climate of Rebellion*; Özel, *The Collapse of Rural Order in Ottoman Anatolia*.

24 Areas producing sheep famous with their meat quality continued to send animals to Istanbul. Greenwood, "Istanbul's Meat Provisioning," pp. 144–154 and 224–243.

25 Uzun, *İstanbul'un İaşesinde*, pp. 27, 57–58, 71, and 78. Although Moldavia and Wallachia were exempted from the *celepkeşan* system and the *ondalık ağnam* tax, they were well integrated with the Istanbul market. In the late sixteenth century, these two principalities sent some 200,000 sheep to the capital per year. See Kokdaş, "Celeps, Butchers, and the Sheep," pp. 53–54.

26 A similar tax to ondalık ağnam, called *bedel-i ağnam*, was applied in some parts of Anatolia, though it imposed a lighter burden on herders. See Uzun, *İstanbul'un İaşesinde*, pp. 55–56.

27 Kokdaş, "Celeps, Butchers, and the Sheep," pp. 19–21. Kokdaş notes that the Ottomans categorized three different varieties of sheep bred in Rumelia under the taxonomy of *Kıvırcık*. See Ibid., p. 25.

28 Köksal and Polatel, "A Tribe as an Economic Actor," p. 101.

29 Greenwood, "Istanbul's Meat Provisioning," pp. 28–29. White, "The Little Ice Age Crisis of the Ottoman Empire," pp. 73–78.

30 Uzun, *İstanbul'un İaşesinde*, pp. 22–23 and 27–28. Shipments from Anatolia to Istanbul continued during the seventeenth and first half of the eighteenth centuries. However, Greenwood notes that by the 1730s, "Anatolian supply was still not considered critical to the city's provisioning, although definitely worth encouraging." See Greenwood, "Istanbul's Meat Provisioning," p. 29.

31 "Report by Vice-Consul Wrench on the Trade and Commerce of Constantinople for the Year 1873," in Commercial No. 15 (1874), *Reports from Her Majesty's Consuls on the Manufactures, Commerce, & c., of Their Consular Districts, Part III*, p. 1555.

32 BOA, ŞD 757/31, doc. 24, 27 Mart 1307 (8 April 1891); BOA, ŞD 774/14, doc.17, 3 Nisan 1311 (15 April 1895).

33 Şevket Pamuk calls state interventions in times of crisis as selective interventionism. See Pamuk, "Institutional Change and the Longevity of the Ottoman Empire," p. 236.

34 Klein, *The Margins of Empire*, pp. 20–94 and 128–169.

35 Between 1863 and 1904, the total length of telegraph wires in the empire increased more than five times and reached 36,640 kilometers. Davison, *Essays in Ottoman and Turkish History*, p. 138.

36 The Ottoman state was familiar with draining wetlands as a method to control local populations in different regions. In Baghdad, for instance, draining marshlands became a way to bring the Khaza'il tribe under state control in the eighteenth century. Likewise, in the latter half of the nineteenth century, the government developed plans for reclaiming swamp to expand cotton-growing lands and enhance the settlement of tribes in Çukurova. See Husain, "In the Bellies of the Marshes," pp. 638–664; Toksöz, *Nomads, Migrants and Cotton*, p. 145.

37 Some recent studies on this topic include Gündoğdu, "The State and the Stray Dogs in Late Ottoman Istanbul," pp. 555–574; Çelik, "It's a Bad Fate to be Born Near a Forest," pp. 111–133.

38 For state-run textile factories established in the nineteenth century, see Clark, "The Ottoman Industrial Revolution," pp. 65–76.

39 Some of these works include Shields, "Regional Trade and 19th-Century Mosul," pp. 19–37; Quataert, *Ottoman Manufacturing in the Age of Industrial Revolution*; Lapavitsas and Çakıroğlu, *Capitalism in the Ottoman Balkans*; Cora, "The Market as a Means of Post-Violence Recovery," pp. 217–241.

40 Lyberatos, "Men of the Sultan," pp. 55–85.

41 Doğan Çetinkaya criticizes the approach that views the creation of a national (Muslim) bourgeoise as a political project of the Young Turk regime and early Republican state. He argues that a Muslim bourgeoisie already existed, which led to the formation and realization of this political project. See Çetinkaya, "Converting Wealth into Capital," pp. 35–55.

42 Shields, "Sheep, Nomads, and Merchants in Nineteenth-Century Mosul," p. 774. For a recent study on the role of animals as valuable moveable property, and the efforts of the Ottoman state and local actors to create a system for administering this property in southeastern Syria in the late nineteenth and early twentieth centuries, see Barakat, "Marginal Actors," pp. 105–134.

43 BOA, A.MKT.MHM 304/72, doc. 2, 24 Mayıs 1280 (5 June 1864); Lynch, *Armenia*, p. 187.

44 Pehlivan, "El Niño and the Nomads," pp. 316–356.

45 Bulliet, "History and Animal Energy in the Arid Zone," pp. 51–70.

46 Mikhail, *The Animal in Ottoman Egypt*, pp. 19–63.

47 Çelik, "It's a Bad Fate to be Born Near a Forest," pp. 111–133.

48 İnal, "One-Humped History," pp. 57–72.

Chapter 2: Central Anatolia: An Established Supplier of Livestock to Istanbul

1 In the nineteenth century, Angora goats were chiefly raised in the provinces of Ankara, Kastamonu, and Konya. See Texier, *Küçük Asya*, pp. 415–417; Dölek Sever, "Geç Dönem Osmanlı İmparatorluğu'nda," p.168.

2 Quataert, "Limited Revolution," p. 151.

3 Perrot, "Les Kurdes de l'Haimaneh," pp. 620–621.

4 BOA, ŞD 678/43, doc. 4, 2 Safer 1290 (1 April 1873).

5 "Angora: Report by Vice-Consul Barnham on the Trade and Commerce of Angora for the Year 1883," in Commercial No. 19 (1884) (Trade Reports), *Reports from Her Majesty's Consuls on the Manufactures, Commerce, & c., of Their Consular Districts, Part IV*, p. 574; Diplomatic and Consular Reports on Trade and Finance, *Report for the Year 1895 on the Trade and Agriculture of Angora*, p. 11; Diplomatic and Consular Reports, *Report for the Year 1897 on the Trade and Commerce of Angora and District*, p. 10; Diplomatic and Consular Reports, *Report for the Year 1898 on the Trade and Commerce of Angora and District*, p. 9.

6 Ankara sharia court registers, Defter No (Dft.). 700, Hüküm No (Hk.). 165

7 Between 1934 and 1938, annual rainfall in Konya ranged from only 262 to 378 millimeters. About five decades later, average annual rainfall in central Anatolia was recorded as 420 millimeters, about 35 percent below Turkey's average. See Altan, *Konyanın İktisadi Bünyesine*, pp. 96–98; Gülbahar, "Supplemental Irrigation in Turkey," p. 538.

8 Köksal, *The Ottoman Empire in the Tanzimat Era*, pp. 32 and 84.

9 In the provinces of Hüdavendigar, Aydın, and Adana, this ratio exceeded 10 percent. See Güran, *19. Yüzyıl Osmanlı Tarımı*, p. 65.

10 *1307 Sene-i Maliyesine Mahsus Ankara Vilayet Salnamesi*, p. 267; *Ankara Vilayeti Salname-i Resmisi, 1325 (1907)*, p.140; BOA, MVL 378/20, doc.1, 7 Rabiulevvel 1278 (12 September 1861); BOA, DH.MKT 615/60, doc.5, 10 Teşrinisani 1318 (23 November 1902); Seyyah Kandemir, *Ankara Vilayeti*, p. 245.

11 *1322 Sene-i Maliyesine Mahsus Konya Vilayet Salnamesi*, p. 249.

12 Huntington, "Physical Environment," p. 475.

13 Ibid., 474.

14 Şerif, *Anadolu'da Tanin*, pp. 93–94.

15 Trak, *İktisadi ve Ticari Türkiye*, p. 58.

16 BOA, İ.MMS 65/3070, doc.3; Ankara Vilayeti Salname-i Resmisi, 1325 (1907), pp. 103–274; Ticaret ve Ziraat Nezareti İstatistik İdare-i Umumiyesi Müdüriyeti, *Memalik-i Osmaniye'nin 1329 Senesine Mahsus Ziraat İstatistiği*, pp. 565–568.

17 Diplomatic and Consular Reports, *Report for the Year 1906 on the Trade of Constantinople and District*, p. 26; BOA, İ.ŞE 22/1, doc.2, 17 Mayıs 1323 (30 May 1907).

18 Tahir, *Göl İnsanları*, pp. 73–77.

19 Ibid., 74. It also took no less than a month to reach Istanbul from the southeastern parts of Ankara province. In 1883, a shepherd who was driving a large herd of sheep from Kırşehir to the capital noted that his total journey "would occupy forty-five days." See Ramsay, "The Drovers' Road," p. 801.

20 For instance, on 10 June 1891, a certain Osman Efendi moved 1,970 of his sheep from Haymana to Abant. BOA, ŞD 349/11, docs. 10–15, 29 Mayıs 1307 (10 June 1891).

21 Ankara sharia court registers, Dft. 728 Hk. 60, 1840; BOA, MVL 605/50, doc.1, 17 Rabiulahir 1277 (2 November 1860); BOA, ŞD 349/11, docs. 8, 10, 11 and 12, 15 and 29 Mayıs 1307 (27 May and 10 June 1891); BOA, A.MKT.MHM 553/30, doc. 1, 9 Ağustos 1310 (21 August 1894); Perrot, "Les Kurdes de l'Haimaneh," p. 621.

22 BOA, ŞD 828/26, doc. 4, 20 Ağustos 1321 (2 September 1905); *Sabah*, 1 Şubat 1305 (13 February 1890).

23 Diplomatic and Consular Reports, *Report for the Year 1893 on the Trade, & c. of Angora*, p. 3; Diplomatic and Consular Reports, *Report for the Year 1894 on the Trade, & c. of Angora*, pp. 2 and 8.

24 In 1895 the company was charging about 1,900 piasters per wagon with a carrying capacity of up to 100–120 sheep for a journey from Ankara to Istanbul. Upon the demands of government officials and merchants, this amount was lowered to 1,500 piasters by 1909. See Diplomatic and Consular Reports, *Report for the Year 1895 on the Trade and Agriculture of Angora*, p. 17; BOA, İ.ŞE 22/1, doc. 5, 1 Mayıs 1323 (14 May 1907); Meclis-i Mebusan Zabıt Ceridesi, Period: 1, Year: 2 vol. 1, Meeting: 22 (23 Kanunuevvel 1325/5 January 1910), p. 461.

25 Diplomatic and Consular Reports, *Report for the Year 1906 on the Trade of Constantinople and District*, p. 27; BOA, T.DMİ 1009/52, doc. 1, 28 Mart 1318 (10 April 1902).

26 Diplomatic and Consular Reports, *Report for the Year 1908 on the Trade of Constantinople and District*, p. 27. The available evidence suggests that during this period, rail shipments of sheep from Ankara also declined significantly. While in 1905 trains carried, in total, 324,904 tons of merchandise from there to Istanbul, this number decreased to 277,406 in 1907 and in the following year to 172,855. See Pech, *Manuel des Sociétés*, p. 63.

27 BOA, C.BLD 67/3304, 29 Ramazan 1181 (18 February 1768).

28 Ankara sharia court registers, Dft. 665, Hk. 217, 1205 (1791). Cabbarzade Süleyman rose to the leadership of the famous Çapanoğlu family, which was in control of a significant part of central and southern Anatolia, in the early 1780s. As the family had by then established a reputation for livestock breeding, Süleyman took an active role in the collection of livestock-related taxes. He farmed the fleece wool tax from the government and supervised the tax farmer of the sheep tax in the region. See Özkaya, *Osmanlı İmparatorluğunda Ayanlık*; Ankara sharia court registers, Dft. 669, Hk. 286, 1209 (1795).

29 Ankara sharia court registers, Dft. 666, Hk. 205, 1206 (1792).

30 Köksal and Polatel, "The Cihanbeyli and the Sheep Trade," p. 162.

31 Ankara sharia court registers, Dft. 719, Hk. 171, 1249 (1834); Aksan, *Ottoman Wars*, pp., 385–388.

32 See Ankara sharia court registers, Dft. 686, Hk. 78, 1219 (1805); Ankara sharia court registers, Dft. 719, Hk. 220, 1834.

33 BOA, C.DH 25/1207, doc. 1, 24 Recep 1209 (14 February 1795); BOA, ŞD 2929/14, doc. 1; Köksal and Polatel, "The Cihanbeyli and the Sheep Trade," p. 163.

34 Ankara sharia court registers, Dft. 692, Hk. 463, 1225 (1811); Ankara sharia court registers, Dft. 698, Hk. 188, 1230 (1816).

35 Ankara sharia court registers, Dft. 698, Hk. 188, 1230 (1816); Ankara sharia court registers, Dft. 700, Hk.165, 1231 (1817). In 1817, more than one third of this quota was supplied by the Zeyveli and Cihanbeyli merchants. The former brought 25,000 sheep to Istanbul for slaughter during the Feast of the Sacrifice and the latter 11,000 sheep. See Gratien, "Istanbul's Moveable Feast."

36 Ankara sharia court registers, Dft. 702, Hk. 178, 1233 (1818); Ankara sharia court registers, Dft. 707, Hk. no. 175, 1240 (1825).

37 Ankara sharia court registers, Dft. 708, Hk. no. 83, 1241 (1826).

38 Uzun, *İstanbul'un İaşesinde*, p. 21.

39 BOA, MVL 101/66, 23 Recep 1267 (24 May 1851); BOA C.ML 352/14463, 29 Zilhicce 1216 (2 May 1802).

40 BOA, C.DRB 31/1509, 29 Zilhicce 1255 (4 March 1840). For instance, in 1847, a Reswan merchant from the district of Esbkeşan sold sheep worth 24,000 piasters to the butchers of Bursa. See BOA, MVL 19/28, doc. 3, 26 Şevval 1263 (7 October 1847).

41 Kasaba, *A Moveable Empire*, pp. 3–12; Deringil, "They Live in a State of Nomadism and Savagery," pp. 311–342

42 BOA, HAT 446/22289, 2 Cemazeyilevvel 1245 (7 November 1830).

43 BOA, MVL 32/57, doc.2, 19 Cemazeyilevvel 1265 (12 April 1849); BOA, MB.İ 2/76, 10 Recep 1264 (12 June 1848)

44 Dede, "From Nomadism to Sedentary Life," pp. 67 and 106–110.

45 For example, Abdurrahman Bey, the head of the Mirveys tribe, accused Alişan Bey of intervening in their tax collection and administrative matters. See Köksal, "Coercion and Mediation," p. 483.

46 Köksal, *The Ottoman Empire in the Tanzimat Era*, p. 88.

47 Doğan, "3525 Numaralı Nüfus Defteri'ne Göre," pp. 61–62, 84, and 91–92.

48 Savalan had investments in leech fishing in Rumelia, mining concessions in Karahisar, and several farms in Manisa and Istanbul. See BOA, A.MKT.UM 286/39, 5 Şevval 1271 (21 June 1855) and BOA, BEO 2937/220238, 16 Teşrinievvel 1322 (29 October 1906).

49 One debated cause of this famine and similar contemporary events in other parts of the world, such as India and Ireland, was a decline in precipitation due to solar forcing. See Slavin, "Climate and Famines," pp. 433–447; Sharma, *Famine, Philanthropy and the Colonial State*; Gray, "Famine and Land in Ireland and India," pp. 193–215.

50 Erdoğan, Kılıcı, and Güncl, *Osmanlı'da Ankara*, p. 287; Erler, "Ankara ve Konya Vilayetlerinde," pp. 92–173; Çelik, "Scarcity and Misery," p.159; Çelik, "No Work for Anyone," pp. 155–156; Doğan, "3525 Numaralı Nüfus Defteri'ne Göre," p. 62.

51 Köksal and Polatel, "A tribe as an Economic Actor," pp. 110–120.

52 Ibid., p. 120.

53 During the Crimean War, for instance, large numbers of cattle and sheep from central Anatolia were delivered to military units in combat. This led to a decline in shipments to both Istanbul and local markets, causing a rise in prices. According to the *narh* registers of Ankara, the retail price of mutton reached a high of ninety-six *paras* per *kıyye* in December 1855. See Figure 2.1 and "Report by Mr. Consul Sansidon on the Trade of Brussa during the Year 1855," in *Abstracts of Reports on the Trade of Various Countries and Places for the Year 1855*, p. 188.

54 According to a petition by five Cihanbeyli merchants, the quota system was still in operation in 1867. However, in petitions and official documents from later times, it was not mentioned as being in force. See BOA, MVL 556/7, doc.1 13 Şaban 1284 (10 December 1867); BOA, DH.MKT 1311/14, 15 Kanunusani 1286 (27 January 1871); BOA, ŞD 682/9, doc.2, 25 Mayıs 1290 (6 June 1874).

55 BOA, AE.SSLM.III 341/19693, 29 Zilhicce 1218 (10 April 1804); BOA C.BLD 31/1531, 24 Zilhicce 1235 (2 October 1820).

56 BOA, ŞD 2929/14, doc. 2, 5 Kanunusani 1304 (17 January 1889). This complaint was not without grounds. In 1891, the Ministry of Finance reported that the Cihanbeyli merchants who grazed their sheep on pastures in state forests in Kastamonu were charged a fee of thirty *paras* per head by the government. The imposition of this fee was authorized by the Forest Regulation of 1870. According to this regulation, merchants and non-local herders who wanted to graze their flocks in the state forests were to obtain the authorization of the local forest officials. They were also subjected to the payment of a fee in accordance with the existing rules and regulations. See BOA, ŞD 2929/14, doc. 3, 23 Kanunusani 1306 (4 February 1891); Dursun, "Forest and the State," pp. 249–250.

57 Erler, "Ankara ve Konya Vilayetlerinde," pp. 98 and 108–110; Ertem, "Considering Famine," pp. 154-155; Bayar, "1873–1875 Orta Anadolu Kıtlığı," pp. 5 and 55.

58 In some districts of the province, such as Keskin, livestock populations were almost totally wiped out. In the forty-two villages of this district, there were 81,240 sheep in 1873. Two years later, this number decreased to 3,312. See "Statistics of the Ravages of the Famine in the Provinces of Angora and of the Relief Offered by the Committee," *The Levant Herald*, 3 March 1875.

59 Bayar, "1873–1875 Orta Anadolu Kıtlığı," pp. 36 and 92; Erler, *Ankara ve Konya Vilayetlerinde*, p. 110.

60 *The Levant Herald*, 5 October 1874.

61 Erler, "Ankara ve Konya Vilayetlerinde," p. 110. For the effects of the famine on meat prices in Istanbul, see Chapter 6.

62 "Lieutenant-Colonel Wilson to Sir A. H. Layard," in *Turkey no. 23: Further Correspondence Respecting the Conditions of the Populations in Asia Minor and Syria*, p. 148. According to Ottoman sources, the harsh winter of 1879–80 killed 30–40 percent of the sheep population in Ankara province. See Ghazarian, "A Climate of Confessionalization," p. 493.

63 "Captain Steward to Mr. Goschen," in *Turkey no. 23: Further Correspondence Respecting the Conditions of the Populations in Asia Minor and Syria*, p. 39.

64 "Vice-Consul Gatheral to Mr. Goschen," in *Turkey no. 6: Further Correspondence Respecting the Conditions of the Populations in Asia Minor and Syria*, p. 245.

65 "Angora: Report by Vice-Consul Henry D. Barnham," in *Second Report of the Royal Commission Appointed to Inquire into the Depression of Trade and Industry, Appendix, Part II*, p. 357.

66 BOA, Y.EE 43/37, 25 Zilkade 1295 (20 November 1878); Birdal, *The Political Economy of the Ottoman Public Debt*, p. 44; Tahsin Paşa, *Tahsin Paşa'nın Yıldız Hatıraları*, pp. 215–216; Ghazarian, "A Climate of Confessionalization," p. 495.

67 BOA, HH.THR 125/2, doc. 2, 25 Şubat 1303 (8 March 1888); BOA, ŞD 730/6, doc. 3, 24 Teşrinievvel 1303 (5 November 1887); BOA, İ.DH 1072/84092, doc. 3, 16 Şubat 1303 (28 February 1888); BOA, MV 65/79, 19 Haziran 1307 (1 July 1891); Sürgevil, *İkinci Meşrutiyet Döneminde İzmir*, pp. 185–187; Ak, "Osmanlı Devleti'nde Veba-i Bakari," pp. 220–221.

68 Ayalon, *Natural Disasters in the Ottoman Empire*, p. 202; Bolanos, "The Ottomans During the Global Crises," pp. 603–620; Ayar, "Osmanlı'nın Rumeli Topraklarında," pp. 19–28.

69 BOA, DH.MKT 145/85, 23 Eylül 1309 (5 October 1893).

70 Schweig, "Progressing into Disaster," pp. 1–23; Ayar, "Osmanlı Devleti'nde Kolera Salgını," pp. 90–96 and 100–105.

71 BOA, A.MKT.UM 553/30, doc. 2, 10 Ağustos 1310 (22 August 1894); BOA, BEO 626/46932, doc. 2, 6 Mayıs 1311 (18 May 1895). After this epidemic, another outbreak hit Ankara and Konya provinces in 1911. See BOA, MV 154/90, 9 Temmuz 1327 (22 July 1911).

72 Diplomatic and Consular Reports, *Report for the Year 1907 on the Trade and Commerce of the Consular District of Smyrna*, p. 4; BOA, BEO 2317/173730, doc. 2, 6 Nisan 1320 (19 April 1904); BOA, BEO 2627/196976, 9 Temmuz 1321 (22 July 1905).

73 BOA, İ.ŞE 22/1, doc. 2, 17 Mayıs 1323 (30 May 1907); "Notes on the Turkish Mohair Trade," *The Levant Herald and Eastern Express*, 24 February 1906.

74 Diplomatic and Consular Reports, *Report for the Year 1906 on the Trade of Constantinople and District*, p. 33; Diplomatic and Consular Reports, *Report for the Year 1908 on the Trade of Constantinople and District*, p. 27.

75 BOA, ŞD 730/6, doc. 5, 16 Kanunusani 1303 (28 January 1888).

76 Diplomatic and Consular Reports on Trade and Finance, *Report for the Year 1894 on the Trade & c. of Angora*, p. 2; Diplomatic and Consular Reports on Trade and Finance, *Report for the Year 1895 on the Trade and Agriculture of Angora*, p. 11; Diplomatic and Consular Reports, *Report for the Year 1897 on the Trade and Commerce of Angora and District*, p. 10; Diplomatic and Consular Reports, *Report for the Year 1898 on the Trade and Commerce of Angora and District*, p. 9.

77 BOA, DH.MKT 615/60, docs. 3 and 5, 3 and 10 Teşrinisani 1318 (16 and 23 November 1902); BOA, ŞD 828/26, doc. 4, 20 Ağustos 1321 (2 September 1905).

78 Diplomatic and Consular Reports, *Report for the Year 1907 on the Trade of Constantinople and District*, p. 34.

79 For example, Reswan units settled around the Bozok district complained about tax burden in the absence of pastures and farmlands in their settlement. See BOA, MVL 101/66, 23 Recep 1267 (24 May 1851).

80 BOA, İ.MVL 228/7802, 9 Rabiulahir 1268 (1 February 1852) and BOA, İ.MVL 397/17283, 22 Zilkade 1274 (4 July 1858).

81 These tribal units usually went to Uzunyayla, Çiçekdağı or Haymana where they used to take their livestock to summer pastures. See BOA, A.MKT.UM 409/49, 19 Zilkade 276 (8 June 1860).

82 Perrot, "Les Kurdes de l'Haimaneh," pp. 617–621. According to Ottoman population registers, in the early 1850s, Katrancı had sixty-seven Mikailli households. See Doğan, "3525 Numaralı Nüfus Defteri'ne Göre," p. 82.

83 Seyyah Kandemir, *Ankara Vilayeti*, pp. 246–251. See also Dede, "From Nomadism to Sedentary Life," p. 68.

84 The Zeyveli tribe became the guarantor for the Cihanbeyli's debt to Savalan. See Köksal and Polatel, "A Tribe as an Economic Actor," p. 112.

85 BOA, ŞD 1672/24, docs. 12 and 23, 15 Mayıs 1320 (28 May 1904) and 10 Temmuz 1320 (23 July 1904).

86 BOA, ŞD 1672/24, docs. 12 and 23, 15 Mayıs 1320 (28 May 1904) and 10 Temmuz 1320 (23 July 1904).

87 Between 1859 and 1879, more than 40,000 immigrants were settled in Ankara province. See Şimşir, *Ankara*, p. 26; Pustu, "Osmanlı Döneminde Ankara'ya," p. 614. For an account by a local notable on the increased demand for land in the western districts of Ankara province, see Sazak, *Emin Bey'in Defteri*, pp. 39–40.

88 BOA, ŞD 1672/24, docs. 23 and 27, 10 Temmuz 1320 (23 July 1904) and 1 Rabiulahir 1251 (27 July 1835).

89 BOA, ŞD 3218/5, 7 Mayıs 1319 (20 May 1903).

90 BOA, ŞD 1672/24, doc. 21, 23 Haziran 1320 (6 July 1904).

91 BOA, ŞD 1672/24, doc. 25, 26 Temmuz 1320 (8 August 1904).

92 BOA, ŞD 1672/24, docs. 12 and 21, 15 Mayıs 1320 (28 May 1904) and 23 Haziran 1320 (6 July 1904).

93 BOA, ŞD 1360/2, doc. 1, 5 Nisan 1324 (18 April 1908); BOA, ŞD 1360/4, doc. 1, 27 Mayıs 1324 (10 July 1908).

94 Trak, *İktisadi ve Ticari Türkiye*, pp. 60–61.

95 Perrot, "Les Kurdes de l'Haimaneh," p. 618.

96 Uçak, *Tarih İçinde Haymana*, p. 116.

97 BOA, MVL 378/20, doc. 1, 7 Rabiulevvel 1278 (12 September 1861); BOA, MVL 552/64, doc. 1, 7 Recep 1284 (4 November 1867); BOA, MVL 822/91, doc. 2, 9 Şevval 1275 (12 May 1859); BOA, ŞD 730/6, doc. 7, 2 Mart 1304 (14 March 1888).

98 For instance, in 1861, the head trader Ali Ağa sued two butchers and had them arrested for not paying their debts, amounting to 3,400 piasters, to a merchant named Mehmed. The two were released only after they furnished a guarantor for the payment of that amount. BOA, A.MKT.NZD 387/4, docs. 1 and 2, 1 and 19 Cemazeyilahir 1278 (4 and 22 December 1861).

99 BOA, Y.PRK.AZJ 6/103, doc. 2.

100 BOA, MVL 378/69, 22 Rabiulahir 1278 (27 October 1861).

101 BOA, ŞD 682/9, doc. 3, 8 Mayıs 1290 (21 May 1874). The same point was later made by the leading members of the butchers' guild in Istanbul in a petition addressed to the Istanbul Municipality. See BOA, ŞD 730/6, doc. 2, 27 Şubat 1303 (10 March 1888).

102 One of the first non-Cihanbeyli head traders was a certain Ali Ağa. In 1861, he replaced Süleyman Ağa from the Cihanbeyli tribe who held the post throughout most of the 1850s. See BOA, MVL 378/11, doc. 2, 17 Rabiulahir 1278 (22 October 1861); BOA, MVL 378/20, docs. 1 and 2, 7 Rabiulevvel 1278 (12 September 1861) and 14 Rabiulahir 1278 (19 October 1861).

103 BOA, MVL 552/64, doc. 1, 7 Recep 1284 (4 November 1867); BOA, MVL 556/7, docs. 1 and 3, 13 Şaban 1284 (10 December 1867) and 29 Şaban 1284 (26 December 1867).

104 BOA, ŞD 702/18, docs.1–3, 22 Safer 1300 (2 January 1883) and 8 Kanunuevvel 1298 (20 December 1882); BOA, Y.PRK.AZJ 6/103, docs. 2–3, 11 Zilkade 1300 (13 September 1883).

105 In 1883, twenty sheep merchants, thirteen from the Cihanbeyli district in Konya province and the rest from the Mikailli and Şeyh Bezenli tribes, produced a petition arguing that head traders rendered simple-minded tribal people invaluable assistance in their trading activities in Istanbul. Without such assistance these people would suffer serious financial losses and consequently limit their exports to the capital. See Y.PRK.AZJ 6/103, doc. 3, 11 Zilkade 1300 (13 September 1883).

106 Ali Rıza annually collected between 500 and 700 head of sheep as his head trader's fee and sold them to Üsküdar butchers. BOA, ŞD 730/6, doc. 6, 21 Teşrinisani 1302 (3 December 1887), 30 Teşrinisani 1303 (12 December 1887) and 18 Şubat 1303 (1 March 1888); BOA, ŞD 744/4, docs. 29 and 32, 14 Teşrinievvel 1303 (26 October 1887) and 26 Kanunuevvel 1303 (7 January 1888).

107 Ali Rıza denied that he presented himself as the new head trader but admitted that he received payment in-kind from merchants in return for assisting them in selling their sheep. BOA, ŞD 730/6, doc.9, 14 Mart 1304 (26 March 1888).

108 For example, in 1887, a certain Yanaki from Kalkandelen, who had reportedly operated as a sheep merchant for years, agreed to sell his animals to three Istanbul butchers, whom he did not know, only after he confirmed their good reputation from a municipal official. BOA, ŞD 744/4, docs. 7 and 32, 27 Haziran 1303 (9 July 1887) and 16 Eylül 1303 (28 September 1887).

109 BOA, ŞD 682/9, doc. 6, 21 Teşrinisani 1289 (3 December 1873).

110 BOA, ŞD 682/9, doc.3, 8 Mayıs 1290 (20 May 1874).

111 BOA, ŞD 2432/19, doc.4, 17 Nisan 1296 (29 April 1880). In response to the complaints that he was neglectful of his duties, the Ministry of Interior dismissed Ali Rıza from office in the fall of 1879. For about a year, following his dismissal, he was not allowed to hold a position in the Ottoman bureaucracy. Yet, in October 1880, the Council of State ruled that since allegations made against him were not well founded, he could be appointed as *kaymakam* to a district outside Ankara. Unfortunately, the documents consulted do not mention whether Ali Rıza received an appointment after this decision and how he earned his living until 1884. See BOA, ŞD 2432/19, doc. 2, 22 Zilkade 1297 (26 October 1880).

112 BOA, ŞD 727/9, doc. 4, 25 Mart 1303 (6 April 1887). Merchants of the Mikailli, Şeyh Bezenli, and Reswan tribes added to their signatures their place of residence. They were all from villages in the district of Haymana.

113 BOA, ŞD 727/9, doc. 2, 16 Temmuz 1303 (28 July 1887). Among the Hamidian bureaucrats with whom Ali Rıza had connections were officials in charge of the auction sale of animals brought from the Mihaliç Imperial Farms. In May 1886, they agreed to sell 300 sheep to a butcher named Lütfi Efendi, only after Ali Rıza stood surety for him. BOA, ML.EEM 85/54, doc. 1, 27 Nisan 1302 (9 May 1886). In the spring of 1886, Ali Rıza had also taken part in at least two auctions on behalf of a butcher named Sıddık Efendi. See BOA, ML.EEM 85/27, doc. 1, 31 Mart 1302 (12 April 1886) and BOA, ML.EEM 85/57, doc. 1, 21 Nisan 1302 (3 May 1886).

114 BOA, ŞD 730/6, docs. 3 and 9, 24 Teşrinievvel 1303 (5 November 1887) and 14 Mart 1304 (26 March 1888).

115 BOA, ŞD 730/6, docs. 5 and 6, 16 Kanunusani 1303 (28 January 1888) and 23 Kanunuevvel 1303 (4 January 1888).

116 BOA, ŞD 730/6, doc. 5, 16 Kanunusani 1303 (28 January 1888).

117 BOA İ.TAL 228/51, docs.1, 3, and 6, 11 Eylül 1316 (24 September 1900) and 20 Cemazeyilahir 1318 (15 October 1900).

118 Sarıay, "II. Meşrutiyet Döneminde Eşraf," p. 604; Şener, *Nallıhan*, pp. 105–106; BOA, DH.MKT 1791/66, 1 Kanunuevvel 1306 (13 December 1890).

119 BOA, Y.PRK.AZJ 45/51, 29 Zilhicce 1320 (29 March 1903).

120 BOA, Y.PRK.AZJ 42/35, doc. 2, 6 Mayıs 1317 (19 May 1901); BOA, DH.TMIKM 129/22, doc. 1, 28 Temmuz 1318 (10 August 1902).

121 BOA, Y.PRK.AZJ 42/35, docs. 14 and 17.

122 BOA, Y.PRK.AZJ 42/35, docs. 12 and 13.

123 BOA, DH.TMIK.M 129/22, doc.1, 28 Temmuz 1318 (10 August 1902); BOA, BEO 1901/142521, docs. 2 and 5, 25 Temmuz 1318 (7 August 1902) and 27 Temmuz 1318 (9 August 1902).

124 BOA, DH.MKT 2701/95, doc.1, 1 Haziran 1320 (14 June 1904); Şerif, *Anadolu'da Tanin*, p. 94.

125 The Young Turk Revolution had a similar impact on rural populations in other parts of the empire. Nilay Özok-Gündoğan shows that peasant communities in Diyarbekir province interpreted the principles of the revolution in accordance with their interests, used these interpretations to voice grievances against provincial notables, and pressed their demands on central state elites. See Özok-Gündoğan, "A 'Peripheral' Approach."

126 BOA, DH.MKT 2735/15, doc. 1, 19 Kanunusani 1324 (1 February 1909).

127 Şerif, *Anadolu'da Tanin*, p. 94.

128 When, in 1916, the *kaymakam* of Beypazarı confiscated seed grain from his warehouse, Hilmi Efendi took the issue to Talat Bey. Shortly afterwards, the confiscated grain was returned to him. See Sarıay, "II. Meşrutiyet Döneminde Eşraf," p. 608.

129 BOA, DH.MKT 2769/15, doc. 2, 21 Şubat 1324 (6 March 1909).

130 Çoker, *Türk Parlamento Tarihi*, p. 81.

131 Şerif, *Anadolu'da Tanin*, p. 95.

132 BOA, DH.MKT 2701/95, doc. 5, 14 Kanunusani 1324 (27 January 1909).

133 BOA, DH.İ.UM 98/1, doc. 4, 22 Teşrinisani 1332 (5 December 1916). Available evidence suggests that Hilmi's family was involved in the cultivation of a variety of crops. In a 1914 booklet, he and his brother, Hakkı, were mentioned as grain and rice merchants. See Torun, *Bilinen ve Bilinmeyen Yönleriyle Beypazarı*, pp. 71–72.

134 Sazak, *Emin Bey'in Defteri*, p. 21.

135 Ibid., pp. 89–90.

136 Ibid., pp. 30–32 and 39.

137 Ibid., pp. 73, 86, and 101. He retained his seat in the Grand National Assembly until 1950. See Çoker, *Türk Parlamento Tarihi*, pp. 409–410.

138 Sazak, *Emin Bey'in Defteri*, pp. 182–183.

139 Terzibaşoğlu and Kaya, "19. Yüzyılda Balkanlar'da Toprak Rejimi ve Emek İlişkileri," pp. 98–99.

Chapter 3: Northeastern Anatolia: An 'Excluded' Region

1 Pamuk, *Uneven Centuries*, p. 124.
2 Küçük, "Erzurum," p. 327.
3 Cora, "Transforming Erzurum/Karin," p. 60.
4 Çetin, "The Development of the Transit Trade," pp. 21–52; Tozlu, "Trabzon-Erzurum-Tebriz Yolu," pp. 481–492.
5 Cora, "Transforming Erzurum/Karin," pp. 234–254; Shields, "Sheep, Nomads and Merchants," p. 776; Koç, "Nomadic Pastoral Tribes," pp. 237–253.
6 Küçük, "Erzurum," p. 328.
7 *1294 Erzurum Vilayet Salnamesi*, pp. 68–125; *1299 Erzurum Vilayet Salnamesi*, pp. 99–135; Özkan, "19. Yüzyılda Osmanlı Devleti'nin İdari Taksimatı," pp. 39, 86, 112, and 182.
8 "Baiburt and the Border Ranges," p. 263.
9 Massy, "Exploration in Asiatic Turkey," p. 280. Ottoman provincial yearbooks also mentioned Erzurum as a region of rich pastures. See, for instance, *Salname-i Vilayet-i Erzurum: 1313 Sene-i Maliye*, pp. 166–167.
10 Koç, "Winter-Quartering Tribes," pp. 47–66.
11 Ateş, *The Ottoman-Iranian Borderlands*, p. 124; Koç, "Nomadic Pastoral Tribes," p. 259.
12 BOA, A.MKT 217/86, 19 Ramazan 1265 (8 August 1849); BOA, A.MKT.UM 246/66, doc. 1, 7 Zilkade 1272 (10 July 1856). Exports to Egypt seemed to gain importance in times of calamities. To give one example, when an epizootic decimated large numbers of cattle and left Egyptian peasants unable to plough in the early 1840s, the governor of Egypt asked his superiors in Istanbul to issue an order to the field marshal of Erzurum to purchase cows and oxen from tribes in the region and send them to Egypt. See BOA, İ.MTZ (05) 11/276, doc. 1, 28 Zilkade 1258 (31 December 1842).
13 BOA, A.MKT 217/86, 19 Ramazan 1265 (8 August 1849).
14 Grehan, *Everyday Life and Consumer Culture*, pp. 97–98.
15 *Report on the Commercial Statistics of Syria by John Bowring*, p. 16.
16 BOA, C.BLD 121/6006, 8 Şaban 1182 (18 December 1768).
17 Ankara sharia court registers, Dft. 660, Hk. 310, 11–20 Zilkade 1201 (25 August–3 September 1787).
18 BOA, C.DH. 119/5909, 29 Cemazeyilahir 1212 (19 December 1797).
19 Ankara sharia court registers, Dft. 666, Hk. 205, 10 Muharrem 1206 (9 September 1791). Because they were red or brown in color, the *Karaman* sheep raised in eastern Anatolia were called red sheep. See *Koyun Yetiştimek ve Bakmak Usulü*, p. 8.
20 Ali Yaycıoğlu, for instance, notes that the Ottoman-Russian war had left very little meat for Istanbul butchers by the spring of 1807. See Yaycıoğlu, *Partners of the Empire*, p. 173.
21 BOA, C.BLD 34/1667, 25 Safer 1216 (7 July 1801).
22 While prominent tribal merchants came from the Merdisi and Cizranlı tribes, their non-tribal counterparts were mainly based in Erzurum and Kars. BOA, AE.SSLM.III 344/19806, doc. 2, 20 Cemazeyilahir 1215 (8 November 1800).
23 BOA, C.BLD 11/547, 29 Cemazeyilevvel 1217 (27 September 1802).
24 According to one source, the Istanbul-Erzurum land route took thirty-eight days in 1826. See Çetin, *Tanzimat'tan Cumhuriyet'e Anadolu'da*, p. 233.
25 BOA, C.BLD 72/3567, doc. 1, 13 Cemazeyilahir 1244 (21 December 1828); BOA, MVL 434/21, doc. 1, 21 Recep 1280 (1 January 1864); Yıldırım, *Sakarya Köprüleri*, p. 58.
26 BOA, C.ML 184/7712, 29 Şaban 1249 (11 January 1834). For a similar case see BOA, C.BLD 149/7423, 29 Cemazeyilevvel 1253 (31 August 1837).

27 BOA, MVL 450/75, doc. 2, 21 Kanunusani 1279 (2 February 1864); BOA, MVL 407/91, doc. 1, 11 Recep 1279 (2 January 1863).

28 BOA, AE. SSLM.III 254/14704, 12 Şevval 1206 (3 June 1792). Attacks by central Anatolian tribes against merchants and their flocks continued into the following decades. See, for instance, Perrot, "Les Kurdes de l'Haimaneh," pp. 625–626.

29 Ankara sharia court registers, Dft. 666, Hk. 205, 10 Muharrem 1206 (9 September 1791).

30 BOA, C.BLD 97/4812, 29 Rabiulevvel 1218 (19 July 1803).

31 BOA, C. İKTS 39/1928, doc. 1, 29 Cemazeyilevvel 1261 (5 June 1845).

32 BOA, A.MKT.MHM 128/11, 24 Recep 1274 (10 March 1858); BOA, A.MKT.UM 530/24, 3 Recep 1278 (4 January 1862); BOA, MVL 450/75, doc. 2, 21 Kanunusani 1279 (2 February 1864). These documents suggest that the government began to collect the taxes in question only after the Erzurum merchants fulfilled their annual shipment quota.

33 BOA, C.ML 184/7712, 29 Şaban 1249 (11 January 1834).

34 BOA, A.MKT.MHM 128/11, 24 Recep 1274 (10 March 1858); BOA, MVL 450/75, doc. 2, 8 Haziran 1279 (20 June 1863); Pehlivan, "Beyond the Desert and the Sown," pp. 132–134; Pehlivan, "El Niño and the Nomads," p. 342. As the preceding chapter has revealed, around this time, the Cihanbeyli and affiliated tribes in central Anatolia were required to send around 120,000 sheep per annum to Istanbul.

35 Cora, "Transforming Erzurum/Karin," p. 244.

36 *Report on the Commercial Statistics of Syria by John Bowring*, p. 16; Uzun, *İstanbul'un İaşesinde*, pp. 163–165; BOA, I.DH 7/300, doc. 1, 5 Zilhicce 1255 (9 February 1840).

37 One such year was 1855. While the price of mutton in Aleppo was then 2.5 piasters a *kıyye*, it did not fall below 4.5 piasters in Istanbul for most of the year. See Issawi, *The Fertile Crescent*, p. 427; BOA, İ.MVL 328/14017, doc. 2, 4 Recep 1271 (23 March 1855); Hornby, *Constantinople During the Crimean War*, p. 116.

38 During his journey to Erzurum in 1856, Süleyman Ağa was accompanied by his son Mehmed, a shepherd, and a slave. When they arrived in Homs in mid-June, Mehmed became involved in an argument with the shepherd and wounded him with his rifle. See BOA, A.MKT.UM 246/66, 7 Zilkade 1272 (10 July 1856).

39 As Tolga Cora's work demonstrates, Armenian entrepreneurs in Erzurum played an important role in financing the trade between northeastern Anatolia and Syrian provinces. According to Ottoman official records, loans owed by livestock merchants from Syria to one of these entrepreneurs, Khachatur Pastırmacıyan Efendi, amounted to more than 14,000 liras in 1867. See Cora, "Transforming Erzurum/Karin," p. 256. For the story of a Damascene merchant who was making purchases in Erzurum on credit, see Nacar and Köksal, "Ali Ağa'nın Koyunları ve Borçları."

40 BOA, İ.MVL 276/10715, doc. 2, 29 Şaban 1269 (7 June 1853); BOA, İ.DH 338/22247, doc. 2, 8 Cemazeyilahir 1272 (15 February 1856); BOA, İ.MVL 328/14017, doc. 2, 4 Recep 1271 (23 March 1855); BOA, İ.MMS 25/1077, docs.1 and 2, 27 Şevval 1278 (27 April 1862) and 6 Zilkade 1278 (5 May 1862); *Vak'a-Nüvis Ahmed Lütfi Efendi Tarihi, v. X*, pp. 45 and 75. For the liberalization of regulations concerning the trade in bread and fresh fruits and vegetables, see *Vak'a-Nüvis Ahmed Lütfi Efendi Tarihi, v. IX*, pp. 97–98; Balıkhane Nazırı Ali Bey, *Eski Zamanlarda İstanbul*, p. 267.

41 BOA, İ.MVL 468/21193, doc. 2, 14 Zilkade 1278 (13 May 1862).

42 "Report by Mr. Consul Taylor on the Trade and Condition of the Vilaiet of Erzeroom and Eyalets of Kharput and Diarbekir, composing the Consular District of Koordistan, for the year 1866," in *Commercial Reports Received at the Foreign Office from Her Majesty's Consuls in 1867*, p. 570.

43 BOA, A.MKT.MHM 304/72, doc. 2, 24 Mayıs 1280 (5 June 1864). According to the same report, the merchants also purchased about 10,000 cattle from both within and outside the empire's borders. After being grazed and fattened in the mountain pastures of Erzurum in spring and summer, around

two thirds of these cattle were sold to local farmers and *pastırma* producers. The rest were driven to Kayseri and Tokat to be sold to *pastırma* producers there. The available evidence suggests that cattle exports at times exceeded figures given in this report. For example, in 1861, a single merchant named Hurşid Ağa purchased 5,000 cattle in Erzurum to sell in Kayseri. See BOA, A.MKT.UM 544/58, doc. 2, 26 Recep 1278 (27 January 1862).

44 Cora, "Transforming Erzurum/Karin," p. 241.

45 Uzun, *İstanbul'un İaşesinde*, pp. 118–119; BOA, İ.MMS 14/576, 24 Cemazeyilevvel 1275 (30 December 1858).

46 BOA, A.MKT.UM 466/50, doc. 2, 7 Şevval 1277 (18 April 1861).

47 BOA, MVL 761/23, doc. 2, 4 Recep 1278 (5 January 1862).

48 "Report by Mr. Consul Taylor on the Trade of Diarbekr and Kurdistan for the Year 1863," in *Commercial Reports Received at the Foreign Office from Her Majesty's Consuls between July 1st and December 31st, 1864*, p. 180.

49 BOA, MVL 407/91, docs. 1 and 3, 11 Recep 1279 (2 January 1863) and 4 Muharrem 1280 (21 June 1863).

50 BOA, ŞD 573/13, docs. 4 and 12, 23 Nisan 1294 (5 May 1878) and 26 Mayıs 1298 (7 June 1882).

51 The available statistics for animals in the yearbooks of the province of Erzurum before the war [1288 (1871), 1289 (1872), 1290 (1873), and 1292 (1875)] are used to calculate this average for the *sancak*s of Kars and Çıldır. The two *sancaks* comprised between 15.29 and 23.52 percent of the total sheep and goat population in the province for the given years.

52 Nedim İpek notes that in May 1879, there were more than 15,000 households in Erzurum that had migrated from Kars and nearby districts. See İpek, "Kafkaslar'dan Anadolu'ya Göçler," p. 106. See also *Reports on Subjects of General and Commercial Interest, Russia: Reports on the Provinces of Semirensk and Kars*, p. 8.

53 BOA, ŞD 1174/16, docs.1, 3 and 4, 22 Teşrinisani 1296 (4 December 1880), 23 Eylül 1296 (5 October 1880), and 30 Eylül 1296 (12 October 1880); Erk, "Tarihte Önemli Sığır Vebası Salgınları," p. 230.

54 "Captain Everett to Major Trotter," in *Turkey no.23: Further Correspondence Respecting Condition of the Populations in Asia Minor and Syria*, pp. 199–200.

55 "Vice-Consul Everett to Mr. Goschen," in *Turkey no. 6: Further Correspondence Respecting the Conditions of the Populations in Asia Minor and Syria*, p. 186.

56 Ghazarian, "A Climate of Confessionalization," p. 491.

57 "Report by Vice-Consul Eyre on the Trade and Commerce of Erzeroum for the Year 1882," in Commercial No. 32 (1883), *Reports from Her Majesty's Consuls on the Manufactures, Commerce, &c. of Their Consular Districts, Part X*, pp. 1751–1752; "Report by Consul Everett on the Trade and Commerce of Some of the Districts Comprised in the Consulate of Kurdistan for 1883," in Commercial No. 33 (1884), *Reports from Her Majesty's Consuls on the Manufactures, Commerce, &c. of Their Consular Districts, Part VIII*, p. 1410.

58 Pehlivan, "El Niño and the Nomads," p. 347; Özkan, "A Road in Rebellion," pp. 304–336. According to a 1893 report by the governor of Erzurum, the famine resulted in an increase in the cases of goat and sheep theft. That was probably because under conditions of drought and food shortage, the population of these animals underwent a certain decrease. See Özger, "XIX. Yüzyıl Sonlarında," p. 91.

59 *Russia: Reports on the Provinces of Semirensk and Kars*, pp. 7–8. Consular reports from the late nineteenth century also mentioned imports of sheep from Iran. Here is one example from the year 1889: "It must not hence be concluded that the demand for Persian sheep has fallen off, for several thousands were driven last summer by way of Bayazid to Erzeroum to be sold there to the Aleppo dealers." See Diplomatic and Consular Reports, *Report for the Year 1889–90 on the Trade of of Erzeroum*, p. 8.

60 These figures, obtained mostly from local merchants, likely did not refer to the entire province but rather to the city center and its adjacent districts.

61 Klein, *The Margins of Empire*, p. 139.

62 Diplomatic and Consular Reports, *Report for the Year 1901 on the Trade of the Consular District of Erzeroum*, p. 7.

63 Özbek, "The Politics of Taxation," pp. 770–797; Koç, "Nomadic Pastoral Tribes," pp. 270–272.

64 "Acting Consul Hampson to Sir W. White," in *Turkey no. 1: Further Correspondence Respecting the Condition of the Populations in Asiatic Turkey*, p. 25.

65 In the early twentieth century, two major suppliers for the Syrian markets were the districts of Diyarbekir and Mosul. In 1907, Lloyd George reported that the former sent 120,000 head of sheep annually to Syria, while the latter dispatched around 100,000 heads. See *British Documents on Foreign Affairs*, p. 252.

66 BOA, ŞD 828/26, doc. 4, 20 Ağustos 1323 (2 September 1905). The aforementioned report by Lloyd George also noted that northeastern Anatolia sent between 130,000 and 180,000 sheep annually to Istanbul through the port of Trabzon. See *British Documents on Foreign Affairs*, p. 252.

67 BOA, ŞD 2771/6, doc. 1, 21 Teşrinisani 1322 (4 December 1906); BOA, İ.ŞE 22/1, doc. 6, 10 Şubat 1322 (23 February 1907).

68 Diplomatic and Consular Reports, *Report for the Year 1911 on the Trade of the Consular District of Erzeroum*, p. 6; Diplomatic and Consular Reports, *Report for the Year 1912 on the Trade of the Consular District of Erzeroum*, p. 5.

69 See, for example, BOA, ŞD 686/27, doc. 1, 19 Cemazeyilahir 1295 (20 June 1878); BOA, BEO 181/13532, doc. 2, 8 Mayıs 1309 (20 May 1893); BOA, İ.ŞE 22/1, doc. 2, 17 Mayıs 1323 (30 May 1907).

70 Issawi, "The Tabriz-Trabzon Trade," pp. 18–27; Turgay, "Trabzon," pp. 435–465; Uygun, *Osmanlı Sularında Rekabet*, pp. 247–250.

71 The quantity and value for livestock exports were given in Şaşmaz, *Trade Reports of the Trebizond Province, v. I-III.*

72 A. Billiotti, "Report on the Existing Waggon-Road from Trebizond to Erzeroum, and its Extension to Tabreez, 1883," in Şaşmaz, *Trade Reports of the Trebizond Province, v. II*, p. 1008; Diplomatic and Consular Reports, *Report for the Year 1898 on the Trade and Commerce of the Trebizond Vilayet*, p. 11; Çağman, "Osmanlı Döneminde İstanbul'da Modern Bir Mezbaha," pp. 50–51.

73 "Report on the Trade and Commerce of the Trebizond Vilayet for the Year 1892," in Şaşmaz, *Trade Reports of the Trebizond Province, v. III*, p. 1202; "Report on the Trade and Commerce of the Trebizond Vilayet for the Year 1893," in Şaşmaz, *Trade Reports of the Trebizond Province, v. III*, p. 1215.

74 See, for example, *Sabah*, 1 Şubat 1305 (13 February 1890); BOA, BEO 299/22364, 11 Teşrinievvel 1309 (23 October 1893).

75 Özkan, "A Road in Rebellion," p. 24.

76 BOA, ŞD 1842/15, 22 Kanunusani 1305 (3 February 1890).

77 BOA, BEO 393/29469, 17 Nisan 1310 (29 April 1894); BOA, ŞD 851/22, 28 May 1328 (10 June 1912).

78 Diplomatic and Consular Reports on Trade and Finance, *Report for the Year 1893 on the Trade of the Consular District of Erzeroum*, p. 3; Diplomatic and Consular Reports on Trade and Finance, *Report for the Year 1893 on the Trade, &c., of the Consular District of Trebizond*, p. 5; BOA, DH.MKT 2004/75, 8 Eylül 1308 (20 September 1892); Topuz, "XIX. Yüzyılda Van'da İllet-i Kolera," pp. 297–316.

79 BOA, ŞD 2961/36, doc. 2, 31 Mayıs 1309 (12 June 1893). Likewise, British consular officials reported that sheep exports from Trabzon decreased from about 85,000 heads in 1891 to 32,000 heads in 1892. See Diplomatic and Consular Reports on Trade and Finance, *Report for the Year 1891 on the Trade of the*

Vilayet of Trebizond, p. 8; Diplomatic and Consular Reports on Trade and Finance, *Report for the Year 1893 on the Trade, &c., of the Consular District of Trebizond*, p. 8.

80 BOA, DH.MKT 1999/25, 27 Ağustos 1308 (8 September 1892); BOA, DH.MKT 2004/75, 8 Eylül 1308 (20 September 1892).

81 In 1893, the Erzurum merchants petitioned once again to be exempt from quarantine in Sinop. See BOA, DH.MKT 170/34, 8 Teşrinisani 1309 (20 November 1893).

82 See, for example, BOA, ŞD 757/31, doc. 5, 3 Mart 1305 (15 March 1889).

83 Yarman, *Palu Harput 1878*, p. 385. In his memoirs, Tahsin Uzer, a senior Ottoman official, recounted that by the early twentieth century, many villagers in the Rumelian provinces also had to sell their animals at low prices to fulfill their tax obligations. See Uzer, *Makedonya Eşkiyalık Tarihi*, p. 33.

84 BOA, ŞD 744/4, doc. 35, 3 Teşrinievvel 1303 (15 October 1887).

85 BOA, BEO 388/29083, doc. 2, 18 Nisan 1310 (30 April 1894); BOA DH.MKT 724/1, docs. 3 and 4, 19 Mayıs 1319 (1 June 1903) and 2 Haziran 1319 (15 June 1903); BOA, ŞD 3000/11, doc. 2; Akın, *When the War Came Home*, p. 131; Kara, "Nurettin Topçu'nun Hayatı," p. 13. By the late nineteenth century, Mahmutpaşa and the nearby neighborhood of Tahtakale had become important centers for sheep merchants from both Anatolia and Rumelia. For a newspaper account of the death of an Albanian merchant named Celil in his room at an inn in Tahtakale, see *Sabah*, 9 Şubat 1305 (21 February 1890).

86 BOA, İ.TAL 228/51, docs. 1, 3, and 6, 11 Eylül 1316 (24 September 1900) and 20 Cemazeyilahir 1318 (15 October 1900).

Chapter 4: Hüdavendigar: A 'Model' Province on the Passageways

1 "Report by Mr. Sandison, British Consul at Brussa, on the Trade of that District for the year 1857," in *Abstract of Reports on the Trades of Various Countries and Places for the Years 1857–58–59*, pp. 464–467; *1316 Hüdavendigar Vilayet Salnamesi*, pp. 275 and 336, Mağmuni, *Bir Osmanlı Doktorunun Anıları*, p.106.

2 Çizakça, "Price History and the Bursa Silk Industry," pp. 533–550; Quataert, "The Silk Industry of Bursa," pp. 98 and 115; Quataert, *Ottoman Manufacturing*, p. 131; Diplomatic and Consular Reports, *Report on the Vilayet of Broussa*, p. 18.

3 Quataert, "Machine Breaking and the Changing Carpet Industry," p. 474.

4 The borders of Hüdavendigar province underwent several alterations in the 1870s and 1880s. While, for instance, Kocaeli was one of the *sancaks* of the province in 1870, it was separated in 1872. About fifteen years later, the *sancak* of Ertuğrul, including the districts of Bilecik and İnegöl, was formed as part of Abdülhamid II's policy to stress the important role of this area in the history of the Ottoman Empire. See *1287 Hüdavendigar Vilayet Salnamesi*, p. 71; *1289 Hüdavendigar Vilayet Salnamesi*; *1306 Hüdavendigar Vilayet Salnamesi*, p. 114.

5 Tabak, *The Waning of the Mediterranean*.

6 Küçükceran, "Agriculture and Agricultural Knowledge in Bursa and Mihaliç," p. 3.

7 Ibid., pp. 97-103.

8 *1290 Hüdavendigar Vilayet Salnamesi*, p. 123.

9 "Turkey: Report by Mr. Barron on the Taxation of Turkey," in *Reports by Her Majesty's Secretaries of Embassy and Legation on the Manufactures, Commerce, & c. of the Countries in which They Reside*, p. 228; BOA, İ.MMS 65/3070, doc. 3; *1293 Hüdavendigar Vilayet Salnamesi*, p. 143.

10 *1324 Hüdavendigar Vilayet Salnamesi*, p. 229.

11 Köylü, *Türkiye'de Büyük Arazi Mülkleri*, p. 39; *Koyun Yetiştirmek ve Bakmak Usulü*, pp. 4–5.

12 *The Levant Herald*, 15 November 1870.

13 The provincial yearbook for 1906–07 reported that in 1905, Kirmasti had 21,756 goats and 28,605 sheep, Mihaliç had 10,827 goats and 47,426 sheep, and Atranos had 59,548 goats and 28,036 sheep. Additionally, the same source indicated substantial populations of cattle (buffalo, oxen, and cow) in these districts: 23,163 in Kirmasti, 19,762 in Atranos, and 15,104 in Mihaliç. British consular reports from the mid-nineteenth century also mentioned the presence of cattle populations in the province. For instance, in 1861, Consul Sandison noted that buffaloes in Bursa were "full sized and vigorous for draught." See *1324 Hüdavendigar Vilayet Salnamesi*, pp. 228–229; "Report of Mr. Consul Sandison on the Trade of Brussa for the year 1861," in *Commercial Reports Received at the Foreign Office from Her Majesty's Consuls Between January 1st and June 30th, 1862*, p. 353.

14 Bayar, "Afyonkarahisar İline İskan Olmuş Aşiretler," pp. 180–197 and 210–214; *1316 Hüdavendigar Vilayet Salnamesi*, pp. 367 and 384; *1324 Hüdavendigar Vilayet Salnamesi*, pp. 221–224 and 476.

15 *1290 Hüdavendigar Vilayet Salnamesi*, p. 125. The same year the *sancak* of Bursa paid slightly over 2 million piasters as sheep tax. See Ibid., p. 123.

16 *1293 Hüdavendigar Vilayet Salnamesi*, pp. 144–145.

17 The same year, the *sancak* of Bursa was reported to have 140,933 sheep. *1324 Hüdavendigar Vilayet Salnamesi*, p. 229.

18 BOA, MVL 480/79, doc. 2, 13 Rabiulahir 1282 (5 September 1865); BOA, ŞD 678/43, doc. 4, 2 Safer 1290 (1 April 1873). In the early nineteenth century, animals from Kütahya and Karahisar were also used to supply army units. See, for example, BOA, C.AS 391/16154, 23 Muharrem 1223 (21 March 1808).

19 BOA, MVL 31/42, docs. 1 and 2, 16 and 27 Recep 1265 (7 and 18 June 1849).

20 Günaydın and Kaplanoğlu, *Seyahatnamelerde Bursa*, p. 155; Demiryürek, "II. Meşrutiyet'ten Cumhuriyet'e Bursa'nın Demografik Yapısı," pp. 191–195; Tan, "Osmanlı Devleti'nde Halk Sağlığı" p. 1370.

21 BOA, A.MKT.UM 804/3, doc. 3, 8 Rabiulahir 1281 (10 September 1864).

22 BOA, İ.RSM 25/23, doc. 1, 3 Temmuz 1322 (16 July 1906).

23 Sheep and goats collected from Mihaliç and its environs were also used to supply the army units in the Aegean coastline. In 1807, for instance, Mihaliç, Atranos, Kite, and Kirmasti were required to send 436 sheep and goats to naval forces in the Dardanelles and the Aegean Islands (Bahr-ı Sefid). BOA, C.DH 33/1641, 18 Rabiulevvel 1222 (26 May 1807).

24 BOA, C.BLD 94/4694, 29 Şaban 1240 (18 April 1825).

25 BOA, A.MKT.MHM 84/6, 10 Cemazeyilahir 1272 (17 February 1856).

26 "Report of Mr. Consul Sandison on the Trade of Brussa for the year 1861," in *Commercial Reports Received at the Foreign Office from Her Majesty's Consuls Between January 1st and June 30th, 1862*, p 347; "Report by Mr. Consul Sandison on the Trade and Agriculture of Brussa, for the Year 1863," in *Commercial Reports Received at the Foreign Office from Her Majesty's Consuls Between July 1st 1863, and June 30th 1864*, p. 428; "Report by Mr. Consul Sandison on the Trade of Brussa, for the Year 1864," in *Commercial Reports Received at the Foreign Office from Her Majesty's Consuls During the Year 1865*, p. 785.

27 *1307 Sene-i Maliyesine Mahsus Hüdavendigar Vilayet Salnamesi*, p. 143; *1310 Hüdavendigar Vilayet Salnamesi*, p. 435; Mağmuni, *Bir Osmanlı Doktorunun Anıları*, p. 106.

28 Aktepe, "Mehmed Salahi Bey ve Mecmuasından Bazı Kısımlar," pp. 34–35.

29 Küçükalioğlu, "İdare-i Mahsusa," p. 58; Mağmuni, *Bir Osmanlı Doktorunun Anıları*, p. 106. In the mid-1890s, the freight rate charged by the İdare-i Mahsusa on sheep was four piasters per head. See BOA, ML.EEM 232/61, doc. 10, 19 Mart 1312 (31 March 1896).

30 Çağman, "Osmanlı Döneminde İstanbul'da Modern Bir Mezbaha," p. 53.

31 Mağmuni, *Bir Osmanlı Doktorunun Anıları*, p. 106.

32 *The Levant Herald*, 21 March 1872.

33 *The Levant Herald*, 22 March 1872.

34 *Sabah*, 17 Mayıs 1306 (29 May 1890).

35 BOA, DH.MKT 1918/8, 3 Recep 1309 (2 February 1892); BOA, DH.MKT 917/17, doc. 3, 1 Teşrinisani 1320 (14 November 1904).

36 Küçükceran, "Agriculture and Agricultural Knowledge in Bursa and Mihaliç," p. 100; Yalazı, "Karacabey'in Eski-Eskimeyen Yüzleri," p. 27.

37 Yalazı, "Karacabey Çiftlikleri"; Terzibaşoğlu, "Eleni Hatun'un Zeytin Bahçeleri," pp. 124–125.

38 Terzibaşoğlu, "A Very Important Requirement of Social Life," p. 37.

39 Şerif, *Anadolu'da Tanin*, p. 5; Terzibaşoğlu, "Eleni Hatun'un Zeytin Bahçeleri," p. 125. Together with a number of other Albanian entrepreneurs, Galip seemed to maintain his powerful position over the following years. In the late 1910s, he was still a large land and sheep holder with a considerable say in local politics. See Gingeras, *Sorrowful Shores*, pp. 88–91.

40 Demirel, "XIX. Yüzyılda Bursa'da Göçmen İskanı," p. 38; İpek, *Rumeli'den Anadolu'ya Türk Göçleri*, p. 186.

41 *1310 Hüdavendigar Vilayet Salnamesi*, p. 309.

42 *1301 Hüdavendigar Vilayet Salnamesi*, p. 255; İpek, *Rumeli'den Anadolu'ya Türk Göçleri*, pp. 187–189.

43 Arıkan, "A History of a Western Anatolian Region," pp. 331 and 335; Dölek Sever, "Geç Dönem Osmanlı İmparatorluğu'nda," p.160.

44 BOA, DH.MKT 189/37, 14 Kanunuevvel 1309 (26 December 1893).

45 BOA, DH.MKT 197/64, 6 Kanunusani 1308 (18 January 1894).

46 BOA, BEO 705/52806, 6 Teşrinisani 1311 (18 November 1895).

47 During the Tanzimat period, some of the tax reforms were first tested in the *sancaks* of Gelibolu and Kocaeli, and then in the provinces of Edirne and Hüdavendigar before their empire-wide application. See Demirkol, "Tanzimat Fermanı Bağlamında," pp. 167–182.

48 Deringil, *The Well-Protected Domains*, p. 31.

49 Ibid., pp. 31–32.

50 Uslu, "Ahmed Vefik Paşa ve Bursa'nın Modernleşmesi," pp. 80–82.

51 Arikan, "A History of a Western Anatolian Region," pp. 145–152.

52 BOA, A.MKT.MHM 236/1, 18 Rabiulevvel 1278 (23 September 1861).

53 According to one source, by the early 1890s, 19,161 immigrants had settled in Kirmasti and 16,128 in Mihaliç. Another source reported the number for Kirmasti as around 15,500. See İpek, *Rumeli'den Anadolu'ya Türk Göçleri*, p. 186; Demirel, "XIX. Yüzyılda Bursa'da Göçmen İskanı," pp. 45–46.

54 BOA, ŞD 1540/9, doc. 2, 15 Teşrinievvel 1296 (27 October 1880).

55 Küçükceran, "Agriculture and Agricultural Knowledge in Bursa and Mihaliç," pp. 75–76; Akpınar, "Reclaiming the Empire," pp. 98–99.

56 For instance, in 1892, 300 immigrant families drained marshland near the Manyas Lake, reclaiming 2,179 *dönüm*s of land. See Terzibaşoğlu, "Landlords, Refugees, and Nomads," p. 71.

57 Köylü, *Türkiye'de Büyük Arazi Mülkleri*, p. 55.

58 In 1889, for instance, local officials reported to the Ministry of Interior that malaria, caused by puddles and standing water left after flooding, was widespread in Kirmasti. See BOA, DH.MKT 1647/5, 14 Zilhicce 1306 (11 August 1889).

59 Şerif, *Anadolu'da Tanin*, p. 112; Mağmuni, *Bir Osmanlı Doktorunun Anıları*, p. 98; Mikhail, *The Animal in Ottoman Egypt*, pp. 151–153.

60 BOA, ŞD 573/13, docs. 13 and 18, 19 Temmuz 1298 (31 July 1882) and 15 Şaban 1300 (21 June 1883); Erk, "Tarihte Önemli Sığır Vebası Salgınları," p. 230.

61 BOA, DH.MKT 1702/84, 4 Recep 1307 (24 February 1890); *Sabah*, 17 Temmuz 1307 (29 July 1891), 19 Eylül 1307 (1 October 1891), 25 Eylül 1307 (7 October 1891), and 26 Teşrinievvel 1307 (7 November 1891).

62 These diseases were reported to be common in Ottoman lands by the Ministry of Interior. See *Sabah*, 18 Teşrinisani 1307 (30 November 1891).

63 In the late 1890s, checkpoints were also set up in Hüdavendigar and Edirne provinces. See Şerif, *Anadolu'da Tanin*, p. 116.

64 BOA, DH.MKT 1875/56, 25 Eylül 1307 (7 October 1891); BOA, MV 79/84, 30 Mart 1310 (11 April 1894); BOA, İ.TNF 1/27, 16 Cemazeyilahir 1310 (5 January 1893); Bekman, *Veteriner Tarihi*, pp. 173–174.

65 Samuel Dolbee shows that, building on Ottoman precedents, the post-Ottoman states sought to control cattle plague through quarantine and other place-related measures, which contributed to the consolidation of the newly formed borders in the Middle East in the 1920s. See Dolbee, "Borders, Disease, and Territoriality," pp. 210-217.

66 For the full text of the regulation, see *Bursa*, 5 Recep 1310 (23 January 1893).

67 Şerif, *Anadolu'da Tanin*, pp. 114–115.

68 Diplomatic and Consular Reports, *Report for the Year 1907 on the Trade and Commerce of the Consular District of Smyrna*, p. 4. Cattle plague continued to affect these provinces well into 1910. The decline observed in sheep tax revenues in the early 1900s, as illustrated in Figure 4.1, was at least partly due to this outbreak. See Erk, "Tarihte Önemli Sığır Vebası Salgınları," p. 233.

69 Ayalon, *Natural Disasters in the Ottoman Empire*, p. 203; Yıldırım, "Bakteriyolojihane-i Şahane'de Veteriner Bakteriyolojisi," pp. 175-178; Yılmaz, "Bakterilere Yakından Bakmak," pp. 57–58; Sami and Hüsnü, *İzmir 1905*, p. 187. In 1914, to meet the growing demand for cattle plague serums, another bacteriology institute was established in Istanbul. See Erk, "Tarihte Önemli Sığır Vebası Salgınları," p. 233.

70 Efforts to develop effective medical treatment for cattle plague began long before the foundation of the Imperial Bacteriology Laboratory. To give but one example, in 1840, the government commissioned two Italian doctors to investigate the disease in Anatolia and report their findings. See BOA, C.SH 10/484, 29 Zilhicce 1255 (4 March 1840).

71 *The Levant Herald and Eastern Express*, 27 January 1906 and 26 May 1906.

72 BOA, İ.HUS 147/37, 24 Teşrinievvel 1322 (6 November 1906).

73 BOA, Y.MTV 203/128, 7 Haziran 1316 (20 June 1900); Yıldırım, "Bakteriyolojihane-i Şahane'de Veteriner Bakteriyolojisi," p. 181.

74 Aşkın, "The Environment, Institutions, and Economy," p. 21.

75 In the sixteenth century, there were twenty-three villages in Mihaliç, which were maintained as crown lands. The villagers specialized in cattle and sheep raising. See Barkan, *Türkiye'de Toprak Meselesi*, pp. 631–633.

76 Özbek, *Osmanlı İmparatorluğu'nda Sosyal Devlet*, p. 128; Odabaşı, "Mihaliç Çiftlikat-ı Hümayunu," pp. 63–64.

77 These farms were namely Orta Çiftlik, Çörekli, Göni, Karaağaç, Büyük Gerdeme, Küçük Gerdeme, Melde, Kayseri, Canbaz, Akçasığırlık, and Kepsud. See Odabaşı, "Mihaliç Çiftlikat-ı Hümayunu," p. 81.

78 Ibid., pp. 99 and 111; Köylü, *Türkiye'de Büyük Arazi Mülkleri*, p. 39; Aşkın, "The Environment, Institutions, and Economy," p. 70.

79 Demirtürk, Cellatoğulları, and Arıcı, "Türkiye'de Merinos Koyunu Yetiştiriciliği," pp. 1–21. In 1847, the price of merino sheep brought from abroad was around 2,500 piasters, almost twenty-five times more than the price of a local variety. See Odabaşı, "Mihaliç Çiftlikat-ı Hümayunu," pp. 160–161.

80 Odabaşı, "Mihaliç Çiftlikat-ı Hümayunu," pp. 81–83, 213, and 239.

81 Ibid., pp. 212–213 and 230–233.

82 Bell, *Trends in the Sheep Industry of the United States*; Odabaşı, "Mihaliç Çiftlikat-ı Hümayunu," pp. 212, 231, and 239.

83 Odabaşı, "Mihaliç Çiftlikat-ı Hümayunu," pp. 135–136; Aşkın, "The Environment, Institutions, and Economy," p. 36. Although the sources we consulted often refer to these shepherds as Bulgarians, it seems that there was a considerable number of Albanians among them. See, for example, BOA, ML.EEM 67/9, doc. 4, 4 Haziran 1297 (16 June 1881).

84 Odabaşı notes that to limit labor's mobility, the Mihaliç Imperial Farms increased the shepherds' wages by 60 percent in the early 1850s. Odabaşı, "Mihaliç Çiftlikat-ı Hümayunu," p. 136.

85 Ibid, pp. 181–184; Köylü, *Türkiye'de Büyük Arazi Mülkleri*, pp. 40–42.

86 "Lieutenant-Colonel Wilson to Sir A. H. Layard," in *Turkey no. 23: Further Correspondence Respecting the Conditions of the Populations in Asia Minor and Syria*, p. 148.

87 According to some Ottoman officials, another factor behind the decline in merino population was the poor state of animal husbandry. In a report submitted to Sultan Abdülhamid II in the early 1890s, a veterinary official noted that sheep, unable to derive sufficient nutrients from pastures, were not provided with supplemental food. Furthermore, the existing pens were insufficient to accommodate them, and veterinary services were generally poor. See Odabaşı, "Mihaliç Çiftlikat-ı Hümayunu," p. 219.

88 Ünver, "Courtgi (Gürcü) Bahr-i Sefid (L'egee) Vapur Kumpanyası," pp. 175–210; Quataert, *Miners and the State in the Ottoman Empire*, pp. 29–30.

89 BOA, Y.PRK.HH 6/51, doc. 1, 22 Şaban 1297 (30 July 1880); Odabaşı, "Mihaliç Çiftlikat-ı Hümayunu," pp. 147–150. That was not the first collaboration between Giurgiu Pano and the Zarifi family. In the contracting business, he often worked in partnership with George Zarifi. Likewise, when he rented the management of the Haliç Company, which operated ships in the Golden Horn, in 1880, he named Leonida Zarifi, George's son, as his guarantor. See Ünver, "Courtgi (Gürcü) Bahr-i Sefid (L'egee) Vapur Kumpanyası," pp. 179–181.

90 Zarifi became Abdülhamid II's banker before he took the throne in 1876. Their relationship continued, with occasional conflicts, until the death of Zarifi in 1884. See Zarifi, *Hatıralarım*, p. 75; Akan, "Osmanlı Rum Bankeri Yorgo Zarifi," pp. 43–51; Hulkiender, *Bir Galata Bankerinin Portresi*, pp. 1–148.

91 Odabaşı, "Mihaliç Çiftlikat-ı Hümayunu," p. 146; Terzi, "Hazine-i Hassa," pp. 137–141.

92 Findley, *Turkey, Islam, Nationalism*, pp. 83–84; Terzi, *Sarayda İktidar Mücadelesi*, pp. 174–206.

93 The parties initially negotiated a twelve-year contract and agreed that payments of rent would be made directly to the sultan. Then the contract term was set to three years. See BOA, Y.MTV 4/19, doc. 1, 20 Recep 1297 (28 June 1880); BOA, Y.PRK.HH 6/51, docs. 1–2, 22 Şaban 1297 (30 July 1880).

94 Odabaşı, "Mihaliç Çiftlikat-ı Hümayunu," pp. 230–231. *Koyun Yetiştirmek ve Bakmak Usulü*, pp. 5–7. A 1924 report by a veterinary official suggests that some animals identified as local breed in the documents Odabaşı consulted might be merino crossbreeds. See Köylü, *Türkiye'de Büyük Arazi Mülkleri*, p. 36.

95 BOA, ML.EEM 85/27, docs. 2 and 4, 2 Nisan 1302 (14 April 1886) and 20 Mart 1302 (1 April 1886); BOA, ML.EEM 85/54, doc. 3, 6 Mayıs 1302 (18 May 1886); BOA, ML.EEM 85/56, doc. 1, 5 Mayıs 1302 (17 May 1886); BOA, ML.EEM 85/57, doc. 3, 6 Mayıs 1302 (18 May 1886); BOA, ML.EEM 85/86, doc. 3, 7 Mayıs 1302 (19 May 1886); BOA, ML.EEM 85/87, doc. 3, 29 Nisan 1302 (11 May 1886); BOA, ML.EEM 85/88, doc. 3, 3 Mayıs 1302 (15 May 1886).

96 BOA, ML.EEM 100/35, docs. 2–8, 8 Mart 1304 (20 March 1888), 13 Mart 1304 (25 March 1888), 31 Mart 1304 (12 April 1888), 9 Nisan 1304 (21 April 1888); BOA, ML.EEM 232/61, docs.3–13, 12 Kanunusani 1311 (24 January 1896), 22 Kanunusani 1311 (3 February 1896), 6 Şubat 1311 (18 February 1896), 14 Şubat 1311 (26 February 1896), 20 Şubat 1311 (3 March 1896), 27 Şubat 1311 (10 March 1896), 12 Mart 1312 (24 March 1896), 19 Mart 1312 (31 March 1896), 27 Mart 1312 (8 April 1896), 16 Nisan 1312 (28 April 1896); BOA, ML.EEM 580/32, docs.1–4, 2 Kanunuevvel 1322 (15 December 1906), 27 Kanunuevvel 1322

(9 January 1907), 28 Kanunuevvel 1322 (10 January 1907), 30 Kanunuevvel 1322 (12 January 1907); BOA, ML.EEM 592/28, doc. 41, 14 Şubat 1322 (27 February 1907).

97 BOA, ŞD 767/16, doc. 1, 27 Kanunusani 1304 (8 February 1889); BOA, ML.EEM 113/10, docs.1–3, 1 Şubat 1304 (13 February 1889) and 14 Şubat 1304 (26 February 1889).

98 BOA, ML.EEM 62/48, doc. 2, 24 Teşrinisani 1297 (6 December 1881). For some purchases undertaken by Hrisovergis over the following years, see BOA, ML.EEM 100/35, doc. 1, 12 Nisan 1304 (24 April 1888).

99 BOA, ML.EEM 85/27, doc. 5, 6 Nisan 1302 (18 April 1886); BOA, ML.EEM 85/57, doc. 2, 5 Mayıs 1302 (17 May 1886); BOA, ML.EEM 85/86, doc. 2, 17 Mayıs 1302 (29 May 1886).

100 BOA, ML.EEM 85/54, doc.1, 27 Nisan 1302 (9 May 1886); BOA, ML.EEM 85/87, doc. 3, 22 Mayıs 1302 (3 June 1886); BOA, ML.EEM 85/88, doc. 2, 20 Mayıs 1302 (1 June 1886). The Mihaliç farms generated revenues from the sale of other breeds of animals. In 1889, for instance, they sold 13,369 piasters worth of horses, mules, and donkeys. The same year sheep sales generated about 415,000 piasters. See Odabaşı, "Mihaliç Çiflikat-ı Hümayunu," p. 144.

101 In 1924, the Ministry of Agriculture of Turkey took control of the Mihaliç Imperial Farms and renamed it the Karacabey Stud Farm (*Karacabey Harası*). In the mid-1930s, a few years before the Bursa factory started operating with 7,000 spinning machines, a special farm was established within this enterprise to raise merino sheep. See Odabaşı, "Mihaliç Çiftlikat-ı Hümayunu," p. 4; Köylü, *Türkiye'de Büyük Arazi Mülkleri*, p. 90; Tezel, *Cumhuriyet Döneminin İktisadi Tarihi*, pp. 298 and 303.

Chapter 5: Eastern Mediterranean Ports and Livestock Trade

1 Özkan, "19. Yüzyılda Osmanlı Devleti'nin İdari Taksimatı," p. 175.

2 BOA, A.MKT.MHM 761/59, 23 Rabiulevvel 1278 (28 September 1861). While the exact taxation rate in Aydın province for 1861 remains unknown, as discussed in Chapter 3, by the end of 1858, the tax stood at 1.5 piasters per head throughout Anatolia, and this rate remained consistent in Adana in 1860. See BOA, İ.MMS 14/576, 24 Cemazeyilevvel 1275 (30 Aralık 1858); BOA, İ.ŞD 16/687, 13 Rabiulevvel 1286 (23 June 1869).

3 BOA, İ.MMS 65/3070, doc. 3; *1301 Aydın Vilayet Salnamesi*, p. 261. Likewise, the provincial yearbook for the year of 1884-85 gave the population of sheep and goats as 2,887,000. See *1302 Aydın Vilayet Salnamesi*, p. 224.

4 Reporting on the consequences of the drought in 1889, a British consular official from Ayvalık, located on the northern border of Aydın province, wrote as follows: "Owing to the long continued drought which has prevailed the meadows are almost bare, and the consequent mortality among animals is very great. The only cattle that could be preserved were such as belonged to comparatively rich owners who had to feed their livestock on corn and hay." See Diplomatic and Consular Reports on Trade and Finance, *Report for the Year 1889 on the Trade of Smyrna*, p. 21. For a brief discussion on the consequences of the cattle plague outbreak in 1889, see BOA, DH.MKT 1657/90, 5 Eylül 1305 (17 September 1889).

5 *1314 Aydın Vilayet Salnamesi*, p. 501.

6 Diplomatic and Consular Reports, *Report on the Trade and Commerce of the Consular District of Smyrna for the Year 1906*, pp. 3–4.

7 Diplomatic and Consular Reports, *Report for the Year 1910–11 on the Trade of Smyrna*, p. 15.

8 Ticaret ve Ziraat Nezareti İstatistik İdare-i Umumiyesi Müdüriyeti, *Memalik-i Osmaniye'nin 1329 Senesine Mahsus Ziraat İstatistiği*, pp. 562–567.

9 İpek, *Rumeli'den Anadolu'ya Türk Göçleri*, p. 180.

10 BOA, ŞD 757/31, doc. 24, 27 Mart 1307 (8 April 1891); BOA, Y.A.HUS 257/154, doc. 2, 16 Mart 1308 (28 March 1892); *Koyun Yetiştirmek ve Bakmak Usulü*, p. 5; Dural, *Bize Derler Çakırca*, pp. 111–112; Trak, *İktisadi ve Ticari Türkiye*, pp. 60–61.

11 Kasaba, "İzmir," pp. 387–410.

12 Frangakis-Syrett, "Commerce in the Eastern Mediterranean," pp. 125–154; Goffman, "Izmir: From Village to Colonial Port City," p. 130; Quataert, "The Age of Reforms," p. 781.

13 Mantran, *17. Yüzyılın İkinci Yarısında İstanbul*, pp. 19–21.

14 Rıfat, *İzmir 1914*, pp. 39 and 42; Tan, "Osmanlı Devleti'nde Halk Sağlığı," p. 1370.

15 BOA, T.DMİ 1009/52, doc. 1, 28 Mart 1318 (10 April 1902).

16 Diplomatic and Consular Reports, *Report for the Year 1910–11 on the Trade of Smyrna*, p 10.

17 BOA, C.SM 97/4858, doc. 2, 11 Cemazeyilahir 1217 (9 October 1802). The decree also ordered purchases of sheep to be made in the districts of Kütahya, Karesi, Kocaeli, and Bolu, with prices ranging from forty to seventy *paras*.

18 BOA, C.AS 688/28866, 18 Şevval 1220 (9 January 1806). In early 1806, Selim III sent similar orders to his officials in Kütahya, Kocaeli, Ankara, Karesi, and Teke. It is important to note here that during this period, the districts of Aydın and Saruhan were not only responsible for the provisioning of the imperial palace and army but also for the British forces fighting alongside the Ottomans against the French occupation of Egypt. In 1800, the governor of Aydın, Hacı Hüseyin from the notable Karaosmanzade family, was ordered by the imperial capital to supply 10,000 sheep and goats and 2,000 cattle to British fleet units that would be stationed in Meğri (today's Fethiye). See BOA, C.HR 144/7168, 29 Recep 1215 (16 December 1800); BOA, AE.SSLM.III 69/4123, 23 Şevval 1215 (9 March 1801).

19 BOA, ŞD 757/31, doc. 24, 27 Mart 1307 (8 April 1891).

20 BOA, ŞD 828/26, doc. 4, 20 Ağustos 1321 (2 September 1905).

21 BOA, Y.PRK.UM 81/13, 15 Mart 1324 (28 March 1908); BOA, Y.PRK.UM 81/21, 21 Mart 1324 (3 April 1908).

22 Mikhail, *The Animal in Ottoman Egypt*, pp. 151–153.

23 BOA, İ.MTZ (05) 11/273, doc. 3, 7 Şevval 1258 (11 November 1842); BOA, İ.MTZ (05) 11/276, doc. 4, 7 Zilhicce 1258 (9 January1843).

24 Delmar, "On the Resources, Productions, and Social Conditions of Egypt," p. 244.

25 BOA, A.MKT.UM 804/3, doc. 1, 31 Ağustos 1280 (12 September 1864).

26 BOA, A.MKT.UM 804/3, doc. 3, 8 Rabiulahir 1281 (10 September 1864); BOA, A.MKT.UM 808/41, 4 Cemazeyilevvel 1281 (5 October 1864).

27 Bidwell, *The Cost of Living Abroad*, p. 117; BOA, İ.ŞE 22/1, doc. 2, 17 Mayıs 1323 (30 May 1907).

28 Diplomatic and Consular Reports, *Report for the Year 1904 on the Trade and Commerce of the Vilayets of Aleppo and Adana*, p. 4.

29 BOA, ŞD 1426/2, doc. 4, 6 Nisan 1322 (19 April 1906). Moreover, in the period between mid-March 1905 and mid-January 1906, about 8,500 cattle were exported from the ports of Meğri and Bodrum. See Ibid.

30 BOA, İ.RSM 20/51, doc. 9, 20 Teşrinievvel 1321 (2 November 1904).

31 Diplomatic and Consular Reports, *Report for the Year 1906 on the Trade and Commerce of the Consular District of Smyrna*, p. 14; Diplomatic and Consular Reports, *Report for the Year 1908 on the Trade and Commerce of the Consular District of Smyrna*, p. 18; Diplomatic and Consular Reports, *Report for the Year 1911–12 on the Trade of Smyrna*, p. 23; *The Levant Herald and Eastern Express*, 6 and 13 October 1906; BOA, İ.ŞE 22/1, doc. 2, 17 Mayıs 1323 (30 May 1907).

32 BOA, HR.TH 335/90, 12 Haziran 1322 (25 June 1906).

33 Diplomatic and Consular Reports, *Report for the Year 1908 on the Trade and Commerce of the Consular District of Smyrna*, p. 17. A British consular report for 1907 suggests that the decline was less dramatic because merchants were able to "find some means or other for getting full cargoes

shipped off, principally to Egypt." See Diplomatic and Consular Reports, *Report for the Year 1907 on the Trade and Commerce of the Consular District of Smyrna*, p. 4.

34 According to the telegram, over the last three months, about 6,000 sheep and goats and 1,600 cattle were exported from İzmir to Alexandria. See BOA, ŞD 1426/2, docs. 1 and 4, 10 Teşrinievvel 1321 (23 October 1905) and 6 Nisan 1322 (19 April 1906).

35 BOA, İ.RSM 25/23, doc. 1, 3 Temmuz 1322 (16 July 1906).

36 *The Levant Herald and Eastern Express*, 6 October 1906. In late 1906, the governor of Aydın sent a telegram to the Ministry of Interior, complaining that large scale livestock shipments to Alexandria continued unhindered. See BOA, ŞD 2771/6, doc. 1, 21 Teşrinisani 1322 (4 December 1906).

37 BOA, Y.MTV 302/103, doc. 1, 13 Eylül 1323 (26 September 1907).

38 BOA, BEO 3298/247336, 10 Nisan 1324 (23 April 1908).

39 BOA, İ.ŞE 22/1, doc. 8, 27 Haziran 1323 (10 July 1907).

40 BOA, BEO 3297/247223, 20 Mart 1324 (2 April 1908)

41 While fixed prices on meat were imposed occasionally in Ankara at least until the late 1870s, it was abolished in Bursa in 1881. See "Report on the Population, Industries, Trade, Commerce, Agriculture, Public Works, Land Tenure, and Government of City and Province of Angora, Anatolia, by Vice-Consul Gatheral," in *Turkey no. 23: Further Correspondence Respecting the Conditions of the Populations in Asia Minor and Syria*, p. 127; BOA, BEO 54/3987, doc. 4, 6 Mayıs 1308 (18 May 1892).

42 See BOA, A.MKT.UM 237/11, 11 Ramazan 1272 (16 May 1856).

43 BOA, ŞD 1380/64, 12 Nisan 1300 (24 April 1884).

44 Revenues from the *gabela* fee, levied by the Communal Council on kosher goods such as meat, wine, and cheese, were used to cover the community's expenses, including the payment of rabbinic salaries and the maintenance of schools and synagogues. Disputes over this tax within the Jewish community of İzmir often coincided with climate disruptions and disease outbreaks in Aydın province or other major cattle and sheep suppliers of the city. For instance, the disputes in 1846 and 1888 were preceded by droughts that severely affected central Anatolia, while the one in 1879 occurred concurrently with harsh winters and cattle plague outbreaks across many parts of Anatolia. For a detailed discussion of these and other disputes over *gabela* in the nineteenth and early twentieth centuries, see Danon, *The Jews of Ottoman Izmir*, pp. 123–150.

45 BOA, BEO 88/6572, docs. 2 and 3, 1 Teşrinievvel 1308 (13 October 1892) and 14 Teşrinisani 1308 (26 November 1892).

46 Rıfat, *İzmir 1914*, pp. 55–56.

47 Bergama's pasture lands were not extensive, covering about 60,000 *dönüms* (15,000 acres) in the 1890s. Despite this, the district was an important livestock-raising center. According to a British consular report for 1909, Bergama and Dikili together had some 100,000 sheep, 60,000 goats, 20,000 oxen and buffaloes, and 10,000 horses and donkeys. See *1314 Aydın Vilayet Salnamesi*, p. 213; Diplomatic and Consular Reports, *Report for the Year 1909 on the Trade of Smyrna*, p. 77.

48 BOA, ŞD 1392/42, docs. 5 and 6, 25 Kanunuevvel 1310 (6 January 1895) and 29 Kanunusani 1310 (10 February 1895).

49 Terzibaşoğlu, "A Very Important Requirement of Social Life," pp. 38–42.

50 Diplomatic and Consular Reports, *Report for the Year 1911–12 on the Trade of Smyrna*, pp. 26–27.

51 İnal, "Fruits of Empire," p. 91. A study conducted by the Ministry of Agriculture in the early 1970s similarly identified the conversion of pastures to croplands as a longstanding problem for animal husbandry in the Little Meander basin. See *Küçük Menderes Havzası Toprakları*, p. 25.

52 Diplomatic and Consular Reports, *Report for the Year 1906 on the Trade and Commerce of the Vilayet of Aleppo*, p. 7.

53 Ibid., p. 7, Gratien, *The Unsettled Plain*, p. 66.

54 Ford, *Wool and Manufactures of Wool*, p. 648. Likewise, according to the report of Consul Longworth, there were 1,433,000 sheep, 1,002,000 goats, and 275,000 oxen in the province in 1906. See Diplomatic and Consular Reports, *Report for the Year 1906 on the Trade and Commerce of the Vilayet of Aleppo*, p. 11.

55 Diplomatic and Consular Reports, *Report for the Year 1899 on the Trade of the Consular District of Erzeroum*, pp. 7–8.

56 Diplomatic and Consular Reports, *Report for the Year 1907 on the Trade and Commerce of the Vilayets of Aleppo and Adana*, p. 12.

57 The available evidence suggests that livestock exports from İskenderun remained limited in the earlier periods of the nineteenth century. In 1837, a British consular official reported that the strict protectionist policies of Egyptian authorities, who were then governing the region, prevented the abundant local supplies of sheep and cattle from being subject to "private speculation." Moving forward to 1864, when the Ottoman government authorized the export of 20,000 sheep from İzmir to Egypt, it allowed only 5,500 animals to be shipped from Aleppo province, with İskenderun likely serving as the transit port. See "Mr Hay's Report for the Year 1837," in *Report on the Commercial Statistics of Syria by John Bowring*, p. 70; BOA, A.MKT.UM 804/3, doc. 6.

58 "Report by Vice-Consul Jago on the Trade, Commerce, and Agriculture of the Vilayet of Syria, and on the Trade and Commerce of Beyrout, Lattakia, Tripoli, and Sidon, during the Year 1871," in *Reports from Her Majesty's Consuls on the Manufactures, Commerce, &c., of Their Consular Districts*, p. 850.

59 "Report by Consul Skene on the Trade, Navigation, Agriculture, Manufactures, Public Works, and Revenues of the Provinces of Aleppo, Adana, and the Desert in the Year 1875," in Commercial No. 9 (1876) (Trade Reports), *Reports from Her Majesty's Consuls on the Manufactures, Commerce, &c., of Their Consular Districts, Part IV*, p. 980.

60 BOA, ŞD 2215/68, doc. 4, 16 Temmuz 1295 (28 July 1879). Some in government circles opposed the ban on the grounds that there were large numbers of livestock in the district of Maraş. See Ibid.

61 BOA. İ.DH 1318/2, doc. 1, 5 Teşrinievvel 1310 (18 October 1894). The growth in the volume of exports was also highlighted by foreign observers. In 1887, Stephan Coidan, the US consular agent in İskenderun wrote: "The cattle trade is also progressing, and over 15,000 bullocks and about 45,000 sheep were shipped during the year [1886] for Egypt, Malta, and Greece." See "Alexandretta: Report of Consular Agent Coidan," in *The Executive Documents of the House of Representatives*, p. 1043.

62 Ibid., p. 1045; Diplomatic and Consular Reports, *Report for the Year 1903 on the Trade and Commerce of the Vilayets of Aleppo and Adana*, pp. 6 and 13.

63 BOA. İ.DH 1318/2, docs. 1 and 2, 9 Teşrinisani 1310 (21 November 1894) and 18 Teşrinisani 1310 (30 November 1894); BOA, ŞD 1920/16, doc. 9, 4 Eylül 1311 (16 September 1895).

64 Diplomatic and Consular Reports on Trade and Finance, *Report for the Year 1893 on the Trade of Damascus*, p. 3; Diplomatic and Consular Reports on Trade and Finance, *Report for the Year 1896 on the Trade of Aleppo and Adana*, p. 3; Diplomatic and Consular Reports on Trade and Finance, *Report for the Year 1895 on the Trade, &c., of Aleppo*, p. 2; Diplomatic and Consular Reports, *Report for the Year 1897 on the Trade of Aleppo and Adana*, pp. 3–4; Diplomatic and Consular Reports, *Report for the Year 1899 on the Trade of the Vilayet of Aleppo*, pp. 4–5; Diplomatic and Consular Reports, *Report for the Year 1900 on the Trade of the Vilayet of Aleppo*, p. 4.

65 Diplomatic and Consular Reports, *Report for the Year 1903 on the Trade and Commerce of the Vilayets of Aleppo and Adana*, pp. 4–5; Diplomatic and Consular Reports, *Report for the Year 1904 on the Trade and Commerce of the Vilayets of Aleppo and Adana*, p. 4.

66 Ibid., p. 4.

67 In 1905 and 1906, Austrian, Italian, French, and German merchants acquired more than 17,500 cattle from Mosul, Baghdad, and Amarah, transporting them to İskenderun for shipment to Egyptian

ports. See BOA, MV 111/85, 31 Temmuz 1321 (13 August 1905); BOA, HR.TH 35/90, 12 Haziran 1322 (25 June 1906).

68 BOA İ.RSM 20/51, doc. 12, 24 Teşrinievvel 1320 (6 November 1904); Diplomatic and Consular Reports, *Report for the Year 1905 on the Trade and Commerce of the Vilayet of Aleppo*, p. 4. The available evidence suggests that İskenderun also outstripped İzmir in both volume and value of shipments. For example, in 1904, the volume of cattle exports from İzmir was less than one-sixth of İskenderun's. In the following year the gap narrowed, but İzmir's exports still lagged by approximately 5,000 heads.

69 Diplomatic and Consular Reports, *Report for the Year 1903 on the Trade and Commerce of the Vilayets of Aleppo and Adana*, p. 6.

70 Diplomatic and Consular Reports, *Report for the Year 1905 on the Trade and Commerce of the Vilayet of Aleppo*, p. 4. The decline in the value of cattle and sheep exports was more modest, at about 14 percent, which appears to have been due to increased prices in Egypt. See Ibid., p. 21.

71 Diplomatic and Consular Reports, *Report for the Year 1909 on the Trade of the Vilayet of Aleppo*, p. 5; Der Matossian, *The Horrors of Adana*, pp. 97–125.

72 Diplomatic and Consular Reports, *Report for the Year 1911 on the Trade of the Aleppo Vilayet*, pp. 5–6.

73 Diplomatic and Consular Reports, *Report for the Year 1897 on the Trade of Aleppo and Adana*, p. 4.

74 *Sabah*, 1 Haziran 1324 (14 June 1908).

75 BOA, A.MKT.UM 575/2, 8 Teşrinievvel 1313 (20 October 1897). The settlement of the case took about four years. During this period, the Courts of First Instance and Appeal ruled against the Ministry of Health, ordering a compensation payment of 3,000 liras to Osman Eyüp Ağa. However, the ministry refused to comply with this decision, leading to complaints from the claimant. Eventually, to appease him, the Hamidian government agreed to award a payment of 2,000 liras as the sultan's gift. See Ibid; BOA, BEO 1287/96476, doc. 10, 6 Şubat 1314 (18 February 1899); BOA, İ.ML 32/56, doc. 2, 26 Haziran 1315 (8 July 1899).

76 Although Adana province had several other ports including, Silifke, Karataş, and Yumurtalık, they remained far behind Mersin. For instance, in 1887, exports from Mersin amounted to 404,712 pounds, constituting about 86 percent of the total value of the province's export revenues. Six years later, in 1893, this ratio increased to 91 percent. See Diplomatic and Consular Reports on Trade and Finance, *Report for the Year 1887 on the Trade of the Vilayet of Adana (Aleppo)*, p. 2; Diplomatic and Consular Reports on Trade and Finance, *Report for the Year 1893 on the Trade of Aleppo*, p. 10; Toksöz, *Nomads, Migrants and Cotton*, pp. 93 and 99.

77 Ibid., pp. 89, 93, and 98; Nacar, "Yüksek Bir Liman Kentinde," p. 76.

78 Diplomatic and Consular Reports on Trade and Finance, *Report for the Year 1887 on the Trade of the Vilayet of Adana (Aleppo)*, p. 1; Diplomatic and Consular Reports on Trade and Finance, *Report for the Year 1888 on the Trade of Adana*, pp. 1–2.

79 Diplomatic and Consular Reports on Trade and Finance, *Report for the Year 1891 on the Trade of Aleppo*, pp. 12 and 15; Diplomatic and Consular Reports on Trade and Finance, *Report for the Year 1892 on the Trade of the Consular District of Aleppo*, p. 11; Diplomatic and Consular Reports on Trade and Finance, *Report for the Year 1896 on the Trade of Aleppo and Adana*, p. 9.

80 Gratien, *The Unsettled Plain*, pp. 69–75; BOA, İ.MMS 65/3070, doc. 3; Ticaret ve Ziraat Nezareti İstatistik İdare-i Umumiyesi Müdüriyeti, *Memalik-i Osmaniye'nin 1329 Senesine Mahsus Ziraat İstatistiği*, pp. 562–567.

81 Diplomatic and Consular Reports, *Report for the Year 1903 on the Trade and Commerce of the Vilayets of Aleppo and Adana*, p. 16.

82 Toksöz, *Nomads, Migrants and Cotton*, p. 136. Among the important centers of livestock raising in this region were the districts of Ceyhan and Osmaniye. See *1297 Adana Vilayet Salnamesi*, p. 148.

83 Ibid., pp. 107–109; Ford, *Wool and Manufactures of Wool*, p. 649; Yalgın, *Cenupta Türkmen Oymakları*, p. 195.

84 Between 1864 and 1914, Adana's population grew from about 35,000 to 80,000. In the early 1930s, when its population was slightly below the 1914 level, the city consumed, on average, approximately 37,000 sheep and goats and 2,750 cattle annually. See Gratien, *The Unsettled Plain*, p. 109; Ata, "Nomads, Animal Breeding, and Agriculture," p. 106.

85 It appears that the trade of animals between Mersin and the Egyptian ports also experienced growth during the animal disease outbreak in 1864. At that time, a merchant named Mustafa Gani was reported to have undertaken a shipment of 8,500 sheep. See BOA, A.MKT.UM 804/3, doc. 6.

86 Diplomatic and Consular Reports, *Report for the Year 1903 on the Trade and Commerce of the Vilayets of Aleppo and Adana*, p. 16.

87 BOA, İ.RSM 20/51, docs. 6 and 7, 21 Teşrinievvel 1320 (3 November 1904) and 23 Teşrinievvel 1320 (5 November 1904); BOA, ŞD 828/26, doc. 4, 20 Ağustos 1321 (2 September 1905).

88 *Mediterranean Pilot*, p. 552.

89 Diplomatic and Consular Reports, *Report for the Year 1903 on the Trade and Commerce of the Vilayets of Aleppo and Adana*, p. 17.

90 BOA, ŞD 686/27, doc. 3, 30 Mayıs 1294 (11 June 1878). According to this document, all 4,000 animals were quickly purchased by government meat contractors.

91 BOA, ŞD 2961/36, doc. 1, 29 Kanunusani 1308 (10 February 1893).

92 *1310 Konya Vilayet Salnamesi*, p. 343; Diplomatic and Consular Reports, *Report for the Years 1897–99 on the Trade and Commerce of the Consular District of Smyrna*, p. 28; Ticaret ve Ziraat Nezareti İstatistik İdare-i Umumiyesi Müdüriyeti, *Memalik-i Osmaniye'nin 1329 Senesine Mahsus Ziraat İstatistiği*, pp. 562–567.

93 Antalya was a less active port than İskenderun and Mersin. To give one example, while 374 steamers called at İskenderun in 1907, only 125 did so in Antalya. Most of the latter plied between İzmir, Antalya, and the Aegean islands. See Diplomatic and Consular Reports, *Report for the Year 1907 on the Trade and Commerce of the Vilayets of Aleppo and Adana*, p. 19; Diplomatic and Consular Reports, *Report for the Year 1907 on the Trade and Commerce of the Consular District of Smyrna*, p. 27; *Daily Consular and Trade Reports, volume 4 nos. 229–305: October, November, and December 1913*, p. 1484.

94 Diplomatic and Consular Reports, *Report for the Year 1907 on the Trade and Commerce of the Consular District of Smyrna*, p. 28.

95 Diplomatic and Consular Reports, *Report for the Year 1910–11 on the Trade of Smyrna*, p. 35; Diplomatic and Consular Reports, *Report for the Year 1911–12 on the Trade of Smyrna*, p. 30.

96 Diplomatic and Consular Reports, *Report for the Years 1897–99 on the Trade and Commerce of the Consular District of Smyrna*, p. 29.

97 Diplomatic and Consular Reports, *Report for the Year 1905 on the Trade and Commerce of the Consular District of Smyrna*, p. 18.

98 Diplomatic and Consular Reports, *Report for the Year Ending July 1913 on the Trade of Smyrna*, p. 26.

99 Çağman, "Osmanlı Döneminde İstanbul'da Modern Bir Mezbaha," p. 51.

Chapter 6: Feeding the Imperial Capital

1 Uzun, *İstanbul'un İaşesinde*, p. 4; Grehan, *Everyday Life and Consumer Culture*, p. 68.

2 Greenwood, "Istanbul's Meat Provisioning," p. 20.

3 Uzun, *İstanbul'un İaşesinde*, pp. 92 and 164.

4 Shortly afterward, the previous meat contractor, Hacı İsmail, was also summoned to a meeting where he agreed to supply 3,500 sheep per month during the period in question. See BOA, A.MKT. MHM 96/25, 7 Muharrem 1273 (7 September 1856).

5 In the late eighteenth and early nineteenth centuries, the term butcher typically referred to persons who obtained a license from the butchers' guilds to run a slaughterhouse and/or butcher shop. The sheep and cattle driven to Istanbul were distributed in shares among these licensed butchers. This process was managed together by government officials and guild leaders. See *İstanbul Ahkam Defterleri*, pp. 51, 191, 195, and 223; Greenwood, "Istanbul's Meat Provisioning," pp. 47 and 53–54; BOA, ŞD 678/43, doc. 7, Teşrinievvel 1288 (October-November 1872), BOA, ŞD 702/18, doc. 3, 8 Kanunuevvel 1298 (20 December 1882).

6 BOA, C.BLD 41/2008, 29 Muharrem 1254 (24 April 1838); BOA, İ.DH 57/2812, doc. 1, 29 Safer 1258 (11 April 1842); BOA, İ.DH 101/5069, doc. 1, 25 Rabiulevvel 1261 (3 April 1845); BOA, İ.MVL 166/4927, doc. 2, 25 Safer 1266 (10 January 1850).

7 In 1812, butcher shops remained closed for three months because of lack of supplies. See Beyhan, "Some Records on Price Controls in Istanbul," p. 140.

8 Ibid., pp. 139–140.

9 For a detailed account of the fall of the New Order, see Yaycıoğlu, *Partners of the Empire*, pp. 173–177.

10 Beyhan, "Some Records on Price Controls in Istanbul," p. 141; BOA, İ.MVL 140/3885, doc. 2, 6 Cemazeyilahir 1265 (29 April 1849); BOA, İ.DH 251/15449, doc. 1, 9 Recep 1268 (29 April 1852); BOA, A.MKT.NZD 133/96, 30 Cemazeyilevvel 1271 (18 February 1855).

11 *İstanbul Ahkam Defterleri*, pp. 51, 191–192, and 223–224; BOA, MVL 237/40, doc. 1, 7 Cemazeyilahir 1267 (9 April 1851); BOA, A.MKT.MVL 67/98, 10 Muharrem 1271 (3 October 1854); BOA, A.MKT.NZD 133/96, 30 Cemazeyilevvel 1271 (18 February 1855); BOA, A.MKT.MHM 96/25, 7 Muharrem 1273 (7 September 1856).

12 For instance, taxes imposed on internal land trade began to be reduced from the 1840s onward and were finally eliminated in the early 1870s. Pamuk, *Uneven Centuries*, p. 100.

13 Ibid., p. 104; Robarts, "Russo-Ottoman Wars," pp. 494–499; Çelik, "Scarcity and Misery," pp. 132 and 138; The Veterinary Department of the Privy Council Office, *Report on the Cattle Plague in Great Britain, During the Years 1865, 1866, and 1867*, p. 241; Uzun, *İstanbul'un İaşesinde*, p. 163.

14 White, *Three Years in Constantinople*, p. 107; Kırlı, *Sultan ve Kamuoyu*, p. 117.

15 Uzun, *İstanbul'un İaşesinde*, p. 170; BOA, A.MKT.VL 135/21, 4 Cemazeyilevvel 1278 (7 November 1861); BOA, İ.MVL 276/10715, doc. 3, 3 Ramazan 1269 (10 June 1853); BOA, İ.MVL 328/14017, doc. 2, 4 Recep 1271 (23 March 1855)

16 BOA, İ.MMS 21/926, doc. 1, 5 Recep 1277 (17 January 1861); Hornby, *Constantinople During the Crimean War*, p. 496.

17 BOA, A.MKT.NZD 272/1, 12 Cemazeyilevvel 1275 (18 December 1858); BOA, A.MKT.NZD 276/19, 27 Cemazeyilahir 1275 (1 February 1859); BOA, MVL 843/12, 16 Recep 1277 (28 January 1861); BOA, A.MKT.NZD 407/52, 16 Ramazan 1278 (17 March 1862); BOA, İ.MMS 25/1077, doc. 1, 27 Şevval 1278 (27 April 1862); BOA, MVL 397/38, 27 Muharrem 1279 (25 July 1862); Birdal, *The Political Economy of the Ottoman Public Debt*, p. 33.

18 Saraçoğlu, "Economic Interventionism," p. 80.

19 BOA, İ.MVL 328/14017, docs. 2 and 3, 4 Recep 1271 (23 March 1855) and 10 Recep 1271 (29 March 1855); BOA, A.MKT.UM 226/9, 18 Cemazeyilahir 1272 (25 February 1856). Before this move, in 1854, the bakers' monopoly was abolished in Istanbul, and opening a bakery was liberalized. Around the same time, regulations concerning entry into the butchery market were also liberalized in New York City and Paris. See *Vak'a-Nüvis Ahmed Lütfi Efendi Tarihi, v. IX*, pp. 97–98; Stanziani, *Rules of Exchange*, p. 69; Horowitz, Pilcher, and Watts, "Meat for the Multitudes," pp. 1055–1083.

20 BOA, A.MKT.NZD 407/52, 16 Ramazan 1278 (17 March 1862); BOA, İ.MMS 25/1077, docs.1 and 2, 27 Şevval 1278 (27 April 1862) and 6 Zilkade 1278 (5 May 1862).

21 Karpat, *Studies on Ottoman Social and Political History*, pp. 283–284; Duben and Behar, *Istanbul Households*, p. 25.

22 Uzun, *İstanbul'un İaşesinde*, pp. 27-28; "Report by Vice-Consul Wrench on the Trade and Commerce of Constantinople for the Year 1873," in Commercial No. 15 (1874), *Reports from Her Majesty's Consuls on the Manufactures, Commerce, & c., of Their Consular Districts, Part III*, p. 1555; BOA, İ.ŞE 22/1, doc. 2, 17 Mayıs 1323 (30 May 1907); BOA, İ.DH 137/4, docs. 28 and 56, 28 Haziran 1327 (11 July 1911) and 27 Teşrinievvel 1329 (9 November 1913).

23 Basiretçi Ali Efendi, *İstanbul Mektupları*, pp. 386 and 400–401; *Sabah*, 23 Şubat 1323 (7 March 1908); BOA, İ.ŞE 22/1, doc. 2, 17 Mayıs 1323 (30 May 1907); Diplomatic and Consular Reports, *Report for the Year 1907 on the Trade and Commerce of the Consular District of Smyrna*, p. 4.

24 BOA, Y.EE 43/37, 25 Zilkade 1295 (20 November 1878); Birdal, *The Political Economy of the Ottoman Public Debt*, p. 44; Tahsin Paşa, *Tahsin Paşa'nın Yıldız Hatıraları*, pp. 215–216.

25 BOA, ŞD 573/13, doc. 6, 19 Rabiulevvel 1296 (13 March 1879); Basiretçi Ali Efendi, *İstanbul Mektupları*, pp. 386 and 676–678.

26 *Sabah*, 26 Kanunuevvel 1305 (7 January 1890); BOA, DH.MKT 1657/90, 5 Eylül 1305 (17 September 1889); BOA, DH.MKT 1692/21, 11 Kanunusani 1305 (23 January 1890).

27 BOA, Y.MTV 73/149, 28 Kanunuevvel 1308 (9 January 1893); BOA, BEO 164/12296, doc.1, 20 Şubat 1308 (4 March 1893); BOA, BEO 179/13353, 20 Mart 1309 (1 April 1893).

28 BOA, MVL 481/64, doc. 2, 9 Eylül 1281 (21 September 1865).

29 BOA, Y.MTV 60/107, 16 Mart 1308 (28 March 1892).

30 Toprak, *İttihad-Terakki ve Cihan Harbi*, pp. 141–142, 162–165, and 398–400; Sazak, *Emin Bey'in Defteri*, p. 108. A chief cause of wartime shortages was the imposition of additional taxes to feed the growing army. Half of the sheep brought to Istanbul by livestock merchants were taken in the form of war taxes. In 1915, the Council of Ministers decreased this rate to 15 percent. Another cause was the occupation of the sheep export centers of eastern Anatolia by Russian forces in 1916. See Akın, *When the War Came Home*, pp. 124 and 131; BOA, DH.İ.UM.EK 4/44, doc. 1, 11 Teşrinievvel 1330 (24 October 1914); BOA, DH.İ.UM.EK 5/1, doc. 1, 28 Eylül 1330 (11 October 1914).

31 BOA, ŞD 682/9, doc. 3, 8 Mayıs 1290 (21 May 1874).

32 BOA, ŞD 678/43, doc. 7, Teşrinievvel 1288 (October–November 1872).

33 *The Levant Herald and Eastern Express*, 16 June 1906; Basiretçi Ali Efendi, *İstanbul Mektupları*, p. 377.

34 BOA, ŞD 573/13, docs. 1, 23, and 27, 2 Haziran 1298 (14 June 1882) and 12 Ağustos 1299 (24 August 1883); BOA, ŞD 695/2, docs.4–5; BOA, ŞD 702/18, docs.1–3, 22 Safer 1300 (2 January 1883) and 8 Kanunuevvel 1298 (20 December 1882); BOA, Y.PRK.AZJ 6/103, docs.2–3, 11 Zilkade 1300 (13 September 1883).

35 BOA, DH.MKT 1311/114, 15 Kanunusani 1286 (27 January 1871).

36 While the financial problems worsened following the famine of 1873–75, foreign capital inflows into the empire nearly ceased after the stock exchange crisis of 1873 in Europe and the United States. These factors led first to a partial and later to a total default on loan payments. See Pamuk, *Uneven Centuries*, pp. 104–107; Birdal, *The Political Economy of the Ottoman Public Debt*, pp. 28 and 39.

37 According to a municipal report dated September 1882, during the one-year period between March 1881 and March 1882, Istanbul imported about 200,000 head of sheep from Anatolia. While those animals coming overland from central and eastern Anatolia were driven mostly to Uzunçayır, those arriving by sea from Hüdavendigar province ended up in the meadows on the European side of the city. Six years after this report, a well-informed merchant stated that the number of sheep sold annually in Uzunçayır was about 200,000. See BOA, ŞD 573/13, doc. 23, 21 Ağustos 1298 (2 September 1882); BOA, ŞD 730/6, doc. 5, 16 Kanunusani 1303 (28 January 1888).

38 BOA, ŞD 730/6, doc. 6, 28 Teşrinisani 1303 (10 December 1887); BOA, ŞD 682/9, doc. 2, 25 Mayıs 1290 (6 June 1874).

39 BOA, ŞD 730/6, doc. 9, 14 Mart 1304 (26 March 1888); BOA. ŞD 349/11, docs. 1 and 29, 12 Haziran 1305 (24 June 1889) and 31 Ağustos 1308 (12 September 1892).

40 For instance, in 1906, tax officials tallied 790 sheep and 49 goats owned by residents of the Mustafa Pasha neighbourhood in the bustling Galata port area. See BOA, ML.VRD.d 4449, 20 Mart 1324 (2 April 1908). Cemil Topuzlu, who served as the mayor of Istanbul twice in the 1910s, noted in his memoirs that when driven from the meadows to slaughterhouses in the districts of Fatih and Galata, sheep again passed through the city's busy streets. See Topuzlu, *İstibdat, Meşrutiyet, Cumhuriyet*, p. 88.

41 BOA, BEO 592/44334, doc. 10, 31 Ağustos 1311 (12 September 1895); BOA, BEO 621/46509, doc. 4, 18 Mart 1311 (30 March 1895); BOA, ŞD 744/4, doc. 32, 3 Teşrinievvel 1303 (15 October 1887); BOA, ŞD 573/5, 21 Zilhicce 1300 (23 October 1883); *The Levant Herald and Eastern Express*, 21 July 1906.

42 This was also the case for the guild of porters in Istanbul. See Kırpık, "Loncadan Cemiyete Osmanlı Hamal Teşkilatlarında Değişim," pp. 95–108.

43 After the revolution, the Unionist government passed a regulation dissolving all guilds in Istanbul and authorizing the establishment of occupational associations in their place. Accordingly, in April 1911, the association of livestock merchants was formed and remained active for more than a decade. See; BOA, BEO 3379/253413, doc. 3, 2 Ağustos 1324 (15 August 1908); Toprak, *İttihad-Terakki ve Cihan Harbi*, p. 135; Toprak, "1909 Cemiyetler Kanunu," pp. 205–208.

44 BOA, ŞD 1747/1, doc.1, 11 Mart 1317 (24 March 1901). After the revolution, Faik Bey was subjected to accusations of extortion and spying. See Haydaroğlu, "II. Abdülhamit'in Hafiye Teşkilatı Hakkında Bir Risale," pp. 109–133.

45 BOA, İ.OM 11/39, doc. 2, 21 Teşrinisani 1322 (4 December 1906); BOA, DH.MKT 2610/71, 15 Mayıs 1322 (28 May 1906); *The Levant Herald and Eastern Express*, 21 April 1906.

46 *Sabah*, 7 and 8 Temmuz 1322 (20 and 21 July 1906); *The Levant Herald and Eastern Express*, 21 July 1906.

47 BOA, ŞD 2923/30, doc. 9, 9 Teşrinisani 1303 (21 November 1887); BOA, BEO 4613/345921, doc. 4, 15 Teşrinisani 1335 (15 November 1919).

48 BOA, ŞD 2923/30, docs. 3 and 9, 9 Kanunusani 1303 (21 January 1888) and 9 Teşrinisani 1303 (21 November 1887).

49 BOA, İ.DH 1127/88046, doc. 1; BOA, ŞD 2923/30, docs. 3, 9, and 10, 9 Kanunusani 1303 (21 January 1888) and 9 Teşrinisani 1303 (21 November 1887).

50 BOA, İ.DH 1127/88046, doc. 1; BOA, ŞD 2923/30, docs. 3, 7, and 15, 9 Kanunusanı 1303 (21 January 1888), 17 Nisan 1303 (29 April 1887), and 3 Teşrinievvel 1304 (15 October 1888).

51 For example, a commission appointed by the government in 1906 to discuss measures to curb the recent upswing in meat prices reported that wholesalers counted the lira at 110–112 piasters while making purchases from sheep merchants. BOA, İ.ŞE 22/1, doc.6, 10 Şubat 1322 (23 February 1907).

52 BOA, İ.MMS 103/4394, docs. 1 and 2, 15 and 16 Mart 1305 (27 and 28 March 1889).

53 According to a municipal report dated July 1896, difficulties in collecting their debts sparked discontent among sheep merchants. See BOA, BEO 844/63271, doc. 2, 20 Haziran 1312 (2 July 1896).

54 BOA, ŞD 2556/24, doc. 10, 25 Eylül 1305 (7 October 1889).

55 BOA, ŞD 757/31, docs. 5 and 30, 3 Mart 1305 (17 March 1889) and 4 Safer 1309 (9 September 1891); BOA, ŞD 2556/24, doc. 7; BOA, BEO 844/63271, doc. 2, 20 Haziran 1312 (2 July 1896).

56 Ergin, "İstanbul'un İaşesi," pp. 65–77; BOA, ŞD 757/31, doc. 30, 4 Safer 1309 (9 September 1891); Sefer, "From Class Solidarity to Revolution," pp. 406–425; Nacar, *Labor and Power in the Late Ottoman Empire*, p. 72; Georgeon, *Sultan Abdülhamid*, pp. 210–211.

57 BOA, ŞD 714/27, doc. 8, 11 Mayıs 1301 (23 May 1885); BOA, ŞD 757/31, doc. 30, 4 Safer 1309 (9 September 1891); BOA, BEO 3237/242772, doc. 9, 25 Kanunuevvel 1323 (7 January 1908).

58 BOA, İ.TAL 118/111, 2 Eylül 1313 (14 September 1897); BOA, ML.EEM 441/32, doc. 1, 11 March 1319 (24 March 1903); BOA, BEO 2854/213984, doc. 2, 7 Haziran 1322 (20 June 1906); BOA, BEO 3250/243728, doc. 1, 23 Kanunusani 1323 (5 February 1908); BOA, ŞD 452/28, doc. 3, 20 Şubat 1326 (5 March 1911).

59 BOA, A.MKT.MHM 208/38, 25 Recep 1277 (6 February 1861); BOA, İ.MMS 21/926, doc. 1, 5 Recep 1277 (17 January 1861).

60 Odabaşı, "Mihaliç Çiftlikat-ı Hümayunu," p. 204; BOA, ŞD 2556/24, doc. 10, 25 Eylül 1305 (7 October 1889).

61 BOA, ŞD 714/27, doc. 10, 4 Mayıs 1301 (16 May 1885); BOA, ŞD 2556/24, doc. 10, 25 Eylül 1305 (7 October 1889); *The Levant Herald and Eastern Express*, 24 July 1891 and 19 August 1891; Bozis, *İstanbul'dan Anadolu'ya Rumların Yemek Kültürü*, p. 43.

62 BOA İ.TAL 228/51, docs. 1, 3, and 6, 11 Eylül 1316 (24 September 1900) and 20 Cemazeyilahir 1318 (15 October 1900). Asım Vasfi served in the parliament for three terms until 1935. Then, he became the commissar of the Kars animal market, a post that he held for about a decade. See Çoker, *Türk Parlamento Tarihi*, p. 387.

63 BOA, İ.ŞE 22/1, doc. 2, 17 Mayıs 1323 (30 Mayıs 1907); BOA, BEO 3237/242772, doc. 22, 27 Teşrinisani 1323 (10 December 1907); Diplomatic and Consular Reports, *Report for the Year 1907 on the Trade and Commerce of the Consular District of Smyrna*, p. 4.

64 BOA, BEO 3237/242772, doc. 9, 25 Kanunuevvel 1323 (7 January 1908).

65 Yarman, *Palu Harput 1878*, p. 385; Uzer, *Makedonya Eşkiyalık Tarihi*, p. 33.

66 In the Konya sheep market, the Ottoman lira was valued at around 116 piasters in 1907. Therefore, a merchant who purchased 200 head of *Karaman* sheep (worth ninety piasters each) from this province and transported them to Istanbul (at a cost of fifteen piasters per head) spent a total of 21,000 piasters, or slightly over 181 liras. With the addition of taxes and fees charged in Istanbul, his costs amounted to about 184 liras. Moreover, according to established market customs in Istanbul, one of the animals in his flock had to be handed over to the purchaser free of charge. Then, if the merchant sold the remaining 199 sheep at 105 piasters per head, he would receive a payment of 20,895 piasters from his customer. Because the Ottoman lira was valued at 110 piasters in *Karaman* sheep transactions in Istanbul at that time, this amount was equivalent to 190 liras, resulting in a profit of six liras. See BOA, İ.ŞE 22/1, doc. 6, 10 Şubat 1322 (23 February 1907); BOA, ŞD 1747/1, docs. 1 and 6, 11 Mart 1317 (24 March 1901) and 30 Temmuz 1317 (12 August 1901); *The Levant Herald and Eastern Express*, 21 July 1906; Diplomatic and Consular Reports, *Report for the Year 1907 on the Trade and Commerce of Constantinople and District*, p. 34.

67 BOA, ŞD 2923/30, doc. 9, 9 Teşrinisani 1303 (21 November 1887); BOA, İ.ŞE 22/1, doc. 6, 10 Şubat 1322 (23 February 1907).

68 *Sabah*, 16 Mayıs 1307 (28 May 1891).

69 Toprak, *İttihad-Terakki ve Cihan Harbi*, p. 171.

70 Spataris, *Biz İstanbullular Böyleyiz*, pp. 119–120. For an official report dealing with this issue, see BOA, BEO 4613/345921, doc. 3, 18 Teşrinisani 1335 (18 November 1919).

71 *Sabah*, 1 Kanunusani 1307 (13 January 1892).

72 *Dersaadet/İstanbul Ticaret ve Sanayi Odası'nda Kayıtlı Olan Banker, Tüccar ve Komisyoncuların İsimleri (1923)*, pp. 11, 14, 21, 31, 68, 77, 86, 89, 93, and 100.

73 The ones in Tophane and Galata were mainly for cattle. See BOA, ŞD 759/40, 1 Kanunusani 1307 (13 January 1892).

74 Rozen, "A Pound of Flesh," p. 197.

75 Ergin, "İstanbul'un İaşesi," p. 69.

76 Ergin, *Mecelle-i Umur-ı Belediyye*, p. 3315. Istanbul papers frequently reported on the activities of the municipal veterinary officials. For instance, in October 1890, *Sabah* published a news item stating that during the past few days, officials in charge of inspecting cattle slaughterhouses in Tophane seized and destroyed large quantities of meat derived from diseased animals. See *Sabah*, 23 Eylül 1306 (5 October 1890).

77 Tamgörgü, "Ondokuzuncu Yüzyıl Osmanlı İstanbul'unda," pp. 17–22.

78 Ibid., pp. 23–26.

79 For example, see BOA, Y.PRK.ZB 24/97, 4 Şubat 1315 (16 February 1900).

80 The Municipality asked for the removal of a Galata slaughterhouse located next to the water storage of the Sultan Bayezid Mosque because of sanitation concerns. BOA, ZB 336/131, 23 Haziran 1325 (6 July 1909).

81 BOA, DH.İD 215/9, 2 Haziran 1330 (14 June 1914).

82 BOA, ŞD 851/22, 28 Mayıs 328 (10 June 1912)

83 In the late 1880s, sheep flocks transported from Rumelia to Istanbul via rail were disembarked at the Makriköy (today's Bakırköy) station, and from there, they were driven to Feriköy. See BOA, ŞD 1913/44, 22 Eylül 1303 (4 October 1887).

84 Çağman, "Osmanlı Döneminde İstanbul'da Modern Bir Mezbaha," pp. 33–62.

85 BOA, ŞD 851/22, 9 Teşrinievvel 1328 (22 October 1912).

86 Dağdeviren, "İstanbul'da Mezbaha ve Et Ticaretinin Bugününe Dair Gözlemler," pp. 124–125.

Chapter 7: Conclusion

1 For a recent example of this challenge, see Bragg, *Ottoman Notables and Participatory Politics.*

2 For the use of provincial history, see Aymes, *A Provincial History of the Ottoman Empire.*

3 Uzun, *İstanbul'un İaşesinde*; Ağır, "The Evolution of Grain Policy," pp. 571–598.

4 See, for example, Specht, *Red Meat Republic.*

5 For a discussion of such problems among agricultural cultivators, see Aytekin, "Cultivators, Creditors and the State," pp. 292–313.

6 Melikoğlu Gölcü, "Osmanlı Devleti'nde Avrupa'ya Gönderilen Veteriner Hekimliği Öğrencileri," pp. 131–139; Shaw and Kural Shaw, *History of the Ottoman Empire and Modern Turkey*, p. 249.

7 Topuzlu, *İstibdat, Meşrutiyet, Cumhuriyet*, p. 173.

8 Danon, *The Jews of Ottoman Izmir*, pp. 128–129. For an earlier example of challenges to the monopoly of Jewish community butchers in Istanbul, see Rozen, "A Pound of Flesh," pp. 207-208.

Bibliography

Archival Sources

Presidency of the Republic of Türkye, Directorate of State Archives – Department of Ottoman Archives (BOA):

A.MKT (Sadaret Mektubi Kalemi Evrakı) 217/86
A.MKT.MHM (Sadaret Mektubi Kalemi Mühimme Kalemi Evrakı) 84/6, 96/25, 128/11, 208/38, 236/1, 304/72, 553/30, 761/59
A.MKT.MVL (Sadaret Mektubi Kalemi Meclis-i Vala Evrakı) 67/98, 135/21
A.MKT.NZD (Sadaret Mektubi Kalemi Nezaret ve Devair Evrakı) 106/39, 133/96, 272/1, 276/19, 387/4, 407/52
A.MKT.UM (Sadaret Mektubi Kalemi Umum Vilayat Evrakı) 226/9, 237/11, 246/66, 286/39, 409/49, 466/50, 530/24, 544/58, 553/30, 575/2, 804/3, 808/41
AE.SSLM.III (Ali Emiri Selim III) 69/4123, 254/14704, 341/19693, 344/19806
BEO (Bab-ı Ali Evrak Odası) 54/3987, 88/6572, 164/12296, 179/13353, 181/13532, 299/22364, 388/29083, 393/29469, 592/44334, 621/46509, 626/46932, 705/52806, 844/63271, 1287/96476, 1901/142521, 2317/173730, 2627/196976, 2854/213984, 2937/220238, 3237/242772, 3250/243728, 3297/247223, 3298/247336, 3379/253413, 4613/345921
C.AS (Cevdet Askeriye) 391/16154, 688/28866
C.BLD (Cevdet Belediye) 11/547, 31/1531, 34/1667, 41/2008, 67/3304, 72/3567, 94/4694, 97/4812, 121/6006, 149/7423,
C.DH (Cevdet Dahiliye) 25/1207, 33/1641, 119/5909
C.DRB (Cevdet Darphane) 31/1509
C.HR (Cevdet Hariciye) 144/7168
C. İKTS (Cevdet İktisat) 39/1928
C.ML (Cevdet Maliye) 184/7712, 352/14463
C.SH (Cevdet Sıhhiye) 10/484
C.SM (Cevdet Saray) 97/4858
DH.İ.UM (Dahiliye Nezareti İdare-i Umumiye Evrakı) 98/1
DH.İ.UM.EK (Dahiliye Nezareti İdare-i Umumiye Evrakı Ekleri) 4/44, 5/1
DH.İD (Dahiliye Nezareti İdare Kısmı) 215/9
DH.MKT (Dahiliye Nezareti Mektubi Kalemi) 145/85, 170/34, 189/37, 197/64, 615/60, 724/1, 917/17, 1311/114, 1647/5, 1657/90, 1692/21, 1702/84, 1791/66, 1875/56, 1918/8, 1999/25, 2004/75, 2423/76, 2610/71, 2701/95, 2735/15, 2769/15
DH.TMIKM (Dahiliye Nezareti Tesri-i Muamelat ve Islahat Komisyonu) 129/22
HAT (Hatt-ı Hümayun) 446/22289
HH.THR (Hazine-i Hassa Tahrirat Kalemi) 125/2
HRT.h (Haritalar) 959
HR.TH (Hariciye Nezareti Tahrirat) 335/90
İ.DH (İrade Dahiliye) 7/300, 57/2812, 101/5069, 137/4, 251/15449, 338/22247, 1072/84092, 1127/88046, 1318/2
İ.HUS (İrade Hususi) 147/37

İ.ML (İrade Maliye) 32/56
İ.MTZ(05) (İrade Eyalet-i Mümtaze Mısır) 11/273, 11/276
İ.MVL (İrade Meclis-i Vala) 140/3885, 166/4927, 228/7802, 276/10715, 328/14017, 397/17283, 468/21193
İ.MMS (İrade Meclis-i Mahsus) 14/576, 21/926, 25/1077, 65/3070, 103/4394
İ.OM (İrade Orman ve Maadin) 11/39
İ.RSM (İrade Rüsumat) 20/51, 25/23
İ.ŞE (İrade Şehremaneti) 22/1
İ.TAL (İrade Taltifat) 118/111, 228/51
İ.TNF (İrade Ticaret ve Nafia) 1/27
MB.İ (Mabeyn-i Hümayun Evrakı İradeleri) 2/76
ML.EEM (Maliye Nezareti Emlak-ı Emiriyye Müdüriyeti) 62/48, 67/9, 85/27, 85/54, 85/56, 85/57, 85/86, 85/87, 85/88, 100/35, 232/61, 441/32, 580/32, 592/28
ML.VRD.d. (Maliye Nezareti Varidat Defterleri) 4449
MV (Meclis-i Vükela Mazbataları) 21/31, 65/79, 79/84, 111/85, 154/90
MVL (Meclis-i Vala) 19/28, 31/42, 32/57, 101/66, 237/40, 378/11, 378/20, 378/69, 397/38, 407/91, 434/21, 450/75, 481/64, 480/79, 552/64, 556/7, 605/50, 761/23, 822/91, 843/12
ŞD (Şura-yı Devlet) 16/687, 349/11, 452/28, 573/5, 573/13, 678/43, 682/9, 686/27, 695/2, 702/18, 714/27, 727/9, 730/6, 744/4, 753/36, 757/31, 767/16, 774/14, 828/26, 851/22, 1174/16, 1360/2, 1360/4, 1380/64, 1392/42, 1426/2, 1540/9, 1672/24, 1747/1, 1842/15, 1913/44, 1920/16, 2215/68, 2432/19, 2556/24, 2771/6, 2923/30, 2929/14, 2961/36, 3000/11, 3218/5
T.DMİ (Ticaret, Nafia, Ziraat, Orman, Maadin Nezareti, Demiryolları İdaresi) 1009/52
Y.A.HUS (Yıldız Sadaret Hususi Maruzat Evrakı) 257/154
Y.EE (Yıldız Esas Evrakı) 43/37
Y.MTV (Yıldız Mütenevvi Maruzat Evrakı) 4/19, 73/149, 203/128, 302/103
Y.PRK.AZJ (Yıldız Perakende Evrakı Arzuhal Jurnal) 6/103, 42/35, 45/51
Y.PRK.HH (Yıldız Perakende Evrakı Hazine-i Hassa) 6/51
Y.PRK.UM (Yıldız Perakende Evrakı Umumi) 81/13, 81/21
Y.PRK.ZB (Yıldız Perakende Evrakı Zabtiye Nezareti Maruzatı) 24/97
ZB (Zabtiye Nezareti) 336/131

Center for Islamic Studies (ISAM):

Ankara Şeriye Mahkemesi Sicilleri, Defter no. 660, 665, 666, 667, 669, 686, 692, 698, 700, 702, 707, 708, 709, 728

Published Government Documents

Ottoman

Meclis-i Mebusan Zabıt Ceridesi, Period: 1, Year: 2 vol. 1, Meeting: 22 (23 Kanunuevvel 1325/5 January 1910).
Provincial Yearbooks (Salnames):
Adana, 1297 (1879–80).
Ankara, 1293 (1876–77), 1307 (1891–92)
Aydın, 1301 (1883–84), 1302 (1884–85), 1314 (1896–97)

Erzurum, 1288 (1871-72), 1289 (1872-73), 1290 (1873-74), 1292 (1875-76), 1294 (1877–78), 1299 (1881–82), 1313 (1897-98), 1315 (1899–1900)

Hüdavendigar, 1287 (1870–71), 1289 (1872–73), 1290 (1873–74), 1293 (1876–77), 1301 (1883–84), 1306 (1888–89), 1307 (1891–92), 1310 (1892–93), 1316 (1898–99), 1324 (1906–07)

Konya, 1310 (1892–93), 1322 (1906–07)

Ticaret ve Ziraat Nezareti İstatistik İdare-i Umumiyesi Müdüriyeti, Memalik-i Osmaniye'nin 1329 Senesine Mahsus Ziraat İstatistiği. Dersaadet: Osmaniye Matbaası, 1332 [1916].

Great Britain

Abstracts of Reports on the Trade of Various Countries and Places for the Year 1855. London: Harrison and Sons, 1856.

Abstract of Reports on the Trades of Various Countries and Places for the Years 1857–58–59. London: Harrison and Sons, 1860.

British Documents on Foreign Affairs: Reports and Papers from the Foreign Office Confidential Print, Part I, Series B (The Near and Middle East, 1856–1914). London: University Publications of America, 1985.

Commercial No. 15 (1874), Reports from Her Majesty's Consuls on the Manufactures, Commerce, & c., of Their Consular Districts, Part III. London: Harrison and Sons, 1874.

Commercial No. 9 (1876) (Trade Reports), Reports from Her Majesty's Consuls on the Manufactures, Commerce, &c., of Their Consular Districts, Part IV. London: Harrison and Sons, 1876.

Commercial No. 32 (1883) (Trade Reports), Reports from Her Majesty's Consuls on the Manufactures, Commerce, &c. of Their Consular Districts, Part X. London: Harrison and Sons, 1883.

Commercial No. 19 (1884) (Trade Reports), Reports from Her Majesty's Consuls on the Manufactures, Commerce, & c., of Their Consular Districts, Part IV. London: Harrison and Sons, 1884.

Commercial No. 33 (1884) (Trade Reports), Reports from Her Majesty's Consuls on the Manufactures, Commerce, &c. of Their Consular Districts, Part VIII. London: Harrison and Sons, 1884.

Commercial Reports Received at the Foreign Office from Her Majesty's Consuls Between January 1st and June 30th, 1862. London: Harrison and Sons, 1862.

Commercial Reports Received at the Foreign Office from Her Majesty's Consuls Between July 1st, 1863, and June 30th, 1864. London: Harrison and Sons, 1864.

Commercial Reports Received at the Foreign Office from Her Majesty's Consuls between July 1st and December 31st, 1864. London: Harrison and Sons, 1865.

Commercial Reports Received at the Foreign Office from Her Majesty's Consuls During the Year 1865. London: Harrison and Sons, 1866.

Commercial Reports Received at the Foreign Office from Her Majesty's Consuls in 1867. London: Harrison and Sons, 1867.

Diplomatic and Consular Reports on Trade and Finance, Report for the Year 1887 on the Trade of the Vilayet of Adana (Aleppo). London: Harrison and Sons, 1888.

Diplomatic and Consular Reports on Trade and Finance, Report for the Year 1888 on the Trade of Adana. London: Harrison and Sons, 1889.

Diplomatic and Consular Reports on Trade and Finance, Report for the Year 1891 on the Trade of Aleppo. London: Harrison and Sons, 1892.

Diplomatic and Consular Reports on Trade and Finance, Report for the Year 1892 on the Trade of the Consular District of Aleppo. London: Harrison and Sons, 1893.

Diplomatic and Consular Reports on Trade and Finance, Report for the Year 1893 on the Trade of Aleppo. London: Harrison and Sons, 1894.

Diplomatic and Consular Reports on Trade and Finance, Report for the Year 1895 on the Trade, &c., of Aleppo. London: Harrison and Sons, 1896.

Diplomatic and Consular Reports on Trade and Finance, Report for the Year 1896 on the Trade of Aleppo and Adana. London: Harrison and Sons, 1897.

Diplomatic and Consular Reports, Report for the Year 1897 on the Trade of Aleppo and Adana. London: Harrison and Sons, 1898.

Diplomatic and Consular Reports, Report for the Year 1899 on the Trade of the Vilayet of Aleppo. London: Harrison and Sons, 1900.

Diplomatic and Consular Reports, Report for the Year 1900 on the Trade of the Vilayet of Aleppo. London: Harrison and Sons, 1901.

Diplomatic and Consular Reports, Report for the Year 1903 on the Trade and Commerce of the Vilayets of Aleppo and Adana. London: Harrison and Sons, 1904.

Diplomatic and Consular Reports, Report for the Year 1904 on the Trade and Commerce of the Vilayets of Aleppo and Adana. London: Harrison and Sons, 1905.

Diplomatic and Consular Reports, Report for the Year 1905 on the Trade and Commerce of the Vilayet of Aleppo. London: Harrison and Sons, 1906.

Diplomatic and Consular Reports, Report for the Year 1906 on the Trade and Commerce of the Vilayet of Aleppo. London: Harrison and Sons, 1907.

Diplomatic and Consular Reports, Report for the Year 1907 on the Trade and Commerce of the Vilayets of Aleppo and Adana. London: Harrison and Sons, 1908.

Diplomatic and Consular Reports, Report for the Year 1909 on the Trade of the Vilayet of Aleppo. London: Harrison and Sons, 1910.

Diplomatic and Consular Reports, Report for the Year 1911 on the Trade of the Aleppo Vilayet. London: Harrison and Sons, 1912.

Diplomatic and Consular Reports, Report for the Year 1893 on the Trade, & c. of Angora. London: Harrison and Sons, 1894.

Diplomatic and Consular Reports, Report for the Year 1894 on the Trade & c. of Angora. London: Harrison and Sons, 1895.

Diplomatic and Consular Reports, Report for the Year 1895 on the Trade and Agriculture of Angora. London: Harrison and Sons, 1896.

Diplomatic and Consular Reports, Report for the Year 1897 on the Trade and Commerce of Angora and District. London: Harrison and Sons, 1898.

Diplomatic and Consular Reports, Report for the Year 1898 on the Trade and Commerce of Angora and District. London: Harrison and Sons, 1899.

Diplomatic and Consular Reports, Report for the Vilayet of Broussa. London: Harrison and Sons, 1898.

Diplomatic and Consular Reports, Report for the Year 1906 on the Trade of Constantinople and District. London: Harrison and Sons, 1907.

Diplomatic and Consular Reports, Report for the Year 1907 on the Trade and Commerce of Constantinople and District. London: Harrison and Sons, 1908.

Diplomatic and Consular Reports, Report for the Year 1908 on the Trade of Constantinople and District. London: Harrison and Sons, 1909.

Diplomatic and Consular Reports on Trade and Finance, Report for the Year 1893 on the Trade of Damascus. London: Harrison and Sons, 1894.

Diplomatic and Consular Reports, Report for the Year 1889–90 on the Trade of Erzeroum. London: Harrison and Sons, 1891.

Diplomatic and Consular Reports on Trade and Finance, Report for the Year 1893 on the Trade of the Consular District of Erzeroum. London: Harrison and Sons, 1894.

Diplomatic and Consular Reports, Report for the Year 1899 on the Trade of the Consular District of Erzeroum. London: Harrison and Sons, 1900.

Diplomatic and Consular Reports, Report for the Year 1901 on the Trade of the Consular District of Erzeroum. London: Harrison and Sons, 1902.

Diplomatic and Consular Reports, Report for the Year 1911 on the Trade of the Consular District of Erzeroum. London: Harrison and Sons, 1912.

Diplomatic and Consular Reports, Report for the Year 1912 on the Trade of the Consular District of Erzeroum. London: Harrison and Sons, 1913.

Diplomatic and Consular Reports, Report for the Years 1897–99 on the Trade and Commerce of the Consular District of Smyrna. London: Harrison and Sons, 1900

Diplomatic and Consular Reports, Report for the Year 1905 on the Trade and Commerce of the Consular District of Smyrna. London: Harrison and Sons, 1906.

Diplomatic and Consular Reports, Report for the Year 1906 on the Trade and Commerce of the Consular District of Smyrna. London: Harrison and Sons, 1907.

Diplomatic and Consular Reports, Report for the Year 1907 on the Trade and Commerce of the Consular District of Smyrna. London: Harrison and Sons, 1908.

Diplomatic and Consular Reports, Report for the Year 1908 on the Trade and Commerce of the Consular District of Smyrna. London: Harrison and Sons, 1909.

Diplomatic and Consular Reports, Report for the Year 1909 on the Trade of Smyrna. London: Harrison and Sons, 1910.

Diplomatic and Consular Reports, Report for the Year 1910–11 on the Trade of Smyrna. London: Harrison and Sons, 1912.

Diplomatic and Consular Reports, Report for the Year 1911–12 on the Trade of Smyrna. London: Harrison and Sons, 1913.

Diplomatic and Consular Reports, Report for the Year Ending July 1913 on the Trade of Smyrna. London: Harrison and Sons, 1914.

Diplomatic and Consular Reports on Trade and Finance, Report for the Year 1891 on the Trade of the Vilayet of Trebizond. London: Harrison and Sons, 1892.

Diplomatic and Consular Reports on Trade and Finance, Report for the Year 1893 on the Trade, &c., of the Consular District of Trebizond. London: Harrison and Sons, 1894.

Diplomatic and Consular Reports, Report for the Year 1898 on the Trade and Commerce of the Trebizond Vilayet. London: Harrison and Sons, 1899.

Reports by Her Majesty's Secretaries of Embassy and Legation on the Manufactures, Commerce, & c. of the Countries in which They Reside. London: Harrison and Sons, 1870.

Reports from Her Majesty's Consuls on the Manufactures, Commerce, &c., of Their Consular Districts. London: Harrison and Sons, 1872.

Report on the Commercial Statistics of Syria by John Bowring. London: William Cloves and Sons, 1840.

Reports on Subjects of General and Commercial Interest, Russia: Reports on the Provinces of Semirensk and Kars. London: Harrison and Sons, 1888.

Second Report of the Royal Commission Appointed to Inquire into the Depression of Trade and Industry, Appendix, Part II. London: Eyre and Spottiswoode, 1886.

Turkey no. 23: Further Correspondence Respecting the Conditions of the Populations in Asia Minor and Syria. London: Harrison and Sons, 1880.

Turkey no.6: Further Correspondence Respecting the Conditions of the Populations in Asia Minor and Syria. London: Harrison and Sons, 1881.

Turkey no. 1: Further Correspondence Respecting the Condition of the Populations in Asiatic Turkey. London: Harrison and Sons, 1892.

United States

Daily Consular and Trade Reports, volume 4 nos. 229–305: October, November, and December 1913. Washington: Government Printing Office, 1914.

Ford, Worthington C. *Wool and Manufactures of Wool*. Washington: Government Printing Office, 1894.

Mediterranean Pilot, Volume 4: From Cape Matapan (Greece) Eastward, the Mediterranean Archipelago, and the Southern Shore of the Mediterranean Sea, Eastward of Ras Ashdir (Libia). Washington: Government Printing Office, 1916.

The Executive Documents of the House of Representatives for the First Session of the Fifth Congress, 1887–88. Washington: Government Printing Office, 1889.

Newspapers

Bursa, 1893

Sabah, 1890–92, 1906, 1908

The Levant Herald, 1870–75

The Levant Herald and Eastern Express, 1891, 1906

Secondary Sources

Ağır, Seven. "The Evolution of Grain Policy: The Ottoman Experience." *The Journal of Interdisciplinary History* 43, no. 4 (2013): 571–598.

Ak, Mehmet. "Osmanlı Devleti'nde Veba-i Bakari (Sığır Vebası)." *OTAM: Ankara Üniversitesi Osmanlı Tarihi Araştırma ve Uygulama Merkezi Dergisi*, no. 39 (2015): 215–240.

Akan, Seriyye. "Osmanlı Rum Bankeri Yorgo Zarifi." *Toplumsal Tarih*, no. 246 (2014): 43–51.

Akın, Yiğit. *When the War Came Home: The Ottomans' Great War and the Devastation of an Empire*. Stanford: Stanford University Press, 2018.

Akpınar, Özkan. "Reclaiming the Empire: Environment, Marshes, and Hydraulic Engineering in the Late Ottoman Period." PhD diss., Boğaziçi University, 2020.

Aksan, Virginia H. *Ottoman Wars, 1700–1870: An Empire Besieged*. London: Routledge, 2007.

Aktepe, M. Münir. "Mehmed Salahi Bey ve Mecmuasından Bazı Kısımlar." *İÜ Edebiyat Fakültesi Tarih Dergisi* 16, no. 21 (1966): 15–38.

Aktepe, Münir, ed. *Vak'a-Nüvis Ahmed Lütfi Efendi Tarihi, v. IX*. Istanbul: Istanbul Üniversitesi Edebiyat Fakültesi Matbaası, 1984.

Aktepe, Münir, ed. *Vak'a-Nüvis Ahmed Lütfi Efendi Tarihi, v. X*. Ankara: Türk Tarih Kurumu Basımevi, 1988.

Altan, Midhat. *Konyanın İktisadi Bünyesine Bir Bakış*. Istanbul: Hüsnütabiat Basımevi, 1940.

Arıkan, Fatma Melek. "A History of a Western Anatolian Region: Yenişehir and İznik during the Late Ottoman Empire 1855–1909." PhD diss., Sabancı University, 2018.

Aşkın, Anıl. "The Environment, Institutions, and Economy in the Nineteenth-Century Ottoman Empire." MA thesis, Boğaziçi University, 2017.

Ata, Onat Ozan. "Nomads, Animal Breeding, and Agriculture in Post-Settlement Çukurova." MA thesis, Koç University, 2023.

Ateş, Sabri. *The Ottoman-Iranian Borderlands: Making a Boundary, 1843–1914*. Cambridge: Cambridge University Press, 2013.

Ayalon, Yaron. *Natural Disasters in the Ottoman Empire: Plague, Famine, and Other Misfortunes*. Cambridge: Cambridge University Press, 2015.

Ayar, Mesut. "Osmanlı Devleti'nde Kolera Salgını: İstanbul Örneği (1892-1895)." PhD diss., Marmara University, 2005.

Ayar, Mesut. "Osmanlı'nın Rumeli Topraklarında 1892–1895 Kolera Salgını." *Güneydoğu Avrupa Araştırmaları Dergisi*, no.17 (2010): 19–28.

Aygün, Necmettin. "Cihanbeyli-Haymana Sahasındaki Konar-Göçer Toplulukların İdari, Sosyal ve İktisadi Yapıları (1827–1861)." *Mütefekkir: Aksaray Üniversitesi İslami İlimler Fakültesi Dergisi* 6, no.12 (2019): 539–558.

Aymes, Marc. *A Provincial History of the Ottoman Empire: Cyprus and the Eastern Mediterranean in the Nineteenth Century*. London: Routledge, 2017.

Aytekin, Atilla. "Cultivators, Creditors and the State: Rural Indebtedness in the Nineteenth Century Ottoman Empire." *Journal of Peasant Studies* 35, no.2 (2008): 292–313.

"Baiburt and the Border Ranges." *The New Armenia: A Semi-Monthly Periodical* 8, no. 17 (1916): 261–263.

Baics, Gergely. *Feeding Gotham: The Political Economy and Geography of Food in New York, 1790–1860*. Princeton: Princeton University Press, 2016.

Baics, Gergely and Thelle, Mikkel. "Introduction: Meat and the Nineteenth-Century City." *Urban History* 45, no.2 (2018): 184–192.

Balıkhane Nazırı Ali Bey, *Eski Zamanlarda İstanbul Hayatı*. Ed. Ali Şükrü Çoruk. Istanbul: Kitabevi, 2001.

Barak, On. *Powering Empire: How Coal Made the Middle East and Sparked Global Carbonization*. Berkeley: University of California Press, 2020.

Barakat, Nora. "Marginal Actors? The Role of Bedouin in the Ottoman Administration of Animals as Property in the District of Salt, 1870–1912." *Journal of the Economic and Social History of the Orient* 58, no. 1/2 (2015): 105–134.

Barkan, Ömer Lütfi. *Türkiye'de Toprak Meselesi*. Istanbul: Gözlem Yayınları, 1980.

Basiretçi Ali Efendi. *İstanbul Mektupları*. Ed. Nuri Sağlam. Istanbul: Kitabevi, 2001.

Bayar, Muharrem. "Afyonkarahisar İline İskan Olmuş Aşiretler ve Karabağlı Türkmen Aşireti'nin İskanı, Sosyal Kültürel Yaşantıları." In *IV. Afyonkarahisar Araştırmaları Sempozyumu Bildirileri*. Ed. E. Emel Sarlık and Mehmet Sarlık, 179–221. Afyon: Hazer Ofset, 1995.

Bayar, Yener. "1873–1875 Orta Anadolu Kıtlığı." MA thesis, Marmara University, 2013.

Bekman, Muzaffer. *Veteriner Tarihi*. Ankara: Ankara Basım ve Cildevi, 1940.

Bell, Donald S. *Trends in the Sheep Industry of the United States: Effects of Breed Type and Economic Circumstances*. Ohio: Ohio Agricultural Research and Development Center, 1970.

Beyhan, Mehmet Ali. "Some Records on Price Controls in Istanbul at the Beginning of the 19th Century." In *Living in the Ottoman Ecumenical Community*. Ed. Vera Constantini and Markus Koller, 131–146. Leiden: Brill, 2008.

Bidwell, Charles Toll. *The Cost of Living Abroad: Reports and Statistics Showing the Prices of House-Rent, Wages, Commodities, Clerk-Hire, &c., at the Present Time, and Compared with Those of the Year 1858, at Most of the Principal Places in Foreign Countries*. London: Sampson Low, Marston Searle, Rivington, 1876.

Bilgin, Arif. "Osmanlı Sarayının İaşesi." PhD diss., Marmara University, 2000.

Birdal, Murat. *The Political Economy of the Ottoman Public Debt: Insolvency and European Financial Control in the Late Nineteenth Century*. London: I.B. Tauris, 2010.

Bolanos, Isacar A. "The Ottomans During the Global Crises of Cholera and Plague: The View from Iraq and the Gulf." *International Journal of Middle East Studies* 51, no. 4 (2019): 603–620.

Bozis, Sula. *İstanbul'dan Anadolu'ya Rumların Yemek Kültürü.* Istanbul: Yapı Kredi Yayınları, 2012.

Bragg, John. *Ottoman Notables and Participatory Politics.* London: Routledge, 2014.

Bulliet, Richard. "History and Animal Energy in the Arid Zone." In *Water and Sand: Environmental Histories of the Middle East and North Africa.* Ed. Alan Mikhail, 51–70. Oxford: Oxford University Press, 2013.

Çağman, Engin. "Osmanlı Döneminde İstanbul'da Modern Bir Mezbaha Kurma Teşebbüsü." *FSM İlmi Araştırmalar İnsan ve Toplum Bilimleri Dergisi,* no. 15 (2020): 33–62.

Çakmak, Ömer."Narh ve Nizam Kayıtlarına Göre İstanbul'da Koyun Eti Fiyatları ve Ücretlerle Karşılaştırılması (1778–1857)." *Kadim,* no. 2 (2021): 69–90.

Çelik, Semih. "Scarcity and Misery at the time of 'Abundance beyond Imagination': Climate Change, Famines and Empire-Building in Ottoman Anatolia (c. 1800–1850)." PhD diss., European University Institute, 2017.

Çelik, Semih. "'It's a Bad Fate to be Born Near a Forest': Forest, People, and Buffaloes in Mid-Nineteenth Century North-Western Anatolia." In *Seeds of Power: Explorations in Ottoman Environmental History.* Ed. Onul İnal and Yavuz Köse, 111–133. Cambridge: The Whitehorse Press, 2019.

Çelik, Semih. "'No Work for Anyone in this Country of Misery': Famine and Labour Relations in Mid-Nineteenth-Century Anatolia." In *Working in Greece and Turkey: A Comparative Labour History from Empires to Nation-States, 1840–1940.* Ed. Leda Papastefanaki and Erdem Kabadayı, 148–173. New York: Berghahn, 2020.

Çetin, Emrah. *Tanzimat'tan Cumhuriyet'e Anadolu'da Karayolu Ulaşımı.* Ankara: Türk Tarih Kurumu, 2017.

Çetin, Mehmet. "The Development of the Transit Trade of Iran in the Triangle of Russia, Ottoman Empire and Iran in the Second Half of the Nineteenth Century." *Tarih İncelemeleri Dergisi* 36, no.1 (2021): 21–52.

Çetinkaya, Y. Doğan. "Converting Wealth into Capital: Bank Savings Accounts, National Savings Movement, and the *Kumbara* (1929–1938)." *Siyasal: Journal of Political Sciences* 32 (2023): 35–55.

Çizakça, Murat. "Price History and the Bursa Silk Industry: A Study in Ottoman Industrial Decline, 1550–1650." *The Journal of Economic History* 40, no. 3 (1980): 533–550.

Clark, Edward C. "The Ottoman Industrial Revolution." *International Journal of Middle East Studies* 5, no. 1 (1974): 65–76.

Clark, T. D. "Livestock Trade Between Kentucky and the South 1840–1860." *Register of Kentucky State Historical Society* 27, no. 81 (1929): 569–581.

Çoker, Fahri. *Türk Parlamento Tarihi: Milli Mücadele ve TBMM I. Dönem, 1919–1923.* Ankara: Türkiye Büyük Millet Meclisi Vakfı Yayınları, 1994.

Connor, L. G. "A Brief History of the Sheep Industry in the US." *Agricultural History Society Papers* 1 (1921): 89, 91, 93–165, 167–197.

Cora, Yaşar Tolga. "Transforming Erzurum/Karin: The Social and Economic History of a Multi-Ethnic Ottoman City in the Nineteenth Century." PhD diss., The University of Chicago, 2016.

Cora, Yaşar Tolga. "The Market as a Means of Post-Violence Recovery: Armenians and the Oriental Carpets in the Late Ottoman Empire (c. 1890s–1910s)." *International Review of Social History* 66, no. 2 (2021): 217–241.

Dağdeviren, Musa. "İstanbul'da Mezbaha ve Et Ticaretinin Bugününe Dair Gözlemler." *Yemek ve Kültür,* no. 11 (2008): 110–125.

Danon, Dina. *The Jews of Ottoman Izmir: A Modern History.* Stanford: Stanford University Press, 2020.

Davison, Roderic. *Essays in Ottoman and Turkish History, 1774–1923: The Impact of the West.* Austin: The University of Texas Press, 1990.

Dede, Suat. "From Nomadism to Sedentary Life in Central Anatolia: The Case of Reswan Tribe (1830–1932)." MA thesis, Bilkent University, 2011.

Delmar, Alexander. "On the Resources, Productions, and Social Conditions of Egypt." *Proceedings of the American Philosophical Society* 11, no. 93 (1874): 232–255.

Demirel, Muammer. "XIX. Yüzyılda Bursa'da Göçmen İskanı." In *Bursa'nın Zenginliği Göçmenler*. Ed. Zeynep Dörtok-Abacı, 31–58. Bursa: Osmangazi Belediyesi Yayınları, 2008.

Demirkol, Kurtuluş. "Tanzimat Fermanı Bağlamında İspenç Vergisi." *Türk Dünyası Araştırmaları*, no. 231 (2017): 167–182.

Demirtürk, Mehmet, Cellatoğulları, İbrahim, and Arıcı, Deniz. "Türkiye'de Merinos Koyunu Yetiştiriciliği ve Risâle-i Ağnâm." *The Journal of Academic Social Science (ASOS)* 5, no. 51 (2017): 1–21.

Demiryürek, Halim. "II. Meşrutiyet'ten Cumhuriyet'e Bursa'nın Demografik Yapısı." *Vakanüvis: Uluslararası Tarih Araştırmaları Dergisi* 1, no.1 (2016): 190–240.

Der Matossian, Bedross. *The Horrors of Adana: Revolution and Violence in the Early Twentieth Century*. Stanford: Stanford University Press, 2022.

Deringil, Selim. *The Well-Protected Domains: Ideology and Legitimation of Power in the Ottoman Empire, 1876–1909*. London: I. B. Tauris, 1999.

Deringil, Selim. "'They Live in a State of Nomadism and Savagery': The Late Ottoman Empire and the Post-Colonial Debate." *Comparative Studies in Society and History* 45, no. 2 (2003): 311–342.

Doğan, Mustafa. "3525 Numaralı Nüfus Defteri'ne Göre Cihanbeyli Aşireti ve Tabi Aşiretlerin Sosyo-Ekonomik Yapısı." MA thesis, Aksaray University, 2019

Dollbee, Samuel. "Borders, Disease and Territoriality in the Post-Ottoman Middle East." In *Regimes of Mobility: Borders and State Formation in the Middle East, 1918-1946*. Ed. Jordi Tejel and Ramazan Hakkı Öztan, 205-227. Edinburgh: Edinburgh University Press, 2023.

Dölek Sever, Deniz. "Geç Dönem Osmanlı İmparatorluğu'nda Hayvan Hırsızlığı: Kastamonu Vilayeti Örneği." *Cihannüma: Tarih ve Coğrafya Araştırmaları Dergisi* 7, no.2 (2021): 157–193.

Duben, Alan, and Behar, Cem. *Istanbul Households: Marriage, Family, and Fertility, 1880–1940*. Cambridge: Cambridge University Press, 1991.

Dural, Halil. *Bize Derler Çakırca: 19. ve 20. Yüzyılda Ege'de Efeler*. Istanbul: Tarih Vakfı Yurt Yayınları, 1999.

Dursun, Selçuk. "Forest and the State: History of Forestry and Forest Administration in the Ottoman Empire." PhD diss., Sabancı University, 2007.

Emiroğlu, Kudret et al, eds. *Ankara Vilayeti Salname-i Resmisi, 1325 (1907)*. Ankara: Ankara Enstitüsü Vakfı Yayınları, 1995.

Erdoğan, Abdülkerim, Kılıcı, Ali, and Günel, Gökçe. *Osmanlı'da Ankara*. Ankara: Ankara Buyukşehir Belediyesi Kültür ve Sosyal İşler Dairesi Başkanlığı, 2007.

Ergin, Osman Nuri. "İstanbul'un İaşesi: İstanbul'un Bir Senelik Et Sarfiyatı ve Karaağaç Mezbahası." *İstanbul Şehremaneti Mecmuası*, no.4 (1924): 65–77.

Ergin, Osman Nuri. *Mecelle-i Umur-ı Belediyye, vol.6*. Istanbul: Istanbul Büyükşehir Belediyesi Kültür İşleri Daire Başkanlığı, 1995.

Erk, Nihal. "Tarihte Önemli Sığır Vebası Salgınları ve 1920'ye Kadar Memleketimizdeki Durumu." *Ankara Üniversitesi Veterinerlik Fakültesi Dergisi* 10, no. 3–4 (1963): 221–237.

Erler, Mehmet Yavuz. "Ankara ve Konya Vilayetlerinde Kuraklık ve Kıtlık (1845 ve 1874 Yılları)." PhD diss., Ondokuz Mayıs University, 1997.

Ertem, Özge. "Considering Famine in the Late Nineteenth Century Ottoman Empire: A Comparative Framework and Overview." *Collegium* 22, no. 9 (2017): 151-172.

Esslen, J. "On the High Price of Meat in the German Empire in 1905." *The Economic Journal* 16, no. 61 (1906): 130–135.

Findley, Carter V. *Turkey, Islam, Nationalism and Modernity: A Brief History, 1789–2007*. New Haven: Yale University Press, 2010.

Frangakis-Syrett, Elena. "Commerce in the Eastern Mediterranean from the Eighteenth to Early Twentieth Centuries: The City-Port of İzmir and Its Hinterland." *International Journal of Maritime History* 10, no. 2 (1998): 125–154.

Genç, Elif Süreyya. *XIX. Yüzyıl İstanbulu, Bir İngiliz Seyyahın İzlenimleri.* Istanbul: Doğu Kitabevi, 2010.

Genç, Mehmet. *Osmanlı İmparatorluğu'nda Devlet ve Ekonomi.* İstanbul: Ötüken, 2000.

Georgeon, François. *Sultan Abdülhamid.* Istanbul: İletişim Yayınları, 2018.

Ghazarian, Matthew. "A Climate of Confessionalization: Famine and Difference in the Late Ottoman Empire." *International Journal of Middle East Studies* 54, no. 3 (2022): 484–504.

Gingeras, Ryan. *Sorrowful Shores: Violence, Ethnicity, and the End of the Ottoman Empire, 1912–1923*. Oxford: Oxford University Press, 2009.

Goffman, Daniel. "Izmir: From Village to Colonial Port City." In *The Ottoman City between East and West: Aleppo, Izmir, and Istanbul.* Ed. Edhem Eldem, Daniel Goffman, and Bruce Masters, 79-134. Cambridge: Cambridge University Press, 1999.

Goldstone, Jack A. "East and West in the Seventeenth Century: Political Crises in Stuart England, Ottoman Turkey, and Ming China." *Comparative Studies in Society and History* 30, no. 1 (1988): 103–142.

Gratien, Chris. *The Unsettled Plain: An Environmental History of the Late Ottoman Frontier.* Stanford: Stanford University Press, 2022.

Gratien, Chris. "Istanbul's Moveable Feast." Accessed 6 June 2023, http://www.docblog.ottomanhistorypodcast.com.

Gray, Peter. "Famine and Land in Ireland and India, 1845–1880: James Caird and the Political Economy of Hunger." *The Historical Journal* 49, no. 1 (2006): 193–215.

Greenwood, Antony Warren. "Istanbul's Meat Provisioning: A Study of the Celepkeşan System." PhD diss., The University of Chicago, 1988.

Grehan, James. *Everyday Life and Consumer Culture in 18th Century Damascus.* Seattle: University of Washington Press, 2007.

Guardia, Manel, Oyon, Jose Luis, Garriga, Sergi, and Fava, Nadia. "Meat Consumption and Nutrition Transition in Barcelona, 1709-1935" *Urban History* 45, no.2 (2018): 193–213.

Gülbahar, Necati. "Supplemental Irrigation in Turkey," In *Supplemental Irrigation in the Near East and North Africa: Proceedings of a Workshop on Regional Consultation on Supplemental Irrigation. ICARDA and FAO, Rabat, Morocco, 7–9 December, 1987*. Ed. E. R. Perrier and A. B. Salkini, 529–560. Springer, 1991.

Günaydın, Nurşen and Kaplanoğlu, Raif. *Seyahatnamelerde Bursa.* Bursa: Bursa Ticaret Borsası Kültür Yayınları, 2000.

Gündoğdu, Cihangir. "The State and the Stray Dogs in Late Ottoman Istanbul: From Unruly Subjects to Servile Friends." *Middle Eastern Studies* 54, no.4 (2018): 555–574.

Güran, Tevfik. *19. Yüzyıl Osmanlı Tarımı Üzerine Araştırmalar.* Istanbul: Eren Yayıncılık, 1998.

Haydaroğlu, İlknur. "II. Abdülhamit'in Hafiye Teşkilatı Hakkında Bir Risale." *Tarih Araştırmaları Dergisi* 17, no. 28 (1995): 109–133.

Hornby, Edmund. *Constantinople During the Crimean War.* London: Richard Bentley, 1863.

Horowitz, Roger. *Putting Meat on the American Table: Taste, Technology, Transformation.* Baltimore: Johns Hopkins University Press, 2006.

Horowitz, Roger, Pilcher, Jeffrey M., and Watts, Sydney. "Meat for the Multitudes: Market Culture in Paris, New York City, and Mexico over the Long Nineteenth Century." *American Historical Review* 109, no.4 (2004): 1055–1083.

Hulkiender, Murat. *Bir Galata Bankerinin Portresi: George Zarifi, 1806–1884*. Istanbul: Osmanlı Bankası Arşiv ve Araştırma Merkezi, 2003.

Huntington, Ellsworth. "Physical Environment as a Factor in the Present Condition of Turkey." *The Journal of Race Development* 1, no. 4 (1911): 460–481.

Husain, Faisal. "In the Bellies of the Marshes: Water and Power in the Countryside of Ottoman Baghdad." *Environmental History* 19, no. 4 (2014): 638–664.

İnal, Onur. "Fruits of Empire: Figs, Raisins and Transformation of Western Anatolia in the Late Nineteenth Century." In *Seeds of Power: Explorations in Ottoman Environmental History*. Ed. Onur İnal and Yavuz Köse, 81–110. Cambridge: The Whitehorse Press, 2019.

İnal, Onur and Köse, Yavuz. "The Ottoman Environments Revisited." In *Seeds of Power: Explorations in Ottoman Environmental History*. Ed. Onur İnal and Yavuz Köse, 1–16. Cambridge: The Whitehorse Press, 2019.

İnal, Onur. "One-Humped History: The Camel as Historical Actor in the Late Ottoman Empire." *International Journal of Middle East Studies*, 53, no. 1 (2021): 57–72.

İpek, Nedim "Kafkaslar'dan Anadolu'ya Göçler (1877–1900)." *Ondokuz Mayıs Üniversitesi Eğitim Fakültesi Dergisi* 6, no.1 (1991): 101–138.

İpek, Nedim. *Rumeli'den Anadolu'ya Türk Göçleri*. Ankara: Türk Tarih Kurumu Basımevi, 1994.

Issawi, Charles. "The Tabriz-Trabzon Trade, 1830–1900." *International Journal of Middle East Studies* 1, no.1 (1970): 18–27.

Issawi, Charles. *The Fertile Crescent, 1800–1914: A Documentary Economic History* Oxford: Oxford University Press, 1988.

Kala, Ahmet, ed. *İstanbul Ahkam Defterleri: İstanbul Esnaf Tarihi 2*. Istanbul: Istanbul Büyükşehir Belediyesi, 1998.

Kara, İsmail. "Nurettin Topçu'nun Hayatı." In *Nurettin Topçu*. Ed. İsmail Kara, 13–61. Ankara: T.C Kültür ve Turizm Bakanlığı Yayınları, 2009.

Karpat, Kemal. *Studies on Ottoman Social and Political History: Selected Articles and Essays*. Leiden: Brill, 2002.

Kasaba, Reşat. "İzmir." *Review (Fernand Braudel Center)* 16, no.4 (1993): 387-410.

Kasaba, Reşat. *A Moveable Empire: Ottoman Nomads, Migrants, and Refugees*. Seattle: University of Washington Press, 2009.

Kırlı, Cengiz. *Sultan ve Kamuoyu: Osmanlı Modernleşme Sürecinde "Havadis Jurnalleri" (1840–1844)*. Istanbul: İş Bankası Kültür Yayınları, 2009.

Kırpık, Cevdet. "Loncadan Cemiyete Osmanlı Hamal Teşkilatlarında Değişim." *Türk Dünyası Araştırmaları*, no.158 (2005): 95–108.

Klein, Janet. *The Margins of Empire: Kurdish Militias in the Ottoman Tribal Zone*. Stanford: Stanford University Press, 2011.

Koç, Yener. "Nomadic Pastoral Tribes at the Intersection of the Ottoman, Persian and Russian Empires (1820s–1890s)." PhD diss., Boğaziçi University, 2020.

Koç, Yener. "Winter-Quartering Tribes: Nomad-Peasant Relations in the Northeastern Frontiers of the Ottoman Empire (1800s–1850s)." *International Review of Social History* 69, no. 1 (2024): 47–66.

Kokdaş, İrfan. "Celeps, Butchers, and the Sheep: The Worlds of Meat in Istanbul in the Sixteenth-Seventeenth Centuries." MA thesis, Sabancı University, 2007.

Köksal, Yonca. "Coercion and Mediation: Centralization and Sedentarization of Tribes in the Ottoman Empire." *Middle Eastern Studies* 42, no. 3 (2006): 469–491.

Köksal, Yonca. *The Ottoman Empire in the Tanzimat Era: Provincial Perspectives from Ankara and Edirne*. London: Routledge, 2019.

Köksal, Yonca and Polatel, Mehmet. "A Tribe as an Economic Actor: The Cihanbeyli Tribe and the Meat Provisioning of Istanbul in the Early Tanzimat Era." *New Perspectives on Turkey*, no.61 (2019): 97–123.

Köksal, Yonca and Polatel, Mehmet. "The Cihanbeyli and Sheep Trade: From Provisionism and Semi-Nomadism to Liberal Economy and Sedentarization." In *Making a Living in Ottoman Anatolia*. Ed. Kate Fleet and Ebru Boyar, 157–174. Leiden: Brill, 2021.

Köksal Özyaşar, Yonca and Nacar, Can. "Marketing Sheep in the Ottoman Empire: Erzurum and Its Trade Networks (Circa 1780s–1910s)." *Archiv Orientalni* 91, no.1 (2023): 41–67.

Köylü, Kazım. *Türkiye'de Büyük Arazi Mülkleri ve Bunların İşletme Şekilleri*. Ankara: Ankara Yüksek Ziraat Enstitüsü Basımevi, 1947.

Koyun Yetiştirmek ve Bakmak Usulü. Dersaadet: Umum-ı Baytariye Müdüriyeti, 1330 [1914].

Küçük, Cevdet. "Erzurum." In *TDV İslam Ansiklopedisi, vol. 11*. 321–329. Istanbul: Türkiye Diyanet Vakfı, 1995.

Küçük Menderes Havzası Toprakları. Ankara: Topraksu Genel Müdürlüğü, 1974.

Küçükalioğlu, Sema. "İdare-i Mahsusa: Kuruluşu, Faaliyetleri, Sosyo-Ekonomik Etkileri." MA thesis, Marmara University, 1999.

Küçükceran, Zeynep. "Agriculture and Agricultural Knowledge in Bursa and Mihaliç (Karacabey) in the Nineteenth Century." PhD diss., Boğaziçi University, 2019.

Kurşun, Zekeriya, ed. *Dersaadet/İstanbul Ticaret ve Sanayi Odası'nda Kayıtlı Olan: Banker, Tüccar ve Komisyoncuların İsimleri (1923)*. Istanbul: Istanbul Ticaret Odası Yayınları, 2008.

Lapavitsas, Costas and Çakıroğlu, Pınar. *Capitalism in the Ottoman Balkans: Industrialisation and Modernity in Macedonia*. London: I.B Tauris, 2019.

Lyberatos, Andreas. "Men of the Sultan: The *Beğlik* Sheep Tax Collection System and the Rise of a Bulgarian National Bourgeoisie in Nineteenth-Century Plovdiv." *Turkish Historical Review* 1 (2010): 55–85.

Lynch, H.F.B. *Armenia: Travels and Studies, Volume 2*. London: Longmans, Green, and Co., 1901.

Mağmuni, Şerafeddin. *Bir Osmanlı Doktorunun Anıları: Yüzyıl Önce Anadolu ve Suriye*. Istanbul: Büke Yayınları, 2002.

Massy, P.H.H. "Exploration in Asiatic Turkey, 1896 to 1903." *The Geographical Journal* 26, no. 3 (1905): 272–303.

Mazanik, Anna. "'Shiny Shoes' for the City: The Public Abattoir and the Reform of Meat Supply in Imperial Moscow." *Urban History* 45, no.2 (2018): 214–232.

Melikoğlu Gölcü, Berfin. "Osmanlı Devleti'nde Avrupa'ya Gönderilen Veteriner Hekimliği Öğrencileri." *Ankara Üniversitesi Veterinerlik Fakültesi Dergisi*, no. 66 (2019): 131–139.

Mikhail, Alan. *The Animal in Ottoman Egypt*. Oxford: Oxford University Press, 2014.

Mikhail, Alan. *Under Osman's Tree: The Ottoman Empire, Egypt, and Environmental History*. Chicago: The University of Chicago Press, 2017.

Nacar, Can. "Yükselen Bir Liman Kentinde Ekonomik Pastayı Paylaşmak: 20. Yüzyılın Başında Mersin'de Rekabet, Çatışma ve İttifaklar." *Cihannüma: Tarih ve Coğrafya Araştırmaları Dergisi* 3, no. 1 (2017): 71–94.

Nacar, Can. *Labor and Power in the Late Ottoman Empire: Tobacco Workers, Managers, and the State, 1872–1912*. Cham: Palgrave Macmillan, 2019.

Nacar, Can and Köksal, Yonca. "Ali Ağa'nın Koyunları ve Borçları: Erzurum-Şam-Mısır Hattında Hayvan Ticareti." *Toplumsal Tarih*, no. 323 (2020): 60–65.

Odabaşı, Necmi "Mihaliç Çiflikat-ı Hümayunu ve İdaresi." PhD diss., Uludağ University, 2014.

Olson, K. C. "Development of the National Cattle Trade." *Rangelands*, 23, no.5 (2001): 3–6.

Özbek, Nadir. *Osmanlı İmparatorluğu'nda Sosyal Devlet: Siyaset, İktidar ve Meşrutiyet, 1876–1914*. Istanbul: İletişim Yayınları, 2002.

Özbek, Nadir. "The Politics of Taxation and the 'Armenian Question' during the Late Ottoman Empire, 1876–1908." *Comparative Studies in History and Society* 54, no. 4 (2012): 770–797.

Özel, Oktay. *The Collapse of Rural Order in Ottoman Anatolia: Amasya, 1576–1643*. Leiden: Brill, 2016.

Özger, Yunus. "XIX. Yüzyıl Sonlarında Meydana Gelen Bir Kuraklık ve Kıtlık Hadisesi ile Bunun Sosyo-Ekonomik Sonuçları." *Karadeniz Araştırmaları*, no. 19 (2008): 87–96.

Özkan, Ela. "19. Yüzyılda Osmanlı Devleti'nin İdari Taksimatı, 1839–1914." PhD diss., Fırat University, 2017.

Özkan, Fulya. "A Road in Rebellion, A History on the Move: The Social History of the Trabzon-Bayezid Road and The Formation of the Modern State in Late Ottoman World." PhD diss., Binghamton University, 2012.

Özkaya, Yücel. *Osmanlı İmparatorluğunda Ayanlık*. Ankara: Türk Tarih Kurumu Yayınevi, 1994.

Özok-Gündoğan, Nilay. "A 'Peripheral' Approach to the 1908 Revolution in the Ottoman Empire: Land Disputes in Peasant Petitions in Post-revolutionary Diyarbekir." In *Social Relations in Ottoman Diyarbekir. 1870–1915*. Ed. Joost Jongerden and Jelle Verheij, 179–216. Leiden: Brill, 2012.

Pamuk, Şevket, "Institutional Change and the Longevity of the Ottoman Empire." *Journal of Interdisciplinary History* 35, no. 2 (2004): 225-247.

Pamuk, Şevket. *Uneven Centuries: Economic Development of Turkey since 1820*. Princeton: Princeton University Press, 2018.

Pech, Edgar. *Manuel des Sociétés Anonymes Fonctionnant en Turquie*. Constantinople: Imprimerie Gérard Frères, 1911.

Pehlivan, Zozan. "Beyond 'the Desert and the Sown': Peasants, Pastoralists, and Climate Crises in Ottoman Diyarbekir, 1840–1890." PhD diss., Queen's University, 2016.

Pehlivan, Zozan. "El Niño and the Nomads: Global Climate, Local Environment, and the Crisis of Pastoralism in Late Ottoman Kurdistan." *Journal of the Economic and Social History of the Orient* 63, no. 3 (2020): 316–356.

Perren, Richard. "The Meat and Livestock Trade in Britain, 1850–70." *The Economic History Review* 28, no. 3 (1975): 385–400.

Perrot, Georges. "Les Kurdes de l'Haimaneh." *Revue des Deux Mondes* 55, no.3 (1865): 607–631.

Pustu, Yunus. "Osmanlı Döneminde Ankara'ya Muhacir İskanı (1856–1918)." *Ankara Anadolu ve Rumeli Araştırmaları Dergisi* 1, no.2 (2020): 591–636.

Quataert, Donald. "Limited Revolution: The Impact of the Anatolian Railway on Turkish Transportation and the Provisioning of Istanbul, 1890–1908." *The Business History Review* 51, no. 2 (1977): 139–160.

Quataert, Donald. "Machine Breaking and the Changing Carpet Industry of Western Anatolia, 1860–1908." *Journal of Social History* 19, no. 3 (1986): 473–489.

Quataert, Donald. *Ottoman Manufacturing in the Age of Industrial Revolution*. Cambridge: Cambridge University Press, 1993.

Quataert, Donald. "The Silk Industry of Bursa, 1880–1914." In *Workers, Peasants and Economic Change in the Ottoman Empire 1730–1914*. Ed. Donald Quataert, 97–115. Istanbul: Isis Press, 1993.

Quataert, Donald. "The Age of Reforms, 1812–1914." In *An Economic and Social History of the Ottoman Empire, vol. 2: 1600–1914*. Ed. Halil İnalcık and Donald Quataert,749–943. Cambridge: Cambridge University Press, 1997.

Quataert, Donald. *Miners and the State in the Ottoman Empire: The Zonguldak Coalfield, 1820–1920*. New York: Berghahn Books, 2006.

Ramsay, W. M. "The Drovers' Road." *Chambers's Journal, Seventh Series* 16 (1926): 801–804.

Rıfat, Hüseyin. *İzmir 1914: Aydın Vilayeti 1330 Sene-i Maliyesi Ticaret Rehberi*. Ed. Erkan Serçe. İzmir: Akademi Kitabevi, 1997.

Robarts, Andrew. "Russo-Ottoman Wars." In *Encyclopedia of the Ottoman Empire*. Ed. Gabor Agoston and Bruce Masters, 494–499. New York: Facts on File, 2009.

Rozen, Minna. "A Pound of Flesh: The Meat Trade and Social Struggle of Jewish Istanbul, 1700–1923." In *Crafts and Craftsmen of the Middle East: Fashioning the Individual in the Muslim Mediterranean*. Ed. Suraiya Faroqhi and Randi Deguilhem, 195–234. London: I. B. Tauris, 2005.

Sami, Cevat and Hüsnü, Hüseyin. *İzmir 1905*. Ed. Erkan Serçe. İzmir: İzmir Büyükşehir Belediyesi, 2000.

Saraçoğlu, M. Safa. "Economic Interventionism, Islamic Law and Provincial Government in the Ottoman Empire." In *Law and Legality in the Ottoman Empire and Republic of Turkey*. Ed. Kent F. Schull, M. Safa Saraçoğlu, and Robert Zens, 65–91. Bloomington: Indiana University Press, 2016.

Sarıay, Erciment. "II. Meşrutiyet Döneminde Eşraf ve Köylü İlişkisi Üzerine Örnek Bir Olay: Çayırhan Köylüleri ile Hilmi Bey Arasındaki Arazi Anlaşmazlığı." *Bilecik Şeyh Edebali Üniversitesi Sosyal Bilimler Enstitüsü Dergisi* 4, no. 2 (2019): 602–610.

Şaşmaz, Musa. *Trade Reports of the Trebizond Province on British Documents 1830–1914, v. I–III*. Ankara: Türk Tarih Kurumu 2014.

Sazak, M. Emin. *Emin Bey'in Defteri: Hatıralar*. Ankara: Tolkun, 2007.

Schweig, Alexander. "Progressing into Disaster: The Railroad and the Spread of Cholera in a Provincial Ottoman Town." *History of Science* (2022): 1–23.

Sefer, Akın. "From Class Solidarity to Revolution: The Radicalization of Arsenal Workers in the Late Ottoman Empire." *International Review of Social History* 58, no.3 (2013): 406–425.

Şener, Mesut. *Nallıhan*. Ankara: Star Ajans Matbaacılık, 1988.

Şerif, Ahmet. *Anadolu'da Tanin*. Ed. Mehmet Çetin Börekçi. Ankara: Türk Tarih Kurumu, 1999.

Seyyah Kandemir. *Ankara Vilayeti*. Ankara: Türk Maarif Cemiyeti, 1932.

Sharma, Sanjay. *Famine, Philanthropy and the Colonial State: North India in the Early Nineteenth Century*. Delhi: Oxford University Press, 2001.

Shaw, Stanford J. and Kural Shaw, Ezel. *History of the Ottoman Empire and Modern Turkey, Volume 2: Reform, Revolution, and the Republic, The Rise of Modern Turkey, 1808–1975*. Cambridge: Cambridge University Press, 1977.

Shields, Sarah. "Regional Trade and 19th-Century Mosul: Revising the Role of Europe in the Middle East Economy." *International Journal of Middle East Studies* 23, no. 1 (1991): 19–37.

Shields, Sarah. "Sheep, Nomads and Merchants in Nineteenth-Century Mosul: Creating Transformations in an Ottoman Society." *Journal of Social History* 25, no.4 (1992): 773–789.

Şimşir, Bilal N. *Ankara...Ankara: Bir Başkentin Doğuşu*. Istanbul: Bilgi Yayınevi, 1988.

Slavin, Philip "Climate and Famines: A Historical Reassessment." *WIREs Climate Change* 7 (2016): 433–447.

Spataris, Haris. *Biz İstanbullular Böyleyiz! Fener'den Anılar, 1906–1922*. Istanbul: Kitap Yayınevi, 2004.

Specht, Joshua. *Red Meat Republic: A Hoof-to-Table History of How Beef Changed America*. Princeton: Princeton University Press, 2019.

Stanziani, Alessandro. *Rules of Exchange: French Capitalism in Comparative Perspective, Eighteenth to Early Twentieth Centuries*. Cambridge: Cambridge University Press, 2012.

Sürgevil, Sabri. *İkinci Meşrutiyet Döneminde İzmir*. İzmir: İzmir Büyükşehir Belediyesi, 2009.

Tabak, Faruk. *The Waning of the Mediterranean 1550–1870: A Geohistorical Approach*. Baltimore: Johns Hopkins University Press, 2008.

Tahir, Kemal. *Göl İnsanları*. Ankara: Bilgi Yayınevi, 1969.

Tahsin Paşa. *Tahsin Paşa'nın Yıldız Hatıraları*. Isparta: Genç Osman Yayınları, 2017.

Tamgörgü, Ahmet Bulut. "Ondokuzuncu Yüzyıl Osmanlı İstanbul'unda Bir Sorunsal Olarak Çöp." MA thesis, Ege University, 2020.

Tan, Seda. "Osmanlı Devleti'nde Halk Sağlığı Uygulamalarına Önemli Bir Örnek: Salhanelerin Şehir Dışına Nakilleri." In *XVIII. Türk Tarih Kongresi, 1–5 Ekim 2018/Ankara: Kongreye Sunulan Bildiriler, Vol. 3*. Ed. Semiha Nurdan and Muhammed Özler, 1363–1385. Ankara: Türk Tarih Kurumu Yayınları, 2022.

Terzi, Arzu. "Hazine-i Hassa." In *TDV İslam Ansiklopedisi, vol. 17*. 137-141. Istanbul: TDV Yayınları, 1998.

Terzi, Arzu. *Sarayda İktidar Mücadelesi: Saray, Mücevher ve İktidar*. Istanbul: Timaş Yayınları, 2009.

Terzibaşoğlu, Yücel. "Landlords, Refugees, and Nomads: Struggles for Land Around Late-Nineteenth-Century Ayvalık." *New Perspectives on Turkey*, no. 24 (2001): 51–82.

Terzibaşoğlu Yücel. "Eleni Hatun'un Zeytin Bahçeleri: 19. Yüzyılda Anadolu'da Mülkiyet Hakları Nasıl İnşa Edildi?" *Tarih ve Toplum, Yeni Yaklaşımlar*, no. 4 (2006): 121–147.

Terzibaşoğlu, Yücel. "'A Very Important Requirement of Social Life': Privatisation of Land, Criminalisation of Custom and Land Disputes in Nineteenth-Century Anatolia.' In *Les acteurs des Transformations Foncières Autour de la Méditerranée XIXe Siècle*. Ed. V. Guéno and D. Guignard, 25–48. Paris: Karthala, 2013.

Terzibaşoğlu, Yücel and Kaya, Alp Yücel. "19. Yüzyılda Balkanlar'da Toprak Rejimi ve Emek İlişkileri." In *İktisat Tarihinin Dönüşü: Yeni Yaklaşımlar, Yeni Tartışmalar*. Ed. Ulaş Karakoç and Alp Yücel Kaya, 49-107. Istanbul: İletişim Yayınları, 2021.

Texier, Charles. *Küçük Asya: Coğrafyası, Tarihi ve Arkeolojisi, v. 2*. Trans. Ali Suat. Ankara: Enformasyon ve Dökümantasyon Hizmetleri Vakfı, 2002.

Tezel, Yahya S. *Cumhuriyet Döneminin İktisadi Tarihi (1923–1950)*. Istanbul: Tarih Vakfı Yurt Yayınları, 2000.

The Veterinary Department of the Privy Council Office. *Report on the Cattle Plague in Great Britain, During the Years 1865, 1866, and 1867*. London: George Edward Eyre and William Spottiswoode, 1868.

Thelle, Mikkel. "The Meat City: Urban Space and Provision in Industrial Copenhagen, 1880–1914." *Urban History* 45, no.2 (2018): 233–252.

Tignor, Robert. *Modernization and British Colonial Rule in Egypt, 1882–1914*. Princeton: Princeton University Press, 1966.

Toksöz, Meltem. *Nomads, Migrants and Cotton in the Eastern Mediterranean: The Making of the Adana-Mersin Region, 1850–1908*. Leiden: Brill, 2010.

Toprak, Zafer "1909 Cemiyetler Kanunu." In *Tanzimat'tan Cumhuriyet'e Türkiye Ansiklopedisi, v. 1*. 205–208. Istanbul: İletişim Yayınları, 1985.

Toprak, Zafer. *İttihad-Terakki ve Cihan Harbi: Savaş Ekonomisi ve Türkiye'de Devletçilik*. Istanbul: Homer Kitabevi, 2003.

Topuz, Ercüment. "XIX. Yüzyılda Van'da İllet-i Kolera ile Mücadelede Karantina Usulü ve Kordon Uygulaması." *Van Yüzüncü Yıl Üniversitesi Sosyal Bilimler Enstitüsü Dergisi*, no.48 (2020): 297–316.

Topuzlu, Cemil. *İstibdat, Meşrutiyet, Cumhuriyet Devirlerinde 80 Yıllık Hatıralarım*. Istanbul: Istanbul Üniversitesi Cerrahpaşa Tıp Fakültesi Yayınları, 1982.

Torun, Ethem. *Bilinen ve Bilinmeyen Yönleriyle Beypazarı*. Ankara: Bey Ofset, 2004.

Tozlu, Selahattin. "Trabzon-Erzurum-Tebriz Yolu (XIX. Yüzyılda Sosyal ve Ekonomik Bakımdan Bir İnceleme)." In *Türkler v.14*. Ed. Hasan Celal Güzel, Kemal Çiçek, and Salim Koca, 481–492. Ankara: Yeni Türkiye Yayınları, 2002.

Trak, Selçuk T. *İktisadi ve Ticari Türkiye, vol. 1*. İzmir: Ticaret Matbaacılık T.A.Ş., 1960.

Turgay, Üner. "Trabzon." *Review (Fernand Braudel Center)* 16, no.4 (1993): 435–465.

Uçak, Halil İbrahim. *Tarih İçinde Haymana*. Ankara: Haymanalılar Yardımlaşma ve Tanışma Derneği, 1986.

Ünver, Metin. "Courtgi (Gürcü) Bahr-i Sefid (L'egee) Vapur Kumpanyası, 1883–1911." *Çanakkale Araştırmaları Türk Yıllığı* 16, no. 24 (2018):175–210.

Uslu, Kübra. "Ahmed Vefik Paşa ve Bursa'nın Modernleşmesi Üzerine Bir İnceleme." MA thesis, Marmara University, 2019.

Uygun, Süleyman. *Osmanlı Sularında Rekabet: Mesajeri Maritim Vapur Kumpanyası,1851–1914*. Istanbul: Kitap Yayınevi, 2015.

Uzer, Tahsin. *Makedonya Eşkiyalık Tarihi ve Son Osmanlı Yönetimi.* Ankara: Türk Tarih Kurumu, 1999.

Uzun, Ahmet. *İstanbul'un İaşesinde Devletin Rolü: Ondalık Ağnam Uygulaması, 1783–1857.* Ankara: Türk Tarih Kurumu Yayınları, 2006.

White, Charles. *Three Years in Constantinople or, Domestic Manners of the Turks in 1844.* London: Henry Colburn Publishers, 1845.

White, Sam. *The Climate of Rebellion in the Early Modern Ottoman Empire.* Cambridge: Cambridge University Press, 2011.

Wishnitzer, Avner. *Reading Clock, Alla Turca: Time and Society in the Late Ottoman Empire.* Chicago: The University of Chicago Press, 2015.

Woods, Rebecca J. H. "Breed, Culture, and Economy: The New Zealand Frozen Meat Trade, 1880–1914." *The Agricultural History Review* 60, no. 2 (2012): 288–308.

Yalazı, Şaban. "Karacabey'in Eski-Eskimeyen Yüzleri." *Bursa Araştırmaları: Kent Tarihi ve Kültürü Dergisi,* no. 24 (2009): 26–32.

Yalazı, Şaban. "Karacabey Çiftlikleri." Accessed 1 February 2024, https://www.belgeseltarih.com/karacabey-ciftlikleri/

Yalgın, Ali Rıza. *Cenupta Türkmen Oymakları, v. 1.* Ankara: Kültür Bakanlığı Yayınları, 1977.

Yarman, Arsen. *Palu Harput 1878: Çarsancak, Çemişgezek, Çapakçur, Erzincan, Hizan ve Civar Bölgeler, v. 1.* Istanbul: Belge Yayınları, 2010.

Yaycıoğlu, Ali. *Partners of the Empire: The Crisis of the Ottoman Empire in the Age of Revolutions.* Stanford: Stanford University Press, 2016.

Yıldırım, Fahri *Sakarya Köprüleri.* Adapazarı: Sakarya Büyükşehir Belediyesi, 2008.

Yıldırım Nuran, "Bakteriyolojihane-i Şahane'de Veteriner Bakteriyolojisi, 1893-1901." In *I. Ulusal Veteriner Hekimliği Tarihi ve Mesleki Etik Sempozyumu Bildirileri.* Ed. Abdullah Özen, 171-184. Elazığ: 2006.

Yılmaz, Seçil. "Bakterilere Yakından Bakmak: Bilim ve Siyaset Arasında Bakteriyolojihane-yi Şahane." *Hayat Sağlık: Sağlık ve Sosyal Bilimler Dergisi,* no. 13 (2015): 54-59.

Zarifi, Yorgo L. *Hatıralarım: Kaybolan Bir Dünya İstanbul, 1800–1920.* Istanbul: Literatür, 2005.

Index

FSC
www.fsc.org
MIX
Papier | Fördert
gute Waldnutzung
FSC® C083411

Kolibri 360 GmbH
Ferdinand-Jühlke-Straße 7
99095 Erfurt, Deutschland
produktsicherheit@kolibri360.de